THE TWO SOURCES OF
MORALITY AND RELIGION

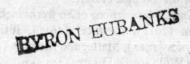

THE TWO SOURCES OF

MORALITY AND RELIGION

By HENRI BERGSON

Translated by R. Ashley Audra and
Cloudesley Brereton
With the assistance of W. Horsfall Carter

Doubleday Anchor Books, 1954

DOUBLEDAY & COMPANY, INC., GARDEN CITY, N.Y.

In undertaking to place before the English public M. Henri Bergson's great work, which since its publication in March 1932 has gone through seventeen editions, the translators were confronted at the outset with great difficulties. An example, of the utmost importance, was the word "morale," which has a wider meaning in French than in English, conveying both morality and ethics. There are obvious disadvantages in attempting to use now the one now the other of these two terms, though this has in some cases been done. But we have in most cases kept to the word "morality," and therefore consider it advisable to inform our readers of the wide sense in which we use it. As Monsieur Bergson himself says more than once, "You may attribute what meaning you like to a word, provided you start by clearly defining that meaning."

The path of all translation is strewn with stumbling-blocks. This is especially true of *The Two Sources of Morality and Religion*. Here the thought is the outcome of twenty-five years' reflection and research, cast with unfailing skill in the language in which it was conceived; the language becomes inseparable from the thought it expresses. That is why the reader who cares to compare the English with the French text will find a certain number of passages which might appear at first sight to have been altered from the original. A closer study will reveal that this is not the case and that in almost every instance an effort has been made to convey the meaning of the French sentence more accurately still than would have been possible by a word-for-word translation. Monsieur

Bergson realized the difficulties with which the translators were confronted, and with the kindly courtesy which is characteristic of him helped them in their task. At his particular request, and under his guidance, these passages have been re-written and even re-thought in English. Once recast in this way, they have been submitted to his final approval. The translators and the reader owe him a debt of gratitude for his generous and careful collaboration.

The translators also wish particularly to thank Mr. W. Horsfall Carter, who has helped them with his advice throughout the work of translation, has taken over from Dr. Cloudesley Brereton the work of final revision (owing to the latter's ill-health), and has undertaken the arduous and delicate task of re-reading the book as a whole, with a fresh mind. Owing to his remarkable command of his own language, together with a consummate knowledge of French, his assistance has been of the greatest value.

R. Ashley Audra
Cloudesley Brereton

CONTENTS

The remembrance of forbidden fruit is the earliest thing
in the memory of each of us, as it is in that of mankind.
We should notice this, were not this recollection overlaid by others which we are more inclined to dwell upon.
What a childhood we should have had if only we had
been left to do as we pleased! We should have flitted
from pleasure to pleasure. But all of a sudden an obstacle
arose, neither visible nor tangible: a prohibition. Why
did we obey? The question hardly occurred to us. We
had formed the habit of deferring to our parents and
teachers. All the same we knew very well that it was
because they were our parents, because they were our
teachers. Therefore, in our eyes, their authority came
less from themselves than from their status in relation
to us. They occupied a certain station; that was the
source of the command which, had it issued from some
other quarter, would not have possessed the same weight.
In other words, parents and teachers seemed to act by
proxy. We did not fully realize this, but behind our
parents and our teachers we had an inkling of some
enormous, or rather some shadowy, thing that exerted
pressure on us through them. Later we would say it was
society. And speculating upon it, we should compare it
to an organism whose cells, united by imperceptible
links, fall into their respective places in a highly developed hierarchy, and for the greatest good of the whole
naturally submit to a discipline that may demand the
sacrifice of the part. This, however, can only be a comparison, for an organism subject to inexorable laws is one
thing, and a society composed of free wills another. But,

once these wills are organized, they assume the guise of an organism; and in this more or less artificial organism habit plays the same rôle as necessity in the works of nature. From this first standpoint, social life appears to us a system of more or less deeply rooted habits, corresponding to the needs of the community. Some of them are habits of command, most of them are habits of obedience, whether we obey a person commanding by virtue of a mandate from society, or whether from society itself, vaguely perceived or felt, there emanates an impersonal imperative. Each of these habits of obedience exerts a pressure on our will. We can evade it, but then we are attracted towards it, drawn back to it, like a pendulum which has swung away from the vertical. A certain order of things has been upset, it *must be* restored. In a word, as with all habits, we feel a sense of obligation.

But in this case the obligation is immeasurably stronger. When a certain magnitude is so much greater than another that the latter is negligible in comparison, mathematicians say that it belongs to another order. So it is with social obligation. The pressure of it, compared to that of other habits, is such that the difference in degree amounts to a difference in kind. It should be noted that all habits of this nature lend one another mutual support. Although we may not speculate on their essence and on their origin, we feel that they are interrelated, being demanded of us by our immediate surroundings, or by the surroundings of those surroundings, and so on to the uttermost limit, which would be society. Each one corresponds, directly or indirectly, to a social necessity; and so they all hang together, they form a solid block. Many of them would be trivial obligations if they appeared singly. But they are an integral part of obligation in general, and this whole, which is what it is owing to the contributions of its parts, in its turn confers upon each one the undivided authority of the totality. Thus the sum-total comes to the aid of each of its parts, and the general sentence "do what duty bids" triumphs over the hesitations we might feel in the presence of a single duty. As a matter of fact, we do not explicitly think of a mass of partial duties added together and constituting a single total obligation. Perhaps there is really not an aggregation of parts. The strength which one obligation derives from all the others is rather to be compared to the breath of life drawn, complete and invisible, by each of the cells from the depths of the organism of which it is an element. Society, present within each of its members, has claims which, whether great or small, each express the sum-total of its vitality. But let us again repeat that this is only a comparison. A human community is a collectivity of free beings. The obligations which it lays down, and which enable it to subsist, introduce into it a regularity which has merely some analogy to the inflexible order of the phenomena of life.

And yet everything conspires to make us believe that this regularity is comparable with that of nature. I do not allude merely to the unanimity of mankind in praising certain acts and blaming others. I mean that, even in those cases where moral precepts implied in judgments of values are not observed, we contrive that they should appear so. Just as we do not notice disease when walking along the street, so we do not gauge the degree of possible immorality behind the exterior which humanity presents to the world. It would take a good deal of time to become a misanthrope if we confined ourselves to the observation of others. It is when we detect our own weaknesses that we come to pity or despise mankind. The human nature from which we then turn away is the human nature we have discovered in the depths of our own being. The evil is so well screened, the secret so universally kept, that in this case each individual is the dupe of all: however severely we may profess to judge other men, at bottom we think them better than ourselves. On this happy illusion much of our social life is grounded.

It is natural that society should do everything to encourage this idea. The laws which it promulgates and which maintain the social order resemble, moreover, in certain aspects, the laws of nature. I admit that the difference is a radical one in the eyes of the philosopher. To him the law which enunciates facts is one thing, the law which commands, another. It is possible to evade the latter; here we have obligation, not necessity. The former is, on the contrary, unescapable, for if any fact diverged from it we should be wrong in having assumed it to be a law; there would exist another one, the true one, formulated in such a way as to express everything we observe and to which the recalcitrant fact would then conform like the rest. True enough; but to the majority of people the distinction is far from being so clear. A law, be it physical, social or moral—every law—is in their eyes a command. There is a certain order of nature which finds expression in laws: the facts are presumed to "obey" these laws so as to conform with that order. The scientist himself can hardly help believing that the law "governs" facts and consequently is prior to them, like the Platonic Idea on which all things had to model themselves. The higher he rises in the scale of generalizations the more he tends, willy-nilly, to endow the law with this imperative character; it requires a very real struggle against our own prepossessions to imagine the principles of mechanics otherwise than as inscribed from all eternity on the transcendent tables that modern science has apparently fetched down from another Sinai. But if physical law tends to assume in our imagination the form of a command when it attains to a certain degree of generality, in its turn an imperative which applies to everybody appears to us somewhat like a law of nature. The two ideas, coming against each other in our minds, effect an exchange. The law borrows from the command its prerogative of compulsion; the command receives from the law its inevitability. Thus a breach of the social order assumes an anti-natural character; even when frequently repeated, it strikes us as an exception, being to society what a freak creation is to nature.

And suppose we discern behind the social imperative a religious command? No matter the relation between the two terms: whether religion be interpreted in one way or another, whether it be social in essence or by accident, one thing is certain, that it has always played a social rôle. This part, indeed, is a complex one: it varies with time and place; but in societies such as our own the first effect of religion is to sustain and reinforce the claims of society. It may go much further. It goes at least thus far. Society institutes punishments which may strike the innocent and spare the guilty; its rewards are few and far between; it takes broad views and is easily satisfied; what human scales could weigh, as they should be weighed, rewards and punishments? But, just as the Platonic Ideas reveal to us, in its perfection and fulness, that reality which we see only in crude imitations, so religion admits us to a city whose most prominent features are here and there roughly typified by our institutions, our laws and our customs. Here below, order is merely approximate, being more or less artificially obtained by man; above, it is perfect and self-creative. Religion therefore, in our eyes, succeeds in filling in the gap, already narrowed by our habitual way of looking at things, between a command of society and a law of nature.

We are thus being perpetually brought back to the same comparison, defective though it be in many ways, yet appropriate enough to the point with which we are dealing. The members of a civic community hold together like the cells of an organism. Habit, served by intelligence and imagination, introduces among them a discipline resembling, in the interdependence it establishes between separate individuals, the unity of an organism of anastomotic cells.

Everything, yet again, conspires to make social order an imitation of the order observed in nature. It is evident that each of us, thinking of himself alone, feels at liberty to follow his bent, his desire or his fancy, and not consider his fellow-men. But this inclination has no sooner taken shape than it comes up against a force composed of the accumulation of all social forces: unlike individual motives, each pulling its own way, this force would result in an order not without analogy to that of natural phenomena. The component cell of an organism, on becoming momentarily conscious, would barely have outlived the wish to emancipate itself when it would be recaptured by necessity. An individual forming part of a community may bend or even break a necessity of the same kind, which to some extent he has helped to create, but to which, still more, he has to yield; the sense of this necessity, together with the consciousness of being able to evade it, is none the less what he calls an obligation. From this point of view, and taken in its most usual meaning, obligation is to necessity what habit is to nature.

It does not come then exactly from without. Each of us belongs as much to society as to himself. While his consciousness, delving downwards, reveals to him, the deeper he goes, an ever more original personality, incommensurable with the others and indeed undefinable in words, on the surface of life we are in continuous contact with other men whom we resemble, and united to them by a discipline which creates between them and us a relation of interdependence. Has the self no other means of clinging to something solid than by taking up its position in that part of us which is socialized? That would be so if there were no other way of escape from a life of impulse, caprice and regret. But in our innermost selves, if we know how to look for it, we may perhaps discover another sort of equilibrium, still more desirable than the one on the surface. Certain aquatic plants as they rise to the surface are ceaselessly jostled by the current: their leaves, meeting above the water, interlace, thus imparting to them stability above. But still more stable are the roots, which, firmly planted in the earth, support them from below. However, we shall not dwell for the present on the effort to delve down to the depths of our being. If possible at all, it is exceptional: and it is on the surface, at the point where it inserts itself into the close-woven tissue of other exteriorised personalities, that our ego generally finds its point of attachment; its solidity lies in this solidarity. But, at the point where it is attached, it is itself socialized. Obligation, which we look upon as a bond between men, first binds us to ourselves.

It would therefore be a mistake to reproach a purely social morality with neglecting individual duties. Even if we were only in theory under a state of obligation towards other men, we should be so in fact towards ourselves, since social solidarity exists only in so far as a social ego is superadded, in each of us, to the individual self. To cultivate this social ego is the essence of our obligation to society. Were there not some part of society in us, it would have no hold on us; and we scarcely need seek it out, we are self-sufficient, if we find it present within us. Its presence is more or less marked in different men; but no one could cut himself off from it completely. Nor would he wish to do so, for he is perfectly aware that the greater part of his strength comes from this source, and that he owes to the ever-recurring demands of social life that unbroken tension of energy, that steadiness of aim in effort, which ensures the greatest return for his activity. But he could not do so, even if he wished to, because his memory and his imagination live on what society has implanted in them, because the soul of society is inherent in the language he speaks, and because even if there is no one present, even if he is merely thinking, he is still talking to himself. Vainly do we try to imagine an individual cut off from all social life. Even materially, Robinson Crusoe on his island remains in contact with other men, for the manufactured objects he saved from the wreck, and without which he could not get along, keep him within the bounds of civilization, and consequently within those of society. But a moral contact is still more necessary to him, for he would be soon discouraged if he had nothing else to cope with his incessant difficulties except an individual strength of which he knows the limitations. He draws energy from the society to which he remains attached in spirit; he may not perceive it, still it is there, watching him: if the individual ego maintains alive and present the social ego, he will effect, even in isolation, what he would with the encouragement and even the support of the whole of society. Those whom circumstances condemn for a time to solitude, and who cannot find within themselves the resources of a deep inner life, know the penalty of "giving way," that is to say of not stabilising the individual ego at the level prescribed by the social ego. They will therefore be careful to maintain the latter, so that it shall not relax for one moment its strictness towards the former. If necessary, they will seek for some material or artificial support for it. You remember Kipling's Forest Officer, alone in his bungalow in the heart of the Indian rukh? He dresses every evening for dinner, so as to preserve his self-respect in his isolation.[1]

We shall not go so far as to say that this social ego is Adam Smith's "impartial spectator," or that it must necessarily be identified with moral conscience, or that we feel pleased or displeased with ourselves according as it is favourably or unfavourably affected. We shall discover deeper sources for our moral feelings. Language here groups under one name very different things: what

[1] Kipling, "In the Rukh," from *Many Inventions*.

is there in common between the remorse of a murderer and that racking, haunting pain, also a remorse, which we may feel at having wounded someone's pride or been unjust to a child? To betray the confidence of an innocent soul opening out to life is one of the most heinous offences for a certain type of conscience, which is apparently lacking in a sense of proportion, precisely because it does not borrow from society its standards, its gauges, its system of measurement. This type of conscience is not the one that is most often at work. At any rate it is more or less sensitive in different people. Generally the verdict of conscience is the verdict which would be given by the social self.

And also, generally speaking, moral distress is a throwing-out of gear of the relations between the social and the individual self. Analyse the feeling of remorse in the soul of a desperate criminal. You might mistake it at first for the dread of punishment, and indeed you find most minute precautions, perpetually supplemented and renewed, to conceal the crime and avoid being found out; at every moment comes the awful thought that some detail has been overlooked and that the authorities will get hold of the tell-tale clue. But look closer: what the fellow wants is not so much to evade punishment as to wipe out the past, to arrange things just as though the crime had never been committed at all. When nobody knows that a thing exists, it is almost as if it were non-existent. Thus it is the crime itself that the criminal wants to erase, by suppressing any knowledge of it that might come to the human ken. But his own knowledge persists, and note how it drives him more and more out of that society within which he hoped to remain by obliterating the traces of his crime. For the same esteem for the man he was is still shown to the man he is no longer; therefore society is not addressing him; it is speaking to someone else. He, knowing what he is, feels more isolated among his fellow-men than he would on a desert island; for in his solitude he would carry with him, enveloping him and supporting him, the image of society; but now he is cut off from the image as well as the thing. He could reinstate himself in society by confessing his crime: he would then be treated according to his deserts, but society would then be speaking to his real self. He would resume his collaboration with other men. He would be punished by them, but, having made himself one of them, he would be in a small degree the author of his own condemnation; and a part of himself, the best part, would thus escape the penalty. Such is the force which will drive a criminal to give himself up. Sometimes, without going so far, he will confess to a friend, or to any decent fellow. By thus putting himself right, if not in the eyes of all, at least in somebody's eyes, he re-attaches himself to society at a single point, by a thread: even if he does not reinstate himself in it, at least he is near it, close to it; he no longer remains alienated from it; in any case he is no longer in complete rupture with it, nor with that element of it which is part of himself.

It takes this violent break to reveal clearly the nexus of the individual to society. In the ordinary way we conform to our obligations rather than think of them. If we had every time to evoke the idea, enunciate the formula, it would be much more tiring to do our duty. But habit is enough, and in most cases we have only to leave well alone in order to accord to society what it expects from us. Moreover, society has made matters very much easier for us by interpolating intermediaries between itself and us: we have a family; we follow a trade or a profession; we belong to our parish, to our district, to our country; and, in cases where the insertion of the group into society is complete, we may content ourselves, if need be, with fulfilling our obligations towards the group and so paying our debts to society. Society occupies the circumference; the individual is at the centre: from the centre to the circumference are arranged, like so many ever-widening concentric circles, the various groups to which the individual belongs. From the circumference to the centre, as the circles grow smaller, obligations are added to obligations, and the individual ends by finding himself confronted with all of them together. Thus obligation increases as it advances; but, if it is more complicated, it is less abstract, and the more easily accepted. When it has become fully concrete, it coincides with a tendency, so habitual that we find it natural, to play in society the part which our station assigns to us. So long as we yield to this tendency, we scarcely feel it. It assumes a peremptory aspect, like all deep-seated habits, only if we depart from it.

It is society that draws up for the individual the programme of his daily routine. It is impossible to live a family life, follow a profession, attend to the thousand and one cares of the day, do one's shopping, go for a stroll, or even stay at home, without obeying rules and submitting to obligations. Every instant we have to choose, and we naturally decide on what is in keeping with the rule. We are hardly conscious of this; there is no effort. A road has been marked out by society; it lies open before us, and we follow it; it would take more initiative to cut across country. Duty, in this sense, is almost always done automatically; and obedience to duty, if we restrict ourselves to the most usual case, might be defined as a form of non-exertion, passive acquiescence. How comes it, then, that on the contrary this obedience appears as a state of strain, and duty itself as something harsh and unbending? Obviously because there occur cases where obedience implies an overcoming of self. These cases are exceptions; but we notice them because they are accompanied by acute consciousness, as happens with all forms of hesitation—in fact consciousness is this hesitation itself; for an action which is started automatically passes almost unperceived. Thus, owing to the interdependence of our duties, and because the ob-

ligation as a whole is immanent in each of its parts, all
duties are tinged with the hue taken on exceptionally
by one or the other of them. From the practical point
of view this presents no inconvenience, there are even
certain advantages in looking at things in this way. For,
however naturally we do our duty, we may meet with
resistance within ourselves; it is wise to expect it, and
not take for granted that it is easy to remain a good
husband, a decent citizen, a conscientious worker, in a
word an honest fellow. Besides, there is a considerable
amount of truth in this opinion; for if it is relatively
easy to keep within the social order, yet we have had to
enrol in it, and this enrolment demands an effort. The
natural disobedience of the child, the necessity of education, are proof of this. It is but just to credit the individual with the consent virtually given to the totality
of his obligations, even if he no longer needs to take
counsel with himself on each one of them. The rider
need only allow himself to be borne along; still he has
had to get into the saddle. So it is with the individual in
relation to society. In one sense it would be untrue, and
in every sense it would be dangerous, to say that duty can
be done automatically. Let us then set up as a practical
maxim that obedience to duty means resistance to self.

But a maxim is one thing, an explanation another.
When, in order to define obligation, its essence and its
origin, we lay down that obedience is primarily a struggle
with self, a state of tension or contraction, we make a
psychological error which has vitiated many theories of
ethics. Thus artificial difficulties have arisen, problems
which set philosophers at variance and which will be
found to vanish when we analyse the terms in which they
are expressed. Obligation is in no sense a unique fact,
incommensurate with others, looming above them like a
mysterious apparition. If a considerable number of philosophers, especially those who follow Kant, have taken
this view, it is because they have confused the sense of

obligation, a tranquil state akin to inclination, with the violent effort we now and again exert on ourselves to break down a possible obstacle to obligation.

After an attack of rheumatism, we may feel some discomfort and even pain in moving our muscles and joints. It is the general sensation of a resistance set up by all our organs together. Little by little it decreases and ends by being lost in the consciousness we have of our movements when we are well. Now, we are at liberty to fancy that it is still there, in an incipient, or rather a subsiding, condition, that it is only on the look-out for a chance to become more acute; we must indeed expect attacks of rheumatism if we are rheumatic. Yet what should we say of a philosopher who saw in our habitual sensations, when moving our arms and legs, a mere diminution of pain, and who then defined our motory faculty as an effort to resist rheumatic discomfort? To begin with, he would thus be giving up the attempt to account for motory habits, since each of these implies a particular combination of movements, and can be explained only by that combination. The general faculty of walking, running, moving the body, is but an aggregation of these elementary habits, each of them finding its own explanation in the special movements it involves. But having only considered the faculty as a whole, and having then defined it as a force opposed to a resistance, it is natural enough to set up rheumatism beside it as an independent entity. It would seem as though some such error had been made by many of those who have speculated on obligation. We have any number of particular obligations, each calling for a separate explanation. It is natural, or, more strictly speaking, it is a matter of habit to obey them all. Suppose that exceptionally we deviate from one of them, there would be resistance; if we resist this resistance, a state of tension or contraction is likely to result. It is this rigidity which we objectify when we attribute so stern an aspect to duty.

It is also what the philosophers have in mind, when they see fit to resolve obligation into rational elements. In order to resist resistance, to keep to the right paths, when desire, passion or interest tempt us aside, we must necessarily give ourselves reasons. Even if we have opposed the unlawful desire by another, the latter, conjured up by the will, could arise only at the call of an idea. In a word, an intelligent being generally exerts his influence on himself through the medium of intelligence. But from the fact that we get back to obligation by rational ways it does not follow that obligation was of a rational order. We shall dwell on this point later; we do not intend to discuss ethical theories for the present. Let us merely say that a tendency, natural or acquired, is one thing, another thing the necessarily rational method which a reasonable being will use to restore to it its force and to combat what is opposing it. In the latter case the tendency which has been obscured may reappear; and then everything doubtless happens as though we had succeeded by this method in re-establishing the tendency anew. In reality we have merely swept aside something that hampered or checked it. It comes to the same thing, I grant you, in practice: explain the fact in one way or another, the fact is there, we have achieved success. And in order to succeed it is perhaps better to imagine that things did happen in the former way. But to state that this is actually the case would be to vitiate the whole theory of obligation. Has not this been the case with most philosophers?

Let there be no misunderstanding. Even if we confine ourselves to a certain aspect of morality, as we have done up to now, we shall find many different attitudes towards duty. They line the intervening space between the extremes of two attitudes, or rather two habits: that of moving so naturally along the ways laid down by society as barely to notice them; or on the contrary hesitating and deliberating on which way to take, how far

to go, the distances out and back we shall have to cover
if we try several paths one after another. In the second
case new problems arise with more or less frequency; and
even in those instances where our duty is fully mapped
out, we make all sorts of distinctions in fulfilling it. But,
in the first place, the former attitude is that of the immense majority of men; it is probably general in backward communities. And, after all, however much we
may reason in each particular case, formulate the maxim,
enunciate the principle, deduce the consequences: if
desire and passion join in the discussion, if temptation
is strong, if we are on the point of falling, if suddenly
we recover ourselves, what was it that pulled us up? A
force asserts itself which we have called the "totality of
obligation": the concentrated extract, the quintessence
of innumerable specific habits of obedience to the countless particular requirements of social life. This force is no
one particular thing and, if it could speak (whereas it
prefers to act), it would say: "You must because you
must." Hence the work done by intelligence in weighing reasons, comparing maxims, going back to first principles, was to introduce more logical consistency into a
line of conduct subordinated by its very nature to the
claims of society; but this social claim was the real root of
obligation. Never, in our hours of temptation, should we
sacrifice to the mere need for logical consistency our
interest, our passion, our vanity. Because in a reasonable
being reason does indeed intervene as a regulator to
assure this consistency between obligatory rules or maxims, philosophy has been led to look upon it as a principle of obligation. We might as well believe that the
fly-wheel drives the machinery.

Besides, the demands of a society dovetail into one
another. Even the individual whose decent behaviour is
the least based on reasoning and, if I may put it so, the
most conventional, introduces a rational order into his
conduct by the mere fact of obeying rules which are

logically connected together. I freely admit that such
logic has been late in taking possession of society. Logical co-ordination is essentially economy. From a whole it
first roughly extracts certain principles and then excludes
everything which is not in accordance with them. Nature, by contrast, is lavish. The closer a community is to
nature, the greater the proportion of unaccountable and
inconsistent rules it lays down. We find in primitive
races many prohibitions and prescriptions explicable at
most by vague associations of ideas, by superstition, by
automatism. Nor are they without their use, since the
obedience of everyone to laws, even absurd ones, assures
greater cohesion to the community. But in that case the
usefulness of the rule accrues, by a kind of reverse action,
solely from the fact of our submission to it. Prescriptions
or prohibitions which are intrinsically useful are those
that are explicitly designed for the preservation or well-
being of society. No doubt they have gradually detached
themselves from the others and survived them. Social
demands have therefore been co-ordinated with each
other and subordinated to principles. But no matter.
Logic permeates indeed present-day communities, and
even the man who does not reason out his conduct will
live reasonably if he conforms to these principles.

But the essence of obligation is a different thing from
a requirement of reason. This is all we have tried to suggest so far. Our description would, we think, correspond
more and more to reality as one came to deal with less
developed communities and more rudimentary stages of
consciousness. It remains a bare outline so long as we
confine ourselves to the normal conscience, such as is
found to-day in the ordinary decent person. But precisely because we are in this case dealing with a strange
complex of feelings, of ideas and tendencies all inter-
penetrating each other, we shall avoid artificial analyses
and arbitrary syntheses only if we have at hand an outline which gives the essential. Such is the outline

we have attempted to trace. Conceive obligation as weighing on the will like a habit, each obligation dragging behind it the accumulated mass of the others, and utilising thus for the pressure it is exerting the weight of the whole: here you have the totality of obligation for a simple, elementary, moral conscience. That is the essential: that is what obligation could, if necessary, be reduced to, even in those cases where it attains its highest complexity.

This shows when and in what sense (how slightly Kantian!) obligation in its elementary state takes the form of a "categorical imperative." We should find it very difficult to discover examples of such an imperative in everyday life. A military order, which is a command that admits neither reason nor reply, does say in fact: "You must because you must." But, though you may give the soldier no reason, he will imagine one. If we want a pure case of the categorical imperative, we must construct one *a priori* or at least make an arbitrary abstraction of experience. So let us imagine an ant who is stirred by a gleam of reflection and thereupon judges she has been wrong to work unremittingly for others. Her inclination to laziness would indeed endure but a few moments, just as long as the ray of intelligence. In the last of these moments, when instinct regaining the mastery would drag her back by sheer force to her task, intelligence at the point of relapsing into instinct would say, as its parting word: "You must because you must." This "must because you must" would only be the momentary feeling of awareness of a tug which the ant experiences—the tug which the string, momentarily relaxed, exerts as it drags her back. The same command would ring in the ear of a sleep-walker on the point of waking, or even actually beginning to wake, from the dream he is enacting: if he lapsed back at once into a hypnotic state, a categorical imperative would express in words, on behalf of the reflexion which had just been on the point of emerging and had instantly disappeared, the inevitableness of the relapse. In a word, an absolutely categorical imperative is instinctive or somnambulistic, enacted as such in a normal state, represented as such if reflexion is roused long enough to take form, not long enough to seek for reasons. But, then, is it not evident that, in a reasonable being, an imperative will tend to become categorical in proportion as the activity brought into play, although intelligent, will tend to become instinctive? But an activity which, starting as intelligent, progresses towards an imitation of instinct is exactly what we call, in man, a habit. And the most powerful habit, the habit whose strength is made up of the accumulated force of all the elementary social habits, is necessarily the one which best imitates instinct. Is it then surprising that, in the short moment which separates obligation merely experienced as a living force from obligation fully realized and justified by all sorts of reasons, obligation should indeed take the form of the categorical imperative: "you must because you must"?

Let us consider two divergent lines of evolution with societies at the extremities of each. The type of society which will appear the more natural will obviously be the instinctive type; the link that unites the bees of a hive resembles far more the link which holds together the cells of an organism, co-ordinate and subordinate to one another. Let us suppose for an instant that nature has intended to produce at the extremity of the second line societies where a certain latitude was left to individual choice: she would have arranged that intelligence should achieve here results comparable, as regards their regularity, to those of instinct in the other; she would have had recourse to habit. Each of these habits, which may be called "moral," would be incidental. But the aggregate of them, I mean the habit of contracting these habits, being at the very basis of societies and a necessary condition of their existence, would have a force comparable to that of instinct in respect of both intensity and regularity. This is exactly what we have called the "totality of obligation." This, be it said, will apply only to human societies at the moment of emerging from the hands of nature. It will apply to primitive and to elementary societies. But, however much human society may progress, grow complicated and spiritualized, the original design, expressing the purpose of nature, will remain.

Now this is exactly what has happened. Without going deeply into a matter we have dealt with elsewhere, let us simply say that intelligence and instinct are forms of consciousness which must have interpenetrated each other in their rudimentary state and become dissociated as they grew. This development occurred on the two main lines of evolution of animal life, with the Arthropods and the Vertebrates. At the end of the former we have the instinct of insects, more especially the Hymenoptera; at the end of the second, human intelligence. Instinct and intelligence have each as their essential object the utilisation of implements: in the first case, organs supplied by nature and hence immutable; in the second, invented tools, and therefore varied and unforeseen. The implement is, moreover, designed for a certain type of work, and this work is all the more efficient the more it is specialized, the more it is divided up between diversely qualified workers who mutually supplement one another. Social life is thus immanent, like a vague ideal, in instinct as well as in intelligence: this ideal finds its most complete expression in the hive or the ant-hill on the one hand, in human societies on the other. Whether human or animal, a society is an organization; it implies a co-ordination and generally also a subordination of elements; it therefore exhibits, whether merely embodied in life or, in addition, specifically formulated, a collection of rules and laws. But in a hive or an ant-hill the individual is riveted to his task by his structure, and the organization is relatively invariable, whereas the human community is variable in form, open to every kind of progress. The result is that in the former each rule is laid down by nature, and is necessary: whereas in the latter only one thing is natural, the necessity of a rule. Thus the more, in human society, we delve down to the root of the various obligations to reach obligation in general, the more obligation will tend to become necessity, the nearer it will draw, in its peremptory aspect, to instinct. And yet we should make a great mistake if we tried to ascribe any particular obligation, whatever it might be, to instinct. What we must perpetually recall is that, no one obligation being instinctive, obligation as a whole *would have been* instinct if human societies were not, so to speak, ballasted with variability and intelligence. It is a virtual instinct, like that which lies behind the habit of speech. The morality of a human society may indeed be compared to its language. If ants exchange signs, which seems probable, those signs are provided by the very instinct that makes the ants communicate with one another. On the contrary, our languages are the product of custom. Nothing in the vocabulary, or even in the syntax, comes from nature. But speech is natural, and unvarying signs, natural in origin, which are presumably used in a community of insects, exhibit what our language would have been, if nature in bestowing on us the faculty of speech had not added that function which, since it makes and uses tools, is inventive and called intelligence. We must perpetually recur to what obligation *would have been* if human society had been instinctive instead of intelligent: this will not explain any particular obligation, we shall even give of obligation in general an idea which would be false, if we went no further; and yet we must think of this instinctive society as the counterpart of intelligent society, if we are not to start without any clue in quest of the foundations of morality.

From this point of view obligation loses its specific

character. It ranks among the most general phenomena of life. When the elements which go to make up an organism submit to a rigid discipline, can we say that they feel themselves liable to obligation and that they are obeying a social instinct? Obviously not; but whereas such an organism is barely a community, the hive and the ant-hill are actual organisms, the elements of which are united by invisible ties, and the social instinct of an ant—I mean the force by virtue of which the worker, for example, performs the task to which she is predestined by her structure—cannot differ radically from the cause, whatever it be, by virtue of which every tissue, every cell of a living body, toils for the greatest good of the whole. Indeed it is, strictly speaking, no more a matter of obligation in the one case than in the other, but rather of necessity. It is just this necessity that we perceive, not actual but virtual, at the foundations of moral obligation, as through a more or less transparent veil. A human being feels an obligation only if he is free, and each obligation, considered separately, implies liberty. But it is necessary that there should be obligations; and the deeper we go, away from those particular obligations which are at the top, towards obligation in general, or, as we have said, towards obligation as a whole, which is at the bottom, the more obligation appears as the very form assumed by necessity in the realm of life, when it demands, for the accomplishment of certain ends, intelligence, choice, and therefore liberty.

Here again it may be alleged that this applies to very simple human societies, that is to say primitive or rudimentary societies. Certainly, but, as we shall have occasion to point out later, civilized man differs from primitive man above all by the enormous mass of knowledge and habits which he has absorbed, since the first awakening of his consciousness, from the social surroundings in which they were stored up. What is natural is in great measure overlaid by what is acquired; but it endures, almost unchangeable, throughout the centuries; habits and knowledge by no means impregnate the organism to the extent of being transmitted by heredity, as used to be supposed. It is true that we could consider what is natural as negligible in our analysis of obligation, if it had been crushed out by the acquired habits which have accumulated over it in the course of centuries of civilization. But it remains in excellent condition, very much alive, in the most civilized society. To it we must revert, not to account for this or that social obligation, but to explain what we have called obligation as a whole. Our civilized communities, however different they may be from the society to which we were primarily destined by nature, exhibit indeed, with respect to that society, a fundamental resemblance.

For they too are closed societies. They may be very extensive compared to the small agglomerations to which we were drawn by instinct and which the same instinct would probably tend to revive to-day if all the material and spiritual acquisitions of civilization were to disappear from the social environment in which we find them stored; their essential characteristic is none the less to include at any moment a certain number of individuals, and exclude others. We have said above, that underlying moral obligation there was a social demand. Of what society were we speaking? Was it of that open society represented by all mankind? We did not settle the matter, any more than one usually does when speaking of a man's duty to his fellows; one remains prudently vague; one refrains from making any assertion, but one would like to have it believed that "human society" is already an accomplished fact. And it is well that we should like to have it believed, for if incontestably we have duties towards man as man (although these duties have an entirely different origin, as we shall see a little later) we should risk undermining them, were we to make a radical distinction between them and our duties to our fellow-citizens. This is right enough so far as action is concerned. But a moral philosophy which does not emphasize this distinction misses the truth; its analyses will thereby be inevitably distorted. In fact, when we lay down that the duty of respecting the life and property of others is a fundamental demand of social life, what society do we mean? To find an answer we need only think what happens in time of war. Murder and pillage and perfidy, cheating and lying become not only lawful, they are actually praiseworthy. The warring nations can say, with Macbeth's witches: "Fair is foul, and foul is fair." Would this be possible, would the transformation take place so easily, generally and instantaneously, if it were really a certain attitude of man towards man that society had been enjoining on us till then? Oh, I know what society says (it has, I repeat, its reasons for saying so); but to know what it thinks and what it wants, we must not listen too much to what it says, we must look at what it does. It says that the duties it defines are indeed, in principle, duties towards humanity, but that under exceptional circumstances, regrettably unavoidable, they are for the time being inapplicable. If society did not express itself thus, it would bar the road to progress for another morality, not derived from it, which it has every inducement to humour. On the other hand, it is consistent with our habits of mind to consider as abnormal anything relatively rare or exceptional, disease for instance. But disease is as normal as health, which, viewed from a certain standpoint, appears as a constant effort to prevent disease or to avoid it. In the same way, peace has always hitherto been a preparation for defence or even attack, at any rate for war. Our social duties aim at social cohesion; whether we will or no they compose for us an attitude which is that of discipline in the face of the enemy. This means that, however much society may endow man, whom it has trained to discipline, with all it has acquired during centuries of civili-

zation, society still has need of that primitive instinct
which it coats with so thick a varnish. In a word, the
social instinct which we have detected at the basis of
social obligation always has in view—instinct being relatively unchangeable—a closed society, however large.
It is doubtless overlaid by another morality which for
that very reason it supports and to which it lends something of its force, I mean of its imperative character. But
it is not itself concerned with humanity. For between
the nation, however big, and humanity there lies the
whole distance from the finite to the indefinite, from
the closed to the open. We are fond of saying that the
apprenticeship to civic virtue is served in the family, and
that in the same way, from holding our country dear,
we learn to love mankind. Our sympathies are supposed
to broaden out in an unbroken progression, to expand
while remaining identical, and to end by embracing all
humanity. This is *a priori* reasoning, the result of a
purely intellectualist conception of the soul. We observe
that the three groups to which we can attach ourselves
comprise an increasing number of people, and we conclude that a progressive expansion of feeling keeps pace
with the increasing size of the object we love. And what
encourages the illusion is that, by a fortunate coincidence, the first part of the argument chances to fit in
with the facts; domestic virtues are indeed bound up
with civic virtues, for the very simple reason that family
and society, originally undifferentiated, have remained
closely connected. But between the society in which we
live and humanity in general there is, we repeat, the
same contrast as between the closed and the open; the
difference between the two objects is one of kind and
not simply one of degree. How much greater it would
be if, passing to the realm of feeling, we compared with
each other the two sentiments, love of country and love
of mankind! Who can help seeing that social cohesion
is largely due to the necessity for a community to protect

itself against others, and that it is primarily as against all other men that we love the men with whom we live? Such is the primitive instinct. It is still there, though fortunately hidden under the accretions of civilization; but even to-day we still love naturally and directly our parents and our fellow-countrymen, whereas love of mankind is indirect and acquired. We go straight to the former, to the latter we come only by roundabout ways; for it is only through God, in God, that religion bids man love mankind; and likewise it is through reason alone, that Reason in whose communion we are all partakers, that philosophers make us look at humanity in order to show us the pre-eminent dignity of the human being, the right of all to command respect. Neither in the one case nor the other do we come to humanity by degrees, through the stages of the family and the nation. We must, in a single bound, be carried far beyond it, and, without having made it our goal, reach it by outstripping it. Besides, whether we speak the language of religion or the language of philosophy, whether it be a question of love or respect, a different morality, another kind of obligation supervenes, above and beyond the social pressure. So far we have only dealt with the latter. The time has come to pass to the other.

We have been searching for pure obligation. To find it we have had to reduce morality to its simplest expression. The advantage of this has been to indicate in what obligation consisted; the disadvantage, to narrow down morality enormously. Not indeed because that part of it which we have left on one side is not obligatory: is there such a thing as a duty which is not compulsory? But it is conceivable that, starting from a primitive basis of obligation pure and simple, such as we have just defined, this obligation should radiate, expand, and even come to be absorbed into something that transfigures it. Let us now see what complete morality would be like. We shall use the same method and once more proceed, not downwards as up to now but upwards, to the extreme limit.

In all times there have arisen exceptional men, incarnating this morality. Before the saints of Christianity, mankind had known the sages of Greece, the prophets of Israel, the Arahants of Buddhism, and others besides. It is to them that men have always turned for that complete morality which we had best call absolute morality. And this very fact is at once characteristic and instructive; this very fact suggests to us the existence of a difference of kind and not merely one of degree between the morality with which we have been dealing up to now and that we are about to study, between the minimum and the maximum, between the two extremes. Whereas the former is all the more unalloyed and perfect precisely in proportion as it is the more readily reduced to impersonal formulae, the second, in order to be fully itself, must be incarnate in a privileged person who becomes an example. The generality of the one consists in the universal acceptance of a law, that of the other in a common imitation of a model.

Why is it, then, that saints have their imitators, and why do the great moral leaders draw the masses after them? They ask nothing, and yet they receive. They have no need to exhort; their mere existence suffices. For such is precisely the nature of this other morality. Whereas natural obligation is a pressure or a propulsive force, complete and perfect morality has the effect of an appeal.

Only those who have come into touch with a great moral personality have fully realized the nature of this appeal. But we all, at those momentous hours when our usual maxims of conduct strike us as inadequate, have wondered what such or such a one would have expected of us under the circumstances. It might have been a relation or a friend whom we thus evoked in thought. But it might quite as well have been a man we had never met, whose life-story had merely been told us, and to whose judgment we in imagination submitted our conduct, fearful of his censure, proud of his approval. It might even be a personality brought up from the depths of the soul into the light of consciousness, stirring into life within us, which we felt might completely pervade us later, and to which we wished to attach ourselves for the time being, as the disciple to his teacher. As a matter of fact this personality takes shape as soon as we adopt a model; the longing to resemble, which ideally generates the form, is an incipient resemblance; the word which we shall make our own is the word whose echo we have heard within ourselves. But the person matters little. Let us merely make the point that, whereas the first morality was the more potent the more distinctly it broke up into impersonal obligation, on the contrary the latter morality, at first dispersed among general precepts to which our intelligence gave its allegiance, but which did not go so far as to set our will in motion, becomes more and more cogent in proportion as the multiplicity and generality of its maxims merge more completely into a man's unity and individuality.

Whence does it derive its strength? What is the principle of action which here takes the place of the natural obligation, or rather which ends by absorbing it? To discover this, let us first see what is tacitly demanded of us. The duties dealt with so far are those imposed on us by social life; they are binding in respect of the city more than in respect of humanity. You might say that the second morality—if we *do* distinguish two—differs from the first in that it is human instead of being merely social. And you would not be entirely wrong. For we have seen that it is not by widening the bounds of the city that you reach humanity; between a social morality and a human morality the difference is not one of degree but of kind. The former is the one of which we are generally thinking when we feel a natural obligation.

Superimposed upon these clearly defined duties we like
to imagine others, the lines of which are perhaps a little
blurred. Loyalty, sacrifice of self, the spirit of renunciation, charity, such are the words we use when we think
of these things. But have we, generally speaking, in mind
at such times anything more than words? Probably not,
and we fully realize this. It is sufficient, we say, that the
formula is there; it will take on its full meaning, the idea
which is to fill it out will become operative, when the
occasion arises. It is true that for many people the occasion will never arise or the action will be put off till
later. With certain people the will does make a feeble
start, but so feeble that the slight shock they feel can in
fact be attributed to no more than the expansion of social duty broadened and weakened into human duty.
But only let these formulae be invested with substance,
and that substance become animate, lo and behold! a
new life is proclaimed; we understand, we feel the advent of a new morality. Consequently, in speaking here
of love of humanity we should doubtless be denoting
this morality. And yet we should not be expressing the
essence of it, for the love of humanity is not a self-sufficient force or one which has a direct efficacy. The
teachers of the young know full well that you cannot
prevail over egoism by recommending "altruism." It
even happens that a generous nature, eager to sacrifice
itself, experiences a sudden chill at the idea that it is
working "for mankind." The object is too vast, the effect
too diffuse. We may therefore conjecture that if a love
of humanity constitutes this morality, it constitutes it in
much the same way as the intention of reaching a certain
point implies the necessity of crossing an intervening
space. In one sense it is the same thing; in another sense
it is something entirely different. If we think only of
the interval and the various points, infinite in number,
which we still have to pass one by one, we shall be discouraged from starting, like Zeno's arrow, and besides

there would be no object, no inducement. But if we step across the intervening space, thinking only of the goal or looking even beyond it, we shall easily accomplish a simple act, and at the same time overcome the infinite multiplicity of which this simplicity is the equivalent. What then, in this case, is the goal, what the direction of the effort? What exactly, in a word, is required of us?

Let us first define the moral attitude of the man we have been considering up to now. He is part and parcel of society; he and it are absorbed together in the same task of individual and social preservation. Both are self-centred. True, it is doubtful whether private interest invariably agrees with public interest: we know against what insurmountable difficulties utilitarian ethics has always come up when it laid down the principle that the individual could seek only his own good, while maintaining that this would lead him to desire the good of others. An intelligent being, pursuing his personal advantage, will often do something quite different from what the general interest demands. Yet, if utilitarian ethics persists in recurring in one form or another, this means that it is not untenable, and if it is tenable the reason is precisely because, beneath the intelligent activity, forced in fact to choose between its own interests and those of others, there lies a substratum of instinctive activity, originally implanted there by nature, where the individual and the social are well-nigh indistinguishable. The cell lives for itself and also for the organism, imparting to it vitality and borrowing vitality from it; it will sacrifice itself to the whole, if need be; and it would doubtless then say, if it were conscious, that it made this sacrifice in its own interest. Such would probably be the state of mind of an ant reflecting on her conduct. She would feel that her activity hinges on something intermediate between the good of the ant and the good of the ant-hill. Now it is just with this fundamental instinct that we have associated obligation as such: it implies at the beginning a state of things in which the individual and society are not distinguishable. This is what enables us to say that the attitude to which it corresponds is that of an individual and a community concentrated on themselves. At once individual and social, the soul here moves round in a circle. It is closed.

The other attitude is that of the open soul. What, in that case, is allowed in? Suppose we say that it embraces all humanity: we should not be going too far, we should hardly be going far enough, since its love may extend to animals, to plants, to all nature. And yet no one of these things which would thus fill it would suffice to define the attitude taken by the soul, for it could, strictly speaking, do without all of them. Its form is not dependent on its content. We have just filled it; we could as easily empty it again. "Charity" would persist in him who possesses "charity," though there be no other living creature on earth.

Once again, it is not by a process of expansion of the self that we can pass from the first state to the second. A psychology which is too purely intellectualist, following the indications of speech, will doubtless define feelings by the things with which they are associated; love for one's family, love for one's country, love of mankind, it will see in these three inclinations one single feeling, growing ever larger, to embrace an increasing number of persons. The fact that these feelings are outwardly expressed by the same attitude or the same sort of motion, that all three *incline* us to something, enables us to group them under the concept "love," and to express them by one and the same word; we then distinguish them by naming three objects, each larger than the other, to which they are supposed to apply. This does in fact suffice to distinguish them. But does it describe them? Or analyse them? At a glance, consciousness perceives between the two first feelings and the third a difference of kind. The first imply a choice, therefore an exclusion; they may act as incentives to strife, they do not exclude hatred. The latter is all love. The former alight directly on an object which attracts them. The latter does not yield to the attraction of its object; it has not aimed at this object; it has shot beyond and reached humanity only by passing through humanity. Has it, strictly speaking, an object? We shall ask this question. But for the present we shall confine ourselves to noting that this psychic attitude, or rather psychic motion, is self-sufficient.

Nevertheless there arises in regard to it a problem which stands ready solved in the case of the other. For that other was ordained by nature; we have just seen how and why we feel bound to adopt it. But the second attitude is acquired; it calls for, has always called for, an effort. How comes it that the men who have set the example have found other men to follow them? And what is the power that is in this case the counterpart of social pressure? We have no choice. Beyond instinct and habit there is no direct action on the will except feeling. The impulse given by feeling can indeed closely resemble obligation. Analyse the passion of love, particularly in its early stages; is pleasure its aim? Could we not as well say it is pain? Perhaps a tragedy lies ahead, a whole life wrecked, wasted, ruined, we know it, we feel it, no matter, we must because we must. Indeed the worst perfidy of a nascent passion is that it counterfeits duty. But we need not go as far as passion. Into the most peaceful emotion there may enter a certain demand for action, which differs from obligation as described above in that it will meet with no resistance, in that it imposes only what has already been acquiesced in, but which none the less resembles obligation in that it does impose something. Nowhere do we see this more clearly than in those cases where the demand ceases to have any practical consequence, thus leaving us the leisure to reflect upon it and analyse what we feel. This is what occurs in musical emotion, for example. We feel, while we listen, as though we could not desire anything else but what the music is suggesting to us, and that that is just as we should naturally and necessarily act did we not refrain from action to listen. Let the music express joy or grief, pity or love, every moment we are what it expresses. Not only ourselves, but many others, nay, all the others, too. When music weeps, all humanity, all nature, weeps with it. In point of fact it does not introduce these feelings into us; it introduces us into them, as passers-by are forced into a street dance. Thus do pioneers in morality proceed. Life holds for them unsuspected tones of feeling like those of some new symphony, and they draw us after them into this music that we may express it in action.

It is through excess of intellectualism that feeling is made to hinge on an object and that all emotion is held to be the reaction of our sensory faculties to an intellectual representation. Taking again the example of music, we all know that it arouses in us well-defined emotions, joy, sorrow, pity, love, that these emotions may be intense and that to us they are complete, though not attached to anything in particular. Are you going to say that we are here in the realm of art and not among real things, that therefore we are playing at emotion, that our feeling is purely imaginative, and that, anyway, the musician could not produce this emotion in us, suggest it without causing it, if we had not already experienced it in real life, where it was caused by an object from which art had merely to detach it? That would be to forget that joy and sorrow, pity and love, are words expressing generalities, words which we must call upon to express what music makes us feel, whereas each new musical work brings with it new feelings, which are created by that music and within that music, are defined and delimited by the lines, unique of their kind, of the melody or symphony. They have therefore not been extracted from life by art; it is we who, in order to express them in words, are driven to compare the feeling created by the artist with the feeling most resembling it in life. But let us then take states of emotion caused in effect by certain things and, as it were, prefigured in them. Those ordained by nature are finite, that is to say limited in number. They are recognizable because they are destined to spur us on to acts answering to needs. The others, on the contrary, are real inventions, comparable to those of the musician, at the origin of which there has always been a man. Thus mountains may, since the beginning of time, have had the faculty of rousing in those who looked upon them certain feelings comparable with sensations, and indeed inseparable from mountains. But Rousseau created in connection with them a new and original emotion. This emotion has become current coin, Rousseau having put it into circulation. And even to-day it is Rousseau who makes us feel it, as much and more than the mountains. True, there are reasons why this emotion, sprung from the heart of Jean-Jacques, should fasten on to mountains rather than any other object; the elementary feelings, akin to sensations, which were directly aroused by mountains must have been able to harmonize with the new emotion. But Rousseau gathered them together, gave them their places, henceforth as mere harmonics in a sound for which he provided, by a true creation, the principal tone. It is the same with love of nature in general. Nature has ever aroused feelings which are almost sensations; people have always enjoyed the pleasant shade, the cool waters, etc., in fine all those things suggested in the word "amoenus" by which the Romans described the charm of the country. But a fresh emotion, surely the creation of some person or persons, has arisen and used these pre-existing notes as harmonics, and produced in this way something to be compared with the fresh tones of a new instrument, what we call in our respective countries the sentiment of nature. The fundamental tone thus introduced might have been different, as is the case in the East, in Japan especially: the *timbre* would then have been different. Feelings akin to sensation, closely bound up with the objects which give rise to them, are indeed just as likely to attract a previously created emotion as they are to connect with an entirely new one. This is what happened with love. From time immemorial woman must have inspired man with an inclination distinct from desire, but in immediate contact, as though welded to it, and pertaining both to feeling and to sensation. But romantic love has a definite date: it sprang up during the Middle Ages on the day when some person or persons conceived the idea of absorbing love into a kind of supernatural feeling, into religious emotion as created by Christianity and launched by the new religion into the world. When critics reproach mysticism with expressing itself in the same terms as passionate love, they forget that it was love which began by plagiarizing mysticism, borrowing from it its fervour, its raptures, its ecstasies: in using the language of a passion it had transfigured, mysticism has only resumed possession of its own. We may add that the nearer love is to adoration, the greater the disproportion between the emotion and the object, the deeper therefore the disappointment to which the lover is exposed—unless he decides that he will ever look at the object through the mist of the emotion and never touch it, that he will, in a word, treat it religiously. Note that the ancients had already spoken of the illusions of love, but these were errors akin to those of the senses, and they concerned the face of the beloved, her figure, her bearing, her character. Think of Lucretius' description: the illusion here applies only to the qualities of the loved one, and not, as with the modern illusion, to what we can expect of love. Between the old illusion and the illusion we have superadded to it there is the same difference as between the primitive feeling, emanating from the object itself, and the religious emotion summoned from without by which it has been pervaded and eventually submerged. The margin left for disappointment is now enormous, for it is the gap between the divine and the human.

That a new emotion is the source of the great creations of art, of science and of civilization in general there seems to be no doubt. Not only because emotion is a stimulus, because it incites the intelligence to undertake ventures and the will to persevere with them. We must go much further. There are emotions which beget thought; and invention, though it belongs to the category of the intellect, may partake of sensibility in its substance. For we must agree upon the meaning of the words "emotion," "feeling" and "sensibility." An emotion is an affective stirring of the soul, but a surface agitation is one thing, an upheaval of the depths another. The effect is in the first case diffused, in the second it remains undivided. In the one it is an oscillation of the parts without any displacement of the whole; in the other the whole is driven forward. Let us, however, get away from metaphors. We must distinguish between two kinds of emotion, two varieties of feeling, two manifestations of sensibility which have this one feature in common, that they are emotional states distinct from sensation, and cannot be reduced, like the latter, to the psychical transposition of a physical stimulus. In the first case the emotion is the consequence of an idea, or of a mental picture; the "feeling" is indeed the result of an intellectual state which owes nothing to it, which is self-sufficient, and which, if it does experience a certain reaction from the feeling, loses more than it gains. It is the stirring of sensibility by a representation, as it were, dropped into it. But the other kind of emotion is not produced by a representation which it follows and from which it remains distinct. Rather is it, in relation to the intellectual states which are to supervene, a cause and not an effect; it is pregnant with representations, not one of which is actually formed, but which it draws or might draw from its own substance by an organic development. The first is infra-intellectual; that is the one with which the psychologist is generally concerned, and it is this we have in mind when we contrast sensibility with intelligence, and when we make of emotions a vague reflection of the representation. But of the other we should be inclined to say that it is supra-intellectual, if the word did not immediately and exclusively evoke the idea of superiority of value: it is just as much a question of priority in time, and of the relation between that which generates and that which is generated. Indeed, the second kind of emotion can alone be productive of ideas.

This is just what the critic overlooks when he qualifies as "feminine," with a touch of contempt, a psychology which accords so extensive and so handsome a place to sensibility. First of all he should be blamed for abiding by the current commonplaces about women, when it is so easy to use one's eyes. I do not intend, for the mere sake of correcting an inappropriate word, to enter upon a comparative study of the two sexes. Suffice it to say that woman is as intelligent as man, but that she is less capable of emotion, and that if there is any faculty or power of the soul which seems to attain less development in woman than in man, it is not intelligence, but sensibility. I mean of course sensibility in the depths, not agitation at the surface.[2] But no matter. When the

[2] We need hardly say that there are many exceptions. Religious fervour, for example, can attain, in women, to undreamt-of depths. But nature has probably ordained, as a general rule, that woman should concentrate on her child and confine within somewhat narrow bounds the best of her sensibility. In this department she is indeed incomparable; here the emotion is supra-intellectual in that it becomes

critic fancies that he would do injustice to man if he related to sensibility the highest faculties of the mind, he is still more to be blamed for not seeing precisely where the difference lies between that intelligence which understands, discusses, accepts or rejects—which in a word limits itself to criticism—and the intelligence which invents.

Creation signifies, above all, emotion, and that not in literature or art alone. We all know the concentration and effort implied in scientific discovery. Genius has been defined as "an infinite capacity for taking pains." True, we think of intelligence as something apart, and, too, as something equally apart a general faculty of attention which, when more or less developed, is supposed to produce a greater or less concentration of intelligence. But how could this indeterminate attention, extraneous to intelligence, bring out of intelligence something which is not there? We cannot help feeling that psychology is once more the dupe of language when, having used the same word to denote all efforts of attention made in all possible cases, and having thus been deceived into assuming them to be all of the same quality, it perceives between them only differences of degree. The truth is that in each case attention takes on a distinctive colouring, as though individualized by the object to which it applies: this is why psychology has already a tendency to use the term "interest" as much as "attention," thus implicitly introducing sensibility, as being capable of more extensive variation according to particular cases. But then this diversity is not sufficiently insisted upon; a general faculty of being interested is posited, which, while always the same faculty, once

divination. How many things rise up in the vision of a mother as she gazes in wonder upon her little one? Illusion perhaps! This is not certain. Let us rather say that reality is big with possibilities, and that the mother sees in the child not only what he will become, but also what he would become, if he were not obliged, at every step in his life, to choose and therefore to exclude.

again affords variety only through a greater or less ap-
lication to its object. So do not let us speak of interest
in general. Let us rather say that the problem which
has aroused interest is a representation duplicated by
an emotion, and that the emotion, being at one and the
same time curiosity, desire and the anticipated joy of
solving a stated problem, is, like the representation,
unique. It is the emotion which drives the intelligence
forward in spite of obstacles. It is the emotion above all
which vivifies, or rather vitalizes, the intellectual elements with which it is destined to unite, constantly col-
lecting everything that can be worked in with them and
finally compelling the enunciation of the problem to
expand into its solution. And what about literature and
art? A work of genius is in most cases the outcome of an
emotion, unique of its kind, which seemed to baffle expression, and yet which *had* to express itself. But is not
this so of all work, however imperfect, into which there
enters some degree of creativeness? Anyone engaged in
writing has been in a position to feel the difference between an intelligence left to itself and that which burns
with the fire of an original and unique emotion, born
of the identification of the author with his subject, that
is to say of intuition. In the first case the mind cold-
hammers the materials, combining together ideas long
since cast into words and which society supplies in a
solid form. In the second, it would seem that the solid
materials supplied by intelligence first melt and mix,
then solidify again into fresh ideas now shaped by the
creative mind itself. If these ideas find words already
existing which can express them, for each of them this
seems a piece of unexpected good luck; and, in truth,
it has often been necessary to assist fortune, and strain
the meaning of a word, to mould it to the thought. In
that event the effort is painful and the result problem-
atical. But it is in such a case only that the mind feels
itself, or believes itself, to be creative. It no longer starts

from a multiplicity of ready-made elements to arrive at a composite unity made up of a new arrangement of the old. It has been transported at a bound to something which seems both one and unique, and which will contrive later to express itself, more or less satisfactorily, in concepts both multiple and common, previously provided by language.

To sum up, alongside of the emotion which is a result of the representation and which is added to it, there is the emotion which precedes the image, which virtually contains it, and is to a certain extent its cause. A play may be scarcely a work of literature and yet it may rack our nerves and cause an emotion of the first kind, intense, no doubt, but commonplace, culled from those we experience in the course of daily life, and in any case devoid of mental content. But the emotion excited within us by a great dramatic work is of quite a distinct character. Unique of its kind, it has sprung up in the soul of the poet and there alone, before stirring our own; from this emotion the work has sprung, to this emotion the author was continually harking back throughout the composition of the work. It was no more than a creative exigency, but it was a specific one, now satisfied once the work is finished, which would not have been satisfied by some other work unless that other had possessed an inward and profound resemblance with the former, such as that which exists between two equally satisfactory renderings, in terms of ideas or images, of one and the same melody.

Which amounts to saying that, in attributing to emotion a large share in the genesis of the moral disposition, we are not by any means enunciating a "moral philosophy of sentiment." For we are dealing with an emotion capable of crystallising into representations and even into an ethical doctrine. From this particular doctrine we could never have elicited the moral disposition any more than from any other; no amount of speculation

will create an obligation or anything like it: the theory
may be all very fine, I shall always be able to say that I
will not accept it; and even if I do accept it, I shall claim
to be free and do as I please. But if the atmosphere of
the emotion is there, if I have breathed it in, if it has
entered my being, I shall act in accordance with it, up-
lifted by it; not from constraint or necessity, but by virtue of an inclination which I should not want to resist.
And instead of explaining my act by emotion itself, I
might in this case just as well deduce it from the theory
built up by the transposition of that emotion into ideas.
We here get a glimpse of the possible reply to a weighty
question which we have just touched on incidentally
and with which we shall be confronted later. People are
fond of saying that if a religion brings us a new morality, it imposes that morality by means of the metaphysics
which it disposes us to accept, by its ideas on God, the
universe, the relation of the one to the other. To which
the answer has been made that it is, on the contrary, by
the superiority of its morality that a religion wins over
souls and reveals to them a certain conception of things.
But would intelligence recognize the superiority of the
proposed morality, since it can appreciate differences
of value only by comparing them with a rule or an ideal,
and this ideal and this rule are perforce supplied by the
morality which is already in occupation? On the other
hand, how could a new conception of the universal order of things be anything but yet another philosophy to
set alongside of those we know? Even if our intelligence
is won over, we shall never see in it anything but an explanation, theoretically preferable to the others. Even if
it seems to enjoin on us, as more in harmony with itself,
certain rules of conduct, there will be a wide gap
between this assent of the intellect and a conversion of
the will. But the truth is that the doctrine cannot, as a
purely intellectual representation, ensure the adoption
and, above all, the practice of the corresponding moral-

ity, any more than the particular morality, considered by intelligence as a system of rules of conduct, can render the doctrine intellectually preferable. Antecedent to the new morality, and also the new metaphysics, there is the emotion, which develops as an impetus in the realm of the will, and as an explicative representation in that of intelligence. Take, for example, the emotion introduced by Christianity under the name of charity: if it wins over souls, a certain behaviour ensues and a certain doctrine is disseminated. But neither has its metaphysics enforced the moral practice, nor the moral practice induced a disposition to its metaphysics. Metaphysics and morality express here the self-same thing, one in terms of intelligence, the other in terms of will; and the two expressions of the thing are accepted together, as soon as the thing is there to be expressed.

That a substantial half of our morality includes duties whose obligatory character is to be explained fundamentally by the pressure of society on the individual will be readily granted, because these duties are a matter of current practice, because they have a clear precise formula, and it is therefore easy for us, by grasping them where they are entirely visible, and then going down to the roots, to discover the social requirements from which they sprang. But that the rest of morality expresses a certain emotional state, that actually we yield not to a pressure but to an attraction, many people will hesitate to acknowledge. The reason is that here we cannot, generally speaking, get back to the original emotion in the depths of our hearts. There exist formulae which are the residue of this emotion, and which have settled in what we may call the social conscience according as, within that emotion, a new conception of life took form —or rather a certain attitude towards life. Precisely because we find ourselves in the presence of the ashes of an extinct emotion, and because the driving power of that emotion came from the fire within it, the formulae which have remained would generally be incapable of rousing our will, if older formulae, expressing the fundamental requirements of social life, did not by contagious influence communicate to them something of their own obligatory character. These two moralities, placed side by side, appear now to be only one, the first having lent to the second something of its imperative character and having, on the other hand, received from it in exchange a connotation less strictly social, more broadly human. But let us stir the ashes, we shall find some of them still warm, and at length the sparks will kindle into flame; the fire may blaze up again; and, if it does, it will gradually spread. I mean that the maxims of the second morality do not work singly, like those of the first: as soon as one of them, ceasing to be abstract, becomes filled with significance and acquires the capacity to act, the others tend to do the same: at last they will fuse in the warm emotion which left them behind long ago, and in the men, now come to life again, who experienced it. Founders and reformers of religions, mystics and saints, obscure heroes of moral life whom we have met on our way and who are in our eyes the equals of the greatest, they are all there: inspired by their example, we follow them, as if we were joining an army of conquerors. They are indeed conquerors: they have broken down natural resistance and raised humanity to a new destiny. Thus, when we dispel appearances to get at reality, when we set aside the common form assumed, thanks to mutual exchanges, by the two moralities in conceptual thought and in speech, then, at the two extremes of the single morality we find pressure and aspiration: the former the more perfect as it becomes more impersonal, closer to those natural forces which we call habit or even instinct, the latter the more powerful according as it is more obviously aroused in us by definite persons, and the more it apparently triumphs over nature. True, if we went down to the roots of nature itself we should perhaps find that the same force which manifests itself directly, rotating on its own axis, in the human species once constituted, also acts later and indirectly, through the medium of privileged persons, in order to drive humanity forward.

But there is no need to resort to metaphysics to determine the relation between this pressure and this aspiration. Once again, there is some difficulty in comparing the two moralities because they are no longer to be found in a pure state. The first has handed on to the second something of its compulsive force; the second has diffused over the other something of its perfume. We find ourselves in the presence of a series of steps up or down, according as we range through the dictates of morality from one extreme or from the other; as to the two extreme limits, they have chiefly a theoretical interest; it is not often that they are actually attained. Let us, nevertheless, consider separately, in themselves, pressure and aspiration. Immanent in the former is the representation of a society which aims only at self-preservation; the circular movement in which it carries round with it individuals, as it revolves on the same spot, is a vague imitation, through the medium of habit, of the immobility of instinct. The feeling which would characterize the consciousness of these pure obligations, assuming they were all fulfilled, would be a state of individual and social well-being similar to that which accompanies the normal working of life. It would resemble pleasure rather than joy. The morality of aspiration, on the contrary, implicitly contains the feeling of progress. The emotion of which we were speaking is the enthusiasm of a forward movement, enthusiasm by means of which this morality has won over a few and has then, through them, spread over the world. "Progress" and "advance," moreover, are in this case indistinguishable from the enthusiasm itself. To become conscious of them it is not necessary that we should picture a goal that we are trying to reach or a perfection to which we are approximating. It is enough that the joy of enthusiasm involves something more than the pleasure of well-being: the pleasure not implying the joy, while the joy does imply and encompass the pleasure. We feel this to be so, and the certainty thus obtained, far from hinging on a metaphysical theory, is what will provide it with its firmest support.

But antecedent to this metaphysical theory, and far nearer to what we have directly experienced, are the simpler representations which in this case spring from the emotion in proportion as we dwell on it. We were speaking of the founders and reformers of religion, the mystics and the saints. Let us hearken to their language; it merely expresses in representations the emotions peculiar to a soul opening out, breaking with nature, which enclosed it both within itself and within the city.

They begin by saying that what they experience is a feeling of liberation. Well-being, pleasures, riches, all those things that mean so much to the common run of men, leave them indifferent. In breaking away from them they feel relief, and then exhilaration. Not that nature was wrong in attaching us by strong ties to the life she had ordained for us. But we must go further, and the amenities which are real comforts at home would become hindrances, burdensome impedimenta, if we had to take them on our travels. That a soul thus equipped for action would be more drawn to sympathize with other souls, and even with the whole of nature, might surprise us, if the relative immobility of the soul, revolving in a circle in an enclosed society, was not due precisely to the fact that nature has split humanity into a variety of individuals by the very act which constituted the human species. Like all acts creative of a species, this was a halt on the road. By a resumption of the forward movement, the decision to halt is broken. True, to obtain a complete effect, the privileged soul would have to carry the rest of humanity with it. But if a few follow, and if the others imagine they would do likewise on occasion, this already means a great deal; henceforth, with the beginning of accomplishment, there will be the hope that the circle may be broken in the end. In any case, we cannot repeat too often that it is not by preaching the love of our neighbour that we can obtain it. It is not by expanding our narrower feelings that we can embrace humanity. However much our intelligence may convince itself that this is the line of advance, things behave differently. What is simple for our understanding is not necessarily so for our will. In cases where logic affirms that a certain road should be the shortest, experience intervenes, and finds that in that direction there is no road. The truth is that heroism may be the only way to love. Now, heroism cannot be preached, it has only to show itself, and its mere presence may stir others to action. For heroism itself is a return to movement, and emanates from an emotion—infectious like all emotions—akin to the creative act. Religion expresses this truth in its own way by saying that it is in God that we love all other men. And all great mystics declare that they have the impression of a current passing from their soul to God, and flowing back again from God to mankind.

Let no one speak of material obstacles to a soul thus freed! It will not answer that we can get round the obstacle, or that we can break it; it will declare that there is no obstacle. We cannot even say of this moral conviction that it moves mountains, for it sees no mountains to move. So long as you argue about the obstacle, it will stay where it is; and so long as you look at it, you will divide it into parts which will have to be overcome one by one; there may be no limit to their number; perhaps you will never exhaust them. But you can do away with the whole, at a stroke, if you deny its existence. That is what the philosopher did who proved movement by walking: his act was the negation pure and simple of the effort, perpetually to be renewed, and therefore fruitless, which Zeno judged indispensable to cover, one by one, the stages of the intervening space. By going deeply into this new aspect of morality, we should find an impression of coincidence, real or imaginary, with the generative effort of life. If seen from outside, the activity of life lends itself, in each of its works, to an analysis which might be carried on indefinitely; there is no end to a description of the structure of an eye such as ours. But what we call a series of means employed is, in reality, but a number of obstacles overcome; the action of nature is simple, and the infinite complexity of the mechanism which it seems to have built up piece by piece to achieve the power of vision is but the endless network of opposing forces which have cancelled one another out to secure an uninterrupted channel for the functioning of the faculty. So, if we took into account only what we saw, the simple act of an invisible hand plunged into iron filings would seem like an inexhaustible interplay of actions and reactions among the filings themselves in order that they might effect an equilibrium. If such is the contrast between the real working of life and the aspect it presents to the senses and the intelligence which analyse it, is it surprising that a soul which no more recognizes any material obstacle should feel itself, rightly or wrongly, at one with the principle of life?

Whatever heterogeneity we may at first find between the effect and the cause, and though the distance is great from a rule of conduct to a power of nature, it has always been from the contact with the generative principle of the human species that a man has felt he drew the strength to love mankind. By this I mean, of course, a love which absorbs and kindles the whole soul. But a more lukewarm love, faint and fleeting, can only be a radiation of the former, if not a still paler and colder image of it, left behind in the mind or deposited in speech. Thus, morality comprises two different parts, one of which follows from the original structure of human society, while the other finds its explanation in the principle which explains this structure. In the former, obligation stands for the pressure exerted by the elements of society on one another in order to maintain the shape of the whole; a pressure whose effect is prefigured in each of us by a system of habits which, so to speak, go to meet it: this mechanism, of which each separate part is a habit, but whose whole is comparable to an instinct, has been prepared by nature. In the second, there is still obligation, if you will, but that obligation is the force of an aspiration or an impetus, of the very impetus which culminated in the human species, in social life, in a system of habits which bears a resemblance more or less to instinct: the primitive impetus here comes into play directly, and no longer through the medium of the mechanisms it had set up, and at which it had provisionally halted. In short, to sum up what has gone before, we should say that nature, setting down the human species along the line of evolution, intended it to be sociable, in the same way as it did the communities of ants and bees; but since intelligence was there, the maintenance of social life had to be entrusted to an all but intelligent mechanism: intelligent in that each piece could be remodelled by human intelligence, yet instinctive in that man could not, without ceasing to be a man, reject all the pieces together and cease to accept a mechanism of preservation. Instinct gave place temporarily to a system of habits, each one of which became contingent, their convergence towards the preservation of society being alone necessary, and this necessity bringing back instinct with it. The necessity of the whole, felt behind the contingency of the parts, is what we call moral obligation in general—it being understood that the parts are contingent in the eyes of society only; to the individual, into whom society inculcates its habits, the part is as necessary as the whole. Now the mechanism designed by nature was simple, like the societies originally constituted by her. Did she foresee the immense development and the endless complexities of societies such as ours? Let us first agree as to the meaning of this question. We do not assert that nature has, strictly speaking, designed or foreseen anything whatever. But we have the right to proceed like a biologist, who speaks of nature's intentions every time he assigns a function to an organ: he merely expresses thus the adequateness of the organ to the function. In spite of humanity's having become civilized, in spite of the transformation of society, we maintain that the tendencies which are, as it were, organic in social life have remained what they were in the beginning. We can trace them back and study them. The result of this investigation is clear; it is for closed, simple societies that the moral structure, original and fundamental in man, is made. I grant that the organic tendencies do not stand out clearly to our consciousness. They constitute, nevertheless, the strongest element of obligation. However complex our morality has grown and though it has become coupled with tendencies which are not mere modifications of natural tendencies, and whose trend is not in the direction of nature, it is to these natural tendencies that we come in the end, when we want to obtain a precipitate of the pure obligation contained in this fluid mass. Such then is the first half of morality. The other had no place in nature's plan. We mean that nature foresaw a certain expansion of social life through intelligence, but it was to be a limited expansion. She could not have intended that this should go on so far as to endanger the original structure. Numerous indeed are the instances where man has thus outwitted nature, so knowing and wise, yet so simple-minded. Nature surely intended that men should beget men endlessly, according to the rule followed by all other living creatures; she took the most minute precautions to ensure the preservation of the species by the multiplication of individuals; hence she had not foreseen, when bestowing on us intelligence, that intelligence would at once find a way of divorcing the sexual act from its consequences, and that man might refrain from reaping without forgoing the pleasure of sowing. It is in quite another sense that man outwits nature when he extends social solidarity into the brotherhood of man; but he is deceiving her nevertheless, for those societies whose design was prefigured in the original structure of the human soul, and of which we can still perceive the plan in the innate and fundamental tendencies of modern man, required that the group be closely united, but that between group and group there should be virtual hostility; we were always to be prepared for attack or defence. Not, of course, that nature designed war for war's sake. Those leaders of humanity drawing men after them, who have broken down the gates of the city, seem indeed thereby to have placed themselves again in the current of the vital impetus. But this impetus inherent in life is, like life, finite. Its path is strewn with obstacles, and the species which have appeared, one after the other, are so many combinations of this force with opposing forces: the former urging us forward, the others making us turn in a circle. Man, fresh from the hands of nature, was a being both intelligent and social, his sociability being devised to find its scope in small communities, his intelligence being designed to further individual and group life. But intelligence, expanding through its own efforts, has developed unexpectedly. It has freed men from restrictions to which they were condemned by the limitations of their nature. This being so, it was not impossible that some of them, specially gifted, should reopen that which was closed and do, at least for themselves, what nature could not possibly have done for mankind. Their example has ended in leading others forward, in imagination at least. There is a genius of the will as there is a genius of the mind, and genius defies all anticipation. Through those geniuses of the will, the impetus of life, traversing matter, wrests from it, for the future of the species, promises such as were out of the question when the species was being constituted. Hence in passing from social solidarity to the brotherhood of man, we break with one particular nature, but not with all nature. It might be said, by slightly distorting the terms of Spinoza, that it is to get back to *natura naturans* that we break away from *natura naturata*.

Hence, between the first morality and the second, lies the whole distance between repose and movement. The first is supposed to be immutable. If it changes, it immediately forgets that it has changed, or it acknowledges no change. The shape it assumes at any given time claims to be the final shape. But the second is a forward thrust, a demand for movement; it is the very essence of mobility. Thus would it prove, thus alone, indeed, would it be able at first to define, its superiority. Postulate the first, you cannot bring the second out of it, any more than you can from one or several positions of a moveable body derive motion. But, on the contrary, movement includes immobility, each position traversed by the moving object being conceived and even perceived as a virtual stop. But a detailed demonstration is unnecessary: the superiority is experienced before ever it is represented, and furthermore could not be demonstrated afterwards if it had not first been felt. There is a difference of vital tone. Those who regularly put into practice the morality of the city know this feeling of well-being, common to the individual and to society, which is the outward sign of the interplay of material resistances neutralizing each other. But the soul that is opening, and before whose eyes material objects vanish, is lost in sheer joy. Pleasure and well-being are something, joy is more. For it is not contained in these, whereas they are virtually contained in joy. They mean, indeed, a halt or a marking time, while joy is a step forward.

That is why the first morality is comparatively easy to formulate, but not the second. For our intelligence and our language deal in fact with things; they are less at home in representing transitions or progress. The morality of the Gospels is essentially that of the open soul: are we not justified in pointing out that it borders upon paradox, and even upon contradiction, in its more definite admonitions? If riches are an evil, should we not be injuring the poor in giving them what we possess? If he who has been smitten on the one cheek is to offer the other also, what becomes of justice, without which, after all, there can be no "charity"? But the paradox disappears, the contradiction vanishes, if we consider the intent of these maxims, which is to create a certain disposition of the soul. It is not for the sake of the poor, but for his own sake, that the rich man should give up his riches: blessed are the poor "in spirit"! The beauty lies, not in being deprived, not even in depriving oneself, but in not feeling the deprivation. The act by which the soul opens out broadens and raises to pure spirituality a morality enclosed and materialized in ready-made rules: the latter then becomes, in comparison with the other, something like a snapshot view of movement. Such is the inner meaning of the antitheses that occur one after the other in the Sermon on the Mount: "Ye have heard that it was said . . . I say unto you . . ." On the one hand the closed, on the other the open. Current morality is not abolished; but it appears like a virtual stop in the course of actual progression. The old method is not given up; but it is fitted into a more general method, as is the case when the dynamic reabsorbs the static, the latter then becoming a mere particular instance of the former. We should need then, strictly

speaking, a means of expressing directly the movement
and the tendency; but if we still want—and we cannot
avoid it—to translate them into the language of the
static and the motionless, we shall be confronted with
formulae that border on contradiction. So we might
compare what is impracticable in certain precepts of the
Gospels to what was illogical in the first explanations of
the differential calculus. Indeed, between the morality
of the ancients and Christianity we should find much
the same relation as that between the mathematics of
antiquity and our own.

The geometry of the ancients may have provided particular solutions which were, so to say, an anticipated
application of our general methods; but it never brought
out these methods; the impetus was not there which
would have made them spring from the static to the
dynamic. But at any rate it carried as far as possible the
imitation of the dynamic by the static. Now, we have
just the same impression when we compare, for example,
the doctrine of the Stoics with Christian morality. The
Stoics proclaimed themselves citizens of the world, and
added that all men were brothers, having come from the
same God. The words were almost the same; but they
did not find the same echo, because they were not
spoken with the same accent. The Stoics provided some
very fine examples. If they did not succeed in drawing
humanity after them, it is because Stoicism is essentially
a philosophy. The philosopher who is so enamoured of
this noble doctrine as to become wrapped up in it doubtless vitalizes it by translating it into practice; just so did
Pygmalion's love breathe life into the statue once it was
carven. But it is a far cry from that to the enthusiasm
which spreads from soul to soul, unceasingly, like a con-
flagration. Such an emotion may indeed develop into
ideas which make up a doctrine, or even several different
doctrines having no other resemblance between them
than a kinship of the spirit; but it precedes the idea in-

stead of following it. To find something of the kind in classical antiquity, we must go not to the Stoics, but rather to the man who inspired all the great philosophers of Greece without contributing any system, without having written anything, Socrates. Socrates indeed exalts the exercise of reason, and particularly the logical function of the mind, above everything else. The irony he parades is meant to dispose of opinions which have not undergone the test of reflection, to put them to shame, so to speak, by setting them in contradiction with themselves. Dialogue, as he understands it, has given birth to the Platonic dialectics and consequently to the philosophical method, essentially rational, which we still practise. The object of such a dialogue is to arrive at concepts that may be circumscribed by definitions; these concepts will become the Platonic Ideas; and the theory of Ideas, in its turn, will serve as a model for the systems, also essentially rational, of traditional metaphysics. Socrates goes further still; virtue itself he holds to be a science, he identifies the practice of good with our knowledge of it; he thus paves the way for the doctrine which will absorb all moral life in the rational function of thought. Reason has never been set so high. At least that is what strikes us at first. But let us look closer. Socrates teaches because the oracle of Delphi has spoken. He has received a mission. He is poor, and poor he must remain. He must mix with the common folk, he must become one of them, his speech must get back to their speech. He will write nothing, so that his thought shall be communicated, a living thing, to minds who shall convey it to other minds. He is indifferent to cold and hunger, though in no way an ascetic; he is merely delivered from material needs, and emancipated from his body. A "daemon" accompanies him, which makes its voice heard when a warning is necessary. He so thoroughly believes in this "daemonic voice" that he dies rather than not follow it; if he refuses to defend himself before the popular tribunal, if he goes to meet his condemnation, it is because the "daemon" has said nothing to dissuade him. In a word, his mission is of a religious and mystic order, in the present-day meaning of the words; his teaching, so perfectly rational, hinges on something that seems to transcend pure reason. But do we not detect this in his teaching itself? If the inspired, or at all events lyrical sayings, which occur throughout the dialogues of Plato, were not those of Socrates, but those of Plato himself, if the master's language had always been such as Xenophon attributes to him, could we understand the enthusiasm which fired his disciples, and which has come down the ages? Stoics, Epicureans, Cynics, all the Greek moralists spring from Socrates—not only, as has always been said, because they develop the teaching of the Master in its various directions, but also, and, above all, because they borrow from him the attitude which is so little in keeping with the Greek spirit and which he created, the attitude of the Sage. Whenever the philosopher, closeted with his wisdom, stands apart from the common rule of mankind—be it to teach them, to serve as a model, or simply to go about his work of perfecting his inner self—Socrates is there, Socrates alive, working through the incomparable prestige of his person. Let us go further. It has been said that he brought philosophy down from heaven to earth. But could we understand his life, and above all his death, if the conception of the soul which Plato attributes to him in the Phaedo had not been his? More generally speaking, do the myths we find in the dialogues of Plato, touching the soul, its origin, its entrance into the body, do anything more than set down in Platonic terms a creative emotion, the emotion present in the moral teaching of Socrates? The myths, and the Socratic conception of the soul to which they stand in the same relationship as the explanatory programme to a symphony, have been preserved along with the Platonic dialectics. They pursue their subterranean way through Greek metaphysics, and rise to the open air again with the Alexandrine philosophers, with Ammonius perhaps, in any case with Plotinus, who claims to be the successor of Socrates. They have provided the Socratic soul with a body of doctrine similar to that into which was to be breathed the spirit of the Gospels. The two metaphysics, in spite, perhaps because, of their resemblance, gave battle to each other, before the one absorbed the best that was in the other; for a while the world may well have wondered whether it was to become Christian or Neo-Platonic. It was Socrates against Jesus. To confine ourselves to Socrates, the question is: what would this very practical genius have done in another society and in other circumstances; if he had not been struck, above all, by the danger of the moral empiricism of his time, and the mental anarchy of Athenian democracy; if he had not had to deal with the most crying need first, by establishing the rights of reason; if he had not therefore thrust intuition and inspiration into the background, and if the Greek he was had not mastered in him the Oriental who sought to come into being? We have made the distinction between the closed and the open: would anyone place Socrates among the closed souls? There was irony running through Socratic teaching, and outbursts of lyricism were probably rare; but in the measure in which these outbursts cleared the road for a new spirit, they have been decisive for the future of humanity.

Between the closed soul and the open soul there is the soul in process of opening. Between the immobility of a man seated and the motion of the same man running there is the act of getting up, the attitude he assumes when he rises. In a word, between the static and the dynamic there is to be observed, in morality too, a transition stage. This intermediate state would pass unnoticed if, when at rest, we could develop the necessary impetus to spring straight into action. But it attracts our attention when we stop short—the usual sign of insufficient impetus. Let us put the same thing in a different way. We have seen that the purely static morality might be called infra-intellectual, and the purely dynamic, supra-intellectual. Nature intended the one, and the other is a contribution of man's genius. The former is characteristic of a whole group of habits which are, in man, the counterpart of certain instincts in animals; it is something less than intelligence. The latter is inspiration, intuition, emotion, susceptible of analysis into ideas which furnish intellectual notations of it and branch out into infinite detail; thus, like a unity which encompasses and transcends a plurality incapable of ever equalling it, it contains any amount of intellectuality; it is more than intelligence. Between the two lies intelligence itself. It is at this point that the human soul would have settled down, had it sprung forward from the one without reaching the other. It would have dominated the morality of the closed soul; it would not have attained to, or rather it would have not have created, that of the open soul. Its attitude, the result of getting up, would have lifted it to the plane of intellectuality. Compared with the position it had just left—described negatively—such a soul would be manifesting indifference or insensibility, it would be in the "ataraxy" or the "apathy" of the Epicureans and the Stoics. Considered in what it positively is, if its detachment from the old sought to be an attachment to something new, its life would be contemplation; it would conform to the Platonic and the Aristotelian ideal. From whatever angle we look at it, its attitude would be upright, noble, truly worthy of admiration and reserved for the chosen few. Philosophies which start from very different principles may find in it a common goal. The reason is that there is only one road leading from action confined in a circle to action developing in the freedom of space, from repetition to creation, from the infra-intellectual to the supra-intellectual. Anyone halting between the two is inevitably in the zone of pure contemplation, and in any case, no longer holding to the one but without having yet reached the other, naturally practises that half-virtue, detachment.

We are speaking of pure intelligence, withdrawing into itself and judging that the object of life is what the ancients called "science" or contemplation. We are speaking, in a word, of what mainly characterizes the morality of the Greek philosophers. But it would no longer be a matter of Greek or Oriental philosophy, we should be dealing with the morality of everybody if we considered intelligence as a mere elaboration or co-ordinating agent of the material, some of it infra-intellectual and some of it supra-intellectual, with which we have been dealing in this chapter. In order to define the very essence of duty, we have in fact distinguished the two forces that act upon us, impulsion on the one hand, and attraction on the other. This had to be done, and it is because philosophy had left it undone, confining itself to the intellectuality which to-day covers both, that it has scarcely succeeded, so it would seem, in explaining how a moral motive can have a hold upon the souls of men. But our description was thereby condemned, as we hinted, to remain a mere outline. That which is aspiration tends to materialize by assuming the form of strict obligation. That which is strict obligation tends to expand and to broaden out by absorbing aspiration. Pressure and aspiration agree to meet for this purpose in that region of the mind where concepts are formed. The result is mental pictures, many of them of a compound nature, being a blend of that which is a cause of pressure and that which is an object of aspiration. But the result is also that we lose sight of pure pressure and pure aspiration actually at work on our wills; we see only the concept into which have been melted the two distinct objects to which pressure and aspiration were respectively attached. The force acting upon us is taken to be this concept: a fallacy which accounts for the failure of strictly intellectualist systems of morality, in other words, of the majority of the philosophical theories of duty. Not, of course, that an idea pure and simple is without influence on our will. But this influence would operate effectively only if it could remain in isolation. It has difficulty in resisting hostile influences, or, if it does triumph over them, it is because the pressure and the aspiration, which had each renounced its own right of action to be represented together in one idea, have reappeared in their individuality and their independence and have exerted their full strength.

We should have to open a very long parenthesis indeed if we had to give their due share to the two forces, the one social, the other supra-social, one of impulsion, the other of attraction, which impart to each moral motive its driving force. An honest man will say, for example, that he acts from self-respect, from a feeling of the dignity of man. Obviously he would not express himself thus, if he did not begin by splitting himself into two selves, the personality he would be if he simply let himself drift, and the one to which his will uplifts him; the ego that respects is not the same as the ego respected. What, then, is the latter? Wherein lies its dignity? Whence comes the respect it inspires? Let us leave aside the task of analysing this respect, in which we should find above all an impulse of self-effacement, the attitude of the apprentice towards the master, or rather, to use the language of Aristotle, of the accident in the presence of the essence. There would remain to be defined the higher ego to which the average personality defers. There is no doubt that it is in the first place the "social ego" within each of us, on which we have already touched. If we posit, simply for the sake of theoretical clearness, a "primitive" mentality, we shall see in it self-

respect coinciding with the feeling of so firm a solidarity
between the individual and the group that the group
remains present in the isolated individual, keeps an eye
on him, encourages or threatens him, demands, in a
word, to be consulted and obeyed; behind society itself
there are supernatural powers on which the group depends, and which make the community responsible for
the acts of the individual; the pressure of the social ego
is exerted with all these accumulated forces. The individual, moreover, does not obey merely from a habit of
discipline or from fear of punishment; the group to
which he belongs must, of course, exalt itself above the
others, if only to rouse his courage in battle, and the
consciousness of this superiority of strength secures for
him greater strength, together with all the satisfactions
that pride can give. If you want to make sure of this, take
a state of mind already more fully "evolved." Think of
all the pride, as well as all the moral energy which is
represented by *civis Romanus sum*: self-respect, in the
Roman citizen, must have been tantamount to what we
call nationalism to-day. But we need not turn to history
or pre-history to see self-respect coinciding with a group-
pride. We need only observe what goes on under our
very eyes in the small societies which form within the
big one, when men are drawn together by a distinguish-
ing badge which emphasizes a real or apparent superiority, separating them from the common herd. To the
self-respect which every man, as a man, professes is then
coupled an additional respect, that of the ego which is
no more than man for an ego that stands out among
men. All the members of the group behave as a group,
and thus a common code of behaviour comes to be observed, a feeling of honour springs up which is identical
with *esprit de corps*. These are the first components of
self-respect. Looked at from this angle, a point of view
which we to-day can isolate only by an effort of abstraction, it "binds" us by the prestige of the social pressure

it brings with it. Now indeed the impulsion would obviously become attraction, if self-respect were the respect
for a person admired and venerated, whose image we
bore in our hearts and with whom we would aspire to
become identified, as the copy to an original. In reality
it is not so, for even if the word merely evokes the idea
of an attitude towards one's self, nevertheless self-respect
is, at the end of its evolution as at the beginning, a
social feeling. But the great moral figures that have
made their mark on history join hands across the centuries, above our human cities; they unite into a divine
city which they bid us enter. We may not hear their
voices distinctly, the call has none the less gone forth,
and something answers from the depth of our soul; from
the real society in which we live we betake ourselves in
thought to this ideal society; to this ideal society we bow
down when we reverence the dignity of man within us,
when we declare that we act from self-respect. It is true
that the influence exerted on us by definite persons
tends to become impersonal. And the impersonal character is still more stressed when a philosopher explains
to us that it is reason, present in each of us, which constitutes the dignity of man. But here we must take care
to know what we mean. That reason is the distinguish-
ing mark of man no one will deny. That it is a thing of
superior value, in the sense in which a fine work of art
is indeed valuable, will also be granted. But we must
explain how it is that its orders are absolute and why
they are obeyed. Reason can only put forward reasons,
which we are apparently always at liberty to counter with
other reasons. Let us not then merely assert that reason,
present in each of us, compels our respect and commands our obedience by virtue of its paramount value.
We must add that there are, behind reason, the men
who have made mankind divine, and who have thus
stamped a divine character on reason, which is the essential attribute of man. It is these men who draw us

towards an ideal society, while we yield to the pressure of the real one.

All moral ideas interpenetrate each other, but none is more instructive than that of justice, in the first place, because it includes most of the others, and next, because it is expressed, in spite of its extraordinary richness, in simpler formulae; lastly and above all, because here the two forms of obligation are seen to dovetail into each other. Justice has always evoked ideas of equality, of proportion, of compensation. *Pensare*, from which we derive "compensation" and "recompense," means *to weigh*. Justice is represented as holding the scales. Equity signifies equality. Rules and regulation, right and righteousness, are words which suggest a straight line. These references to arithmetic and geometry are characteristic of justice throughout its history. The idea must have already taken shape as far back as the days of exchange and barter; however rudimentary a community may be, it barters, and it cannot barter without first finding out if the objects exchanged are really equal in value, that is to say, both exchangeable for a definite third object. Let this equality of value be set up as a rule, this rule be given a place among the customs of the group, the "totality of obligation," as we called it, adding its weight to the rule: here we have justice already, in a clearly defined shape, with its imperative character, and the ideas of equality and reciprocity involved.—But such justice will apply not only to the exchange of objects. It will extend gradually to intercourse between persons, though unable, for a long time to come, to shake off all idea of objects and exchanges. It will then consist mainly in the regulation of natural impulses by the introduction of the idea of a no less natural reciprocity, for example, the expectation of an injury equivalent to the injury done. In primitive societies, assaults on persons concern the community only exceptionally, when the act is likely to injure the community itself by bringing down upon it the wrath of the gods. The injured party or his family has only therefore to obey his instinct, react naturally, and avenge himself; and the reprisals might be out of all proportion to the offence, if this requital of evil for evil was not, to all appearances, vaguely subject to the general law of exchanges and barter. It is true that the quarrel might go on for ever, the "vendetta" might be kept up indefinitely by the two families, if one of them did not make up its mind to accept "damages" in cash; here the idea of compensation, already implied in the idea of exchange and barter, will clearly emerge. Now let the community itself undertake to exact punishment, to repress all acts of violence whatsoever, and it will be said that the community is dispensing justice, if the rule to which individuals and families referred for a settlement of their dispues were already being described by that term. Moreover, the community will assess the penalty according to the gravity of the offence, since otherwise there would be no object in stopping, once we have begun to do wrong; we should not run any greater risk by proceeding to extremities. An eye for an eye, a tooth for a tooth, the injury received must always be equivalent to the injury inflicted.—But is the price of an eye always an eye, the price of a tooth always a tooth? Quality must be borne in mind as well as quantity. The law of retaliation is applied only within a class; the same injury sustained, the same offence received, will call for greater compensation, or heavier punishment, if the victim belong to a higher class. In a word, equality may connote a ratio and become a proportion. Hence, though justice may embrace a greater and greater variety of things, it is always defined in the same way.—Nor will its formula alter when, in a more civilized state, it extends to the relations between the rulers and the ruled, and in a more general way to those between different social categories; into a state of things which only exists *de facto* it will introduce considerations of equality or proportion which

will make of that state something mathematically defined, and, thereby, it would seem, apparently *de jure*.
There is indeed no doubt that force lies at the origin of
the division of ancient societies into classes subordinate
to one another. But a subordination that is habitual ends
by seeming natural, and by seeking for itself an explanation; if the inferior class has accepted its position for a
considerable time, it may go on doing so when it has
virtually become the stronger, because it will attribute to
the governing class a superior value. And this superiority will be real, if the members of this class have taken
advantage of the facilities they may have had for intellectual and moral improvement; but it may quite as well
be a mere carefully-fostered appearance of superiority.
However it may be, whether real or apparent, this superiority needs only to persist in order to seem a matter of
birth; since hereditary privilege is there, there must be,
people say to one another, some innate superiority. Nature, who intended ordered societies, has predisposed
man to this illusion. Plato shared it in his Ideal Republic.
If a class system is understood in this way, responsibilities
and privileges are looked upon as a common stock, to be
eventually distributed among the individuals according
to their worth, consequently according to the services
they render. Justice here still holds her scales, measuring
and proportioning.—Now, from this justice, which,
though it may not express itself in utilitarian terms, is
none the less faithful to its mercantile origins, how shall
we pass to the justice which implies neither exchange
made nor service rendered, being the assertion pure and
simple of the inviolability of right and of the incommen-
surability of the person with any values whatever? Before
answering this question, let us pause to admire the magic
property of speech, I mean the power which a word
bestows on a newly created idea—when it extends to
that idea after having been applied to a pre-existent object—of modifying that object and thus retroactively in-

fluencing the past. In whatever light we view the transition from relative to absolute justice, whether it took place by stages or all at once, there has been creation. Something has supervened which might never have existed, which would not have existed except for certain circumstances, certain men, perhaps one particular man. But instead of realizing that some new thing has come and taken possession of the old and absorbed it into a whole that was up to then unforeseeable, we prefer looking upon the process as if the new thing had always been there, not actually but virtually pre-existing, and as if the old had been a part of it even then, a part of something yet uncreated; and on this showing the conceptions of justice which followed one another in ancient societies were no more than partial, incomplete visions of an integral justice which is nothing more or less than justice as we know it to-day. There is no need to analyse in detail this particular example of a very general illusion, barely noticed by philosophers, which has vitiated a goodly number of metaphysical doctrines and which sets the theory of knowledge insoluble problems. Let us simply say that it is part of our habit of considering all forward movement as a progressive shortening of the distance between the starting-point (which indeed exists) and the goal, which comes into being as a stopping-place only when the moving object has chosen to stop there. It does not follow that, because it can always be interpreted in this sense when it has attained its end, the movement consisted in a progression towards this end: an interval which has still but one extremity cannot diminish little by little, since it is not yet an interval: it *will have diminished* little by little when the moving object has created, by its actual or virtual stopping, a second extremity, and when we consider it in retrospect or even simply trace the movement in its progress while, in anticipation, reconstituting it in that way, backwards. But this is just what we do not realize for the most part;

we introduce into the things themselves, under the guise of the pre-existence of the possible in the real, this retrospective anticipation. This illusion lies at the root of many a philosophical problem; Zeno's Dichotomy has provided the typical example. And it is this same illusion which we find in ethics when the continually expanding forms of relative justice are defined as growing approximations of absolute justice. The most we are entitled to say is that once the latter is stated, the former might be regarded as so many halts along a road which, plotted out retrospectively by us, would lead to absolute justice. And even then we should have to add that there had been, not gradual progress, but at a certain epoch a sudden leap.—It would be interesting to determine the exact point at which this *saltus* took place. And it would be no less instructive to find out how it was that, once conceived (in a vague form), absolute justice long remained no more than a respected ideal, without there being any question of translating it into practice. Let us simply say, in so far as the first point is concerned, that the long-standing inequalities of class, doubtless imposed in the beginning by force, and accepted afterwards as inequalities of merit and services rendered, become more and more exposed to the criticism of the lower classes; the ruling elements *are*, moreover, deteriorating, because, being too sure of themselves, they are guilty of a slackening of that inner tension upon which they had called for a greater effort of intelligence and will, and which had consolidated their supremacy. They could indeed maintain their position if they held together; but because of their very tendency to assert their individuality, there will one day arise ambitious men from among them who mean to get the upper hand and who will seek support in the lower class, especially if the latter already has some share in affairs: on that day is shattered the belief in a native superiority of the upper class; the spell is broken. Thus do aristocracies tend to merge into democracy, simply because political inequality is an unstable thing, as, indeed, political equality, once it is established, will be, if it is only *de facto*, if therefore it admits of exceptions, if, for example, it tolerates slavery within the city.—But it is a far cry from such examples of equilibrium, arrived at mechanically and always transitory, like that of the scales held by the justice of yore, to a justice such as ours, the justice of the "rights of man," which no longer evokes ideas of relativity and proportion, but, on the contrary, of the incommensurable and the absolute. Of this justice we could form a complete idea only if we were to "draw it out to infinity," as the mathematicians say; it is formulated precisely and categorically, at any stated time, only by prohibitions; but on its positive side it proceeds by successive creations, each of them being a fuller realization than the last of personality and consequently of humanity. Such realization is possible only through the medium of laws; it implies the assent of society. It would, moreover, be futile to maintain that it takes place gradually and automatically, as a consequence of the state of mind of society at a given period of its history. It is a leap forward, which can take place only if society has decided to try the experiment; and the experiment will not be tried unless society has allowed itself to be won over, or at least stirred. Now the first start has always been given by someone. It is no use maintaining that this leap forward does not imply a creative effort behind it, and that we have not to do here with an invention comparable with that of the artist. That would be to forget that most great reforms appeared at first sight impracticable, as in fact they were. They could be carried out only in a society whose state of mind was already such as their realization was bound to bring about; and you had a circle from which there would have been no escape, if one or several privileged beings, having expanded the social ego within themselves, had not broken the circle and drawn the society after them. Now this is exactly what occurs in the miracle of artistic creation. A work of genius which is at first disconcerting may create, little by little, by the simple fact of its presence, a conception of art and an artistic atmosphere which bring it within our comprehension; it will then become in retrospect a work of genius; otherwise it would have remained what it was at the beginning, merely disconcerting. In a financial speculation, it is the success that causes the idea to have been a good one. Something much the same occurs in artistic creation, with this difference, that the success, if the work which at first repelled us eventually wins through, is due to a transformation of public taste brought about by the work itself, the latter being then force as well as matter; it has set up an impetus imparted to it by the artist, or rather one which is the very impetus of the artist, invisible and present within the work. The same can be said of moral invention, and more particularly of the creations which more and more enrich, one after the other, the idea of justice. They bear, above all, upon the substance of justice, but they modify its form as well.—To take the latter first, let us lay down that justice has always appeared as obligatory, but that for a long time it was an obligation like other obligations. It met, like the others, a social need; and it was the pressure of society on the individual which made justice obligatory. This being so, an injustice was neither more nor less shocking than any other breach of the rules. There was no justice for slaves, save perhaps a relative, almost an optional, justice. Public safety was not merely the supreme law, as indeed it has remained, it was furthermore proclaimed as such; whereas today we should not dare to lay down the principle that it justifies injustice, even if we accept any particular consequence of that principle. Let us dwell on this point, put to ourselves the famous question: "What should we do if we heard that for the common good, for the very existence of mankind, there was somewhere a man, an innocent man, condemned to suffer eternal torment?" Well, we should perhaps agree to it on the understanding that some magic philtre is going to make us forget it, that we shall never hear anything more about it; but if we were bound to know it, to think of it, to realize that this man's hideous torture was the price of our existence, that it was even the fundamental condition of existence in general, no! a thousand times no! Better to accept that nothing should exist at all! Better let our planet be blown to pieces. Now what has happened? How has justice emerged from social life, within which it had always dwelt with no particular privilege, and soared above it, categorical and transcendent? Let us recall the tone and accents of the Prophets of Israel. It is their voice we hear when a great injustice has been done and condoned. From the depths of the centuries they raise their protest. True, justice has singularly expanded since their time. The justice they preached applied above all to Israel, their indignation against injustice was the very wrath of Jehovah against His disobedient people, or against the enemies of this chosen people. If any of them, like Isaiah, may have thought of universal justice, it was because Israel, the chosen of God among the other peoples, bound to God by a covenant, was so high above the rest of mankind that sooner or later it was destined to be taken as a model. None the less, they imparted to justice the violently imperative character which it has kept, which it has since stamped on a substance grown infinitely more extensive.—But these extensions did not occur spontaneously either. On each one of them a competent historian could put a proper name. Each development was a creation, and indeed the door will ever stand open to fresh creations. The progress which was decisive for the substance of justice, as the era of the prophets had been for its form, consisted in the substitution of a universal republic, embracing all men, for that republic which went no further than the gates of the city, and, within the city, was limited to free men. It is from this that all the rest has followed, for, if the door has remained open to new creations, and probably will for all time stand open, yet it must have been opened. There seems to be no doubt that this second advance, the passage from the closed to the open, is due to Christianity, as the first was due to the Prophets of Judaism. Could it have been brought about by mere philosophy? There is nothing more instructive than to see how the philosophers have skirted round it, touched it, and yet missed it. Let us leave out Plato, who certainly includes the Idea of man among the transcendent Ideas: did it not follow that all men were of the same essence? From this to the idea that all men, *qua* men, were of equal worth and that the common essence conferred on them the same fundamental rights, was but one step. But the step was not taken. It would have meant condemning slavery, giving up the Greek idea that foreigners, being barbarians, could claim no rights. Was it, in fact, an essentially Greek idea? We find it, implied in others, wherever Christianity has not penetrated, in modern as well as in ancient times. In China, for example, there have arisen very noble doctrines, but they have not been concerned with laying down laws for humanity; though they do not expressly say so, they are in fact interested only in the Chinese community. Indeed, before Christianity, we find Stoicism and, among the Stoics, philosophers who proclaim that all men are brothers, and that the wise man is a citizen of the world. But these dicta were the expression of an ideal, an ideal merely conceived, and very likely conceived as impracticable. There is nothing to show that any of the great Stoics, not even the Stoic who was an emperor, considered the possibility of lowering the barrier between the free man and the slave, between the Roman citizen and the barbarian. Humanity had to wait till Christianity for the idea of universal brotherhood, with its implication of equality of rights and the sanctity of the person, to become operative. Some may say that it has been rather a slow process; indeed eighteen centuries elapsed before the rights of man were proclaimed by the Puritans of America, soon followed by the men of the French Revolution. It began, nevertheless, with the teachings of the Gospels, and was destined to go on indefinitely; it is one thing for an idea to be merely propounded by sages worthy of admiration, it is very different when the idea is broadcast to the ends of the earth in a message overflowing with love, invoking love in return. Indeed there was no question here of clear-cut wisdom, reducible, from beginning to end, into maxims. There was rather a pointing of the way, a suggestion of the means; at most an indication of the goal, which would only be temporary, demanding a constant renewal of effort. Such effort was bound to be, in certain individuals at least, an effort of creation. The method consisted in supposing possible what is actually impossible in a given society, in imagining what would be its effect on the soul of society, and then inducing some such psychic condition by propaganda and example: the effect, once obtained, would retrospectively complete its cause; new feelings, evanescent indeed, would call forth the new legislation seemingly indispensable to their appearance, and which would then serve to consolidate them. The modern idea of justice has progressed in this way by a series of individual creations which have succeeded through multifarious efforts animated by one and the same impulse. —Classical antiquity had known nothing of propaganda; its justice had the unruffled serenity of the gods upon Olympus. Spiritual expansion, missionary zeal, impetus, movement, all these are of Judaic-Christian origin.

But because men went on using the same word, they too readily thought they were dealing with the same thing. We cannot too often repeat that successive creations, individual and contingent, will be generally grouped under the same heading, classified under the same idea and labelled by the same name, if each one has given rise to the one that follows it and if they appear, in retrospect, as continuations of one another. Let us go further. The name will not apply only to the terms already existing of the series thus obtained. Encroaching on the future, it will denote the whole series, and it will be placed at the end, nay, be drawn out to infinity; as the designation was created long ago, we shall imagine the idea which it represents as having been also created just as long ago, and indeed existing since the beginning of time, though still open to additions and of undetermined content; thus each advance is imagined to be so much gained over an entity conceived as pre-existing; reality is looked upon as eating its way into the ideal, incorporating into itself, bit by bit, the totality of eternal justice.—Now that is true not only of the idea of justice but also of the ideas which are cognate with it—equality and liberty, for example. We are fond of defining the progress of justice as a forward movement towards liberty and equality. The definition is unimpeachable, but what are we to derive from it? It applies to the past; it can seldom guide our choice for the future. Take liberty, for instance. It is commonly said that the individual is entitled to any liberty that does not infringe the liberty of others. But the granting of a new liberty, which might lead to an encroachment of all the different liberties on one another in present-day society, might produce the opposite effect in a society where feeling and custom had been modified by that very reform. So that it is often impossible to state *a priori* the exact degree of liberty which can be allotted to the individual

without injury to the liberty of his fellow-men; change
the quantity, and the quality is no longer the same. On
the other hand, equality can hardly be obtained, save
at the expense of liberty, so that we should first ask ourselves which of the two is preferable to the other. But
the question admits of no general answer; for the
sacrifice of this or that liberty, if it is fully agreed
upon by the citizens as a whole, partakes still of liberty;
and above all, the liberty which is left may be superior
in quality if the reform, tending towards greater
equality, has led to a society where men breathe more
freely, where greater joy is found in action. Look at it
how you will, you must always come back to the conception of moral creators who see in their mind's eye
a new social atmosphere, an environment in which
life would be more worth living, I mean a society such
that, if men once tried it, they would refuse to go back
to the old state of things. Thus only is moral progress to be defined; but it is only in retrospect that it
can be defined, when some exceptional moral nature
has created a new feeling, like a new kind of music,
and passed it on to mankind, stamping it with his
own vitality. Think in this way of "liberty," of "equality," of "the sanctity of the individual," and you will
see that you have here no mere difference of degree,
but a radical difference of nature between the two
ideas of justice which we have distinguished, the one
closed, the other open. For relatively stable justice,
closed justice, which expresses the automatic equilibrium of a society fresh from the hands of nature, manifests itself in customs to which the totality of obligation
is attached, and this totality of obligation ends by incorporating, as public opinion progressively accepts
them, the decrees of the other justice, the justice which
is open to successive creations. Thus the two sub-
stances, the one supplied by society, the other a product
of man's genius, come to be cast in the same mould.

Indeed, in practice, they may well be indistinguishable. But the philosopher must discriminate the one from the other; if not, he is sure to misunderstand the nature of social evolution as well as the origin of duty. Social evolution is not the evolution of a society which has developed according to a method destined to transform it later. Between the development and the transformation there is here neither analogy nor common measure. Because closed justice and open justice are incorporated in equally peremptory laws, expressing themselves in the same way, and outwardly similar, it does not follow that they must be explained in the same fashion. No example can bring out better than this the twofold origin of morality and the two elements of obligation.

There can be no question that, in the present state of things, reason must appear the sole imperative; that it is to the interest of humanity to attribute an intrinsic force, an authority of their own to moral concepts; in a word that moral activity in a civilized society is essentially rational. How else could we tell what to do in each particular case? There are deep underlying forces here, one of impulsion, the other of attraction; we cannot refer directly to them each time we have to make a decision. To do so would, in most cases, simply amount to doing needlessly over again something which society, on the one hand, and the highest representatives of humanity on the other, have done for us. Their work has resulted in certain rules being laid down and an ideal being set up as a pattern: to live morally will mean to follow these rules, to conform to this ideal. In this way alone can we be sure of remaining in complete accord with ourselves: the rational alone is self-consistent. Only in this way can we compare various lines of conduct with one another; only in this way can we estimate their moral value. The thing is so obvious that we have barely hinted at it, we have nearly always taken it for granted. But the result was that our statement remained a mere diagram and might well appear inadequate. Indeed, on the intellectual plane, all the precepts of morality interpenetrate one another in concepts of which each one, like Leibnitz's monad, is more or less representative of all the others. Above or below this plane, we find forces which, taken singly, correspond only to a part of what has been projected on the intellectual plane. Since this drawback to the method we have adopted is undeniable, and indeed inevitable, since we perceive that we must use this method and since we feel that it cannot fail to raise objections throughout its application, we think it important, in conclusion, to dwell on it once more, define it yet again, even if we are once more obliged to repeat at certain points, and almost in the same terms, what we have already had occasion to say.

A human society with its members linked together like the cells of an organism, or, what amounts almost to the same thing, like ants in an ant-hill, has never existed, but the groupings of primitive humanity were certainly nearer the ants than ours are to-day. Nature, in making man a social animal, intended that this solidarity should be very close, while relaxing it sufficiently to enable the individual to display, in the interests of society itself, the intelligence with which she had provided him. We went no further than this contention in the first part of our argument. It would be of slight importance for any moral philosophy that accepted without question the belief in the heredity of acquired characteristics. Man might in that case be born to-day with very different tendencies from those of his remotest ancestors. But we rely upon experience, which teaches that the hereditary transmission of a contracted habit, assuming that it ever happens, is an exceptional and not a regular or frequent occurrence, sufficient in the long run to bring about a far-reaching alteration in the nature of man. However radical the difference may be between primitive man and civilized man, it is due almost solely to what the child has amassed since the first awakening of its consciousness; all the acquisitions of humanity during centuries of civilization are there, at his elbow, deposited in the knowledge imparted to him, in the traditions, the institutions, the customs, the syntax and vocabulary of the language he learns to speak, and even in the gestures of the people about him. It is this thick humus which covers to-day the bedrock of original nature. It may indeed represent the slowly accumulated effects of an infinite variety of causes; it has, nevertheless, had to follow the general configuration of the soil on which it is deposited. In short, the obligation we find in the depths of our consciousness and which, as the etymology of the word implies, binds us to the other members of society, is a link of the same nature as that which unites the ants in the ant-hill or the cells of an organism; it would take this form in the eyes of an ant, were she to become endowed with man's intelligence, or of an organic cell, were it to become as independent in its movements as an intelligent ant. I refer here of course to obligation taken in this simple form, devoid of matter: it is the irreducible, the ever-present element, even now, in our nature. It goes without saying that the matter wrought into this form becomes more and more intellectual and self-consistent as civilization progresses, and new matter accrues incessantly, not inevitably at the direct bidding of this form, but under the logical pressure of the intellectual matter already introduced into it. And we have seen also how a certain kind of matter which is intended to be run into a different mould, whose introduction is not due, even indirectly, to the need for social preservation, but to an aspiration of individual consciousness, adopts this form by settling down, like the rest of morality, on the intellectual plane. But every time we come back to the strictly imperative element in obligation, and even supposing we found in it everything intelligence had put there to enrich it, everything with which reason has hedged it round to justify it, we find ourselves once again confronted by this fundamental framework. So much for pure obligation.

Now, a mystic society, embracing all humanity and moving, animated by a common will, towards the continually renewed creation of a more complete humanity, is no more possible of realization in the future than was the existence in the past of human societies functioning automatically and similar to animal societies. Pure aspiration is an ideal limit, just like obligation unadorned. It is none the less true that it is the mystic souls who draw and will continue to draw civilized societies in their wake. The remembrance of what they have been, of what they have done, is enshrined in the memory of humanity. Each one of us can revive it, especially if he brings it in touch with the image, which abides ever living within him, of a particular person who shared in that mystic state and radiated around him some of its light. If we do not evoke this or that sublime figure, we know that we *can* do so; he thus exerts on us a virtual attraction. Even if we ignore individuals, there remains the general formula of morality accepted to-day by civilized humanity: this formula includes two things, a system of *orders* dictated by *impersonal* social requirements, and a series of *appeals* made to the conscience of each of us by *persons* who represent the best there is in humanity. The obligation relating to the orders is, in its original and fundamental elements, sub-rational. The potency of the appeal lies in the strength of the emotion it has aroused in times gone by, which it arouses still, or can arouse: this emotion, if only because it can indefinitely be resolved into ideas, is more than idea; it is supra-rational. The two forces, working in different regions of the soul, are projected on to the intermediary plane, which is that of intelligence. They will henceforth be represented by their projections. These intermingle and interpenetrate. The result is a transposition of orders and appeals into terms of pure reason. Justice thus finds itself continually broadened by pity; "charity" assumes more and more the shape of justice; the elements of morality become homogeneous, comparable, and almost commensurable with one another; moral problems are clearly enunciated and methodically solved. Humanity is asked to place itself at a certain level, higher than that of animal society, where obligation would be but the force of instinct, but not so high as an assembly of gods, where everything would partake of the creative impetus. Considering then the manifestations of moral life thus organized, we shall find them perfectly self-consistent, capable therefore of being referred to first principles. Moral life will be rational life.

Everybody will agree on this point. But because we have established the rational character of moral conduct, it does not follow that morality has its origin or even its foundation in pure reason. The important question is to find out why we are "obliged" in cases where following our inclination by no means suffices to ensure that our duty is done.

That in that case it is reason speaking, I am willing to admit; but, if it spoke only in its own name, if it did anything more than rationally express the action of certain forces which dwell behind it, how could it struggle against passion and self-interest? The philosopher who considers that reason is self-sufficient and claims to demonstrate this, succeeds in his demonstration only if he tacitly reintroduces these forces; in fact they have crept back themselves, unbeknown to him, surreptitiously. Just examine the demonstration. It takes two forms, according as it assumes reason to be void or grants it a content of matter, according as it sees in moral obligation the necessity, pure and simple, of remaining logically in agreement with itself, or an invitation logically to pursue a certain end. Let us take these two forms in turn. When Kant tells us that a deposit of money must be handed back because, if the recipient appropriated it, it would no longer be a deposit, he is obviously juggling with words. Either by "deposit" he means the material fact of placing a sum of money in the hands (say) of a friend, with an intimation that it will be called for later. But this material fact alone, with this intimation alone, would have no other effect than that of impelling the holder to give back the sum if he has no need of it, or simply to appropriate it if he is short of money; both proceedings are equally consistent, equally logical, so long as the word deposit evokes only a material image unaccompanied by moral conceptions. Or else moral considerations are involved, there is the idea that the deposit has been "entrusted" and that a trust "must not" be betrayed; the idea that the holder has pledged himself, that he has "given his word;" the idea that, even if he has said nothing, he is bound by a tacit "contract;" the idea that there exists a "right of property," etc. Then indeed it would be self-contradictory to accept a deposit and refuse to give it back; the deposit would no longer be a deposit; the philosopher might say that the breach of morality in this case pertains to the irrational. But it would be because the word "deposit" was taken in the sense that it has in a human group possessing fully developed moral ideas, conventions and obligations; the moral obligation would no longer pertain to the bare and empty necessity of not contradicting oneself, since the contradiction in this case would simply consist in rejecting, after having accepted it, a moral obligation which for this very reason was already there. But enough of these quibbles. It is quite natural that we should meet with a pretension to found morality on a respect for logic among philosophers and scholars, who are accustomed to bow to logic in speculative matters, and are thus inclined to believe that in all matters, and for the whole of humanity, logic must be accepted as the sovereign authority. But because science must respect the logic of things and logic in general if it wants to succeed in its researches, because such is the interest of the scientist as a scientist, it is not to be concluded that we are obliged always to conform to logic in our conduct, as though such were the interest of man in general, or even the interest of the scientist as man. Our admiration for the speculative function of the mind may be great; but when philosophers maintain that it should be sufficient to silence selfishness and passion, they prove to us—and this is a matter for congratulation —that they have never heard the voice of the one or the other very loud within themselves. So much for a morality claiming as its basis reason in the guise of pure form, without matter.—Before considering the morality which adds matter to this form, we must note that people often get no further than the first when they think they have reached the second. That is the case with those philosophers who explain moral obligation by the fact that the idea of the Good forces itself upon us. If they take this idea from organized society, where human actions are already classified according as they are more or less appropriate for maintaining social cohesion and furthering the progress of humanity, and, above all, where certain clearly defined forces produce this cohesion and bring about this progress, they can doubtless say that an activity is more moral, the more it conforms to the Good; and they might also add that the Good is conceived as claiming obedience. But this is because the Good would be merely the heading under which men agree to classify the actions which present one or the other feature and to which they feel themselves prompted by the forces of impulsion and attraction which we have defined. The notion of a graduated scale of these various lines of conduct, and therefore of their respective values, and, on the other hand, the all but inevitable necessity which forces them upon us, must then have existed before the idea of Good, which appeared later simply to provide a label or name; this idea, left to itself, would have lent no assistance to their classification, and still less to their enforcement. But if, on the contrary, it is maintained that the idea of the Good is at the source of all obligation and all aspiration, and that it should also serve to evaluate human actions, we must be told by what sign we shall recognize that a given line of conduct is in conformity with it; we must therefore be furnished with a definition of the Good; and we fail to see how it can be defined without assuming a hierarchy of creatures, or at the very least, of actions, of varying elevation: but if the hierarchy exists by itself, there is no need to call upon the idea of the Good to establish it; besides, we do not see why this hierarchy ought to be maintained, why we should be bound to respect it; you can invoke in its favour only aesthetic reasons, allege that a certain line of conduct is "finer" than another, that it sets us more or less high up in the ranks of living beings: but what could you reply to the man who declared that he places his own interest before all other considerations? Looking more closely, one would see that this morality has never been self-sufficient. It has simply been added on, as an artistic make-weight, to obligations which existed before it, and rendered it possible. When Greek philosophers attributed a pre-eminent dignity to the pure idea of Good, and, more generally, to a life of contemplation, they were speaking for a chosen few, a small group formed within society, which would begin by taking social life for granted. It has been said that this morality was silent about duty and knew nothing of obligation as we understand it. True, it was silent about

it; but that was precisely because it assumed obligation
to be self-evident. The philosopher was supposed to have
begun by doing his duty like anybody else, as demanded
of him by the city. Only then did a morality supervene,
destined to make his life more beautiful by treating it as
a work of art. In a word, and to sum up the discussion,
there can be no question of founding morality on the
cult of reason.—It remains to be seen, as we have said,
whether it could be founded on reason in so far as reason might supply our activity with a definite object, in
conformity with reason, but supplementary to it, an object towards which reason would teach us to strive
systematically. But it is easy to see that no objective—
not even the twofold one we have indicated, not even
the dual preoccupation of maintaining social cohesion
and of furthering the progress of humanity—will impose
itself peremptorily as a mere rational proposition. If certain really active forces, actually influencing our will,
are already in possession, reason could and should intervene to co-ordinate their effects, but it could not contend with them, since one can always reason with reason,
confront its arguments with others, or simply refuse all
discussion and reply by a *"sic volo, sic jubeo."* In truth,
a system of ethics which imagines it is founding obligation on purely rational considerations, unwittingly reintroduces, as we have pointed out already and as we shall
point out again, forces of a different order. That is exactly why it succeeds so easily. Real obligation is already
there, and whatever reason impresses upon it assumes
naturally an obligatory character. Society, with all that
holds it together and drives it forward, is already there,
and that is why reason can adopt as a principle of morality one or the other of the ends towards which social
man is striving; by building up a thoroughly consistent
system of means destined to attain this end, reason will
more or less rediscover morality, such as common sense
conceives it, such as humanity in general practises, or

claims to practise it. For each of these objectives, culled
by reason from society, has been socialized and, by that
very fact, impregnated with all the other aims to be
found there. Thus, even if we set up personal interest
as the moral principle, we shall find no great difficulty
in building up a rational morality sufficiently resembling
current morality, as is proved by the relative success of
utilitarian ethics. Selfishness, indeed, for the man living
among his fellow-men, comprises legitimate pride, the
craving for praise, etc., with the result that purely personal interest has become impossible to define, so large
is the element of public interest it contains, so hard is it
to keep them separate. Think of the amount of deference for others included in what we call self-love, and
even in jealousy and envy! Anyone wanting to practise
absolute egoism would have to shut himself up within
himself, and not care enough for his neighbour to be
jealous or envious of him. There is a touch of sympathy
in these forms of hate, and the very vices of a man living
among his fellows are not without certain implications
of virtue; all are saturated with vanity, and vanity means
sociability. Still easier will it be, then, to draw all moral
maxims, or nearly all, from feelings such as honour, or
sympathy, or pity. Each of these tendencies, in a man
living in society, is laden with all that social morality has
deposited in it; and we should have to unload it first, at
the risk of reducing it to very little indeed, if we wished
to avoid begging the question in using it to explain morality. The ease with which theories of this kind are built
up should make us suspicious: if the most varied aims
can thus be transmuted by philosophers into moral aims,
we may surmise, seeing that they have not yet found
the philosopher's stone, that they had started by putting
gold in the bottom of their crucible. Similarly it is obvious that none of these doctrines will account for obligation. For we may be obliged to adopt certain means
in order to attain such and such ends; but if we choose

to renounce the end, how can the means be forced upon us? And yet, by adopting any one of these ends as the principle of morality, philosophers have evolved from it whole systems of maxims, which, without going so far as to assume an imperative form, come near enough to it to afford satisfaction. The reason is quite simple. They have considered the pursuit of these ends, we repeat, in a society in which there are peremptory pressures, together with aspirations to match them and also to extend them. Pressure and attraction, specifying their objectives, would lead to any one of these systems of maxims, since each of them aims at the attainment of an end both individual and social. Each of these systems then already exists in the social atmosphere when the philosopher arrives on the scene; it comprises maxims which are near enough in substance to those which the philosopher will formulate, the former being obligatory. Rediscovered by philosophy, but no longer in the form of a command since they are now mere suggestions for the intelligent pursuit of an end, such as intelligence might easily repudiate, they are snapped up by the vaguer or perhaps merely virtual maxims which resemble them, but which are laden with obligation. They thus become obligatory, but the obligation has not come *down*, as might be imagined, from above, that is to say, from a principle from which the maxims have been rationally deduced; it has come *up* from below, I mean from that substratum of pressure, capable of being extended into aspiration, which is the basis of society. In a word, the moral theorists take society for granted and consequently also the two forces to which society owes its stability and its mobility. Taking advantage of the fact that all social ends interpenetrate one another, and that each of them, resting as it were on that stability and mobility, seems to be invested with these two forces, they have no difficulty in reconstituting the content of morals with one or other of the ends assumed as a principle, and then showing that such morality is obligatory. For, by taking society for granted, they have also taken for granted the matter of this morality and its form, all it contains and all the obligation with which it is clothed.

If we now delve down beneath that illusion which is common to all theoretical moral systems, this is what we should find. Obligation is a necessity with which one can argue, and which is therefore companioned by intelligence and liberty. This necessity is, in fact, similar to that which accompanies the production of a physiological or even a physical effect; in a humanity which nature had made devoid of intelligence, where the individual had no power to choose, the action destined to maintain the preservation and cohesion of the group would be accomplished inevitably; it would be accomplished under the influence of a definite force, the same that makes each ant toil for the ant-hill and each cell in the tissue work for the organism. But intelligence intervenes with its faculty of choice; this is a new force which maintains the other in a state of virtuality, or rather in a state of reality barely discernible in its action, yet perceptible in its pressure: just as the swinging to and fro of the pendulum in a clock, while it prevents the tension of the spring from manifesting itself by a sudden unwinding, is yet a consequence of this tension, being an effect which exerts an inhibitive or regulating action on its causes. What then will intelligence do? It is a faculty used naturally by the individual to meet the difficulties of life; it will not follow the direction of a force which, on the contrary, is working for the species, and which, if it considers the individual at all, does so in the interest of the species. It will make straight for selfish decisions. But this will be only its first impulse. It cannot avoid reckoning with the force of which it feels the invisible pressure. It will therefore persuade itself into thinking that an intelligent egoism must allow all other egoisms their share. And if the intelligence is that of a philosopher, it will build up a theory of ethics in which the interpenetration of personal and general interests will be demonstrated, and where obligation will be brought back to the necessity, realized and felt, of thinking of others, if we wish intelligently to do good to ourselves. But we can answer that it does not suit us to see our interests in this light, and it is therefore not obvious why we should still feel obliged. Yet we *are* obliged, and intelligence is well aware of it, since this is the very reason why it attempted the demonstration. But the truth is that its demonstration seems successful only because it clears the way for something it does not mention, and which is the essential: a necessity that pertains to experience and feeling, one which some argument has thrust into the background and which an opposing argument reinstates. What is therefore, strictly speaking, obligatory in obligation does not come from intelligence. The latter only supplies the element of hesitation in obligation. When it appears to be the basis of obligation, it is merely sustaining it in its resistance to a resistance, in the operation of inhibiting itself from inhibiting. And we shall see in the next chapter what helpers it enlists. For the present, let us revert to a comparison we have found useful. An ant, accomplishing her heavy task as if she never thought of herself, as if she lived only for the ant-hill, is very likely in a somnambulistic state; she is yielding to an irresistible necessity. Imagine her suddenly becoming intelligent. She would reason about what she had done, wonder why she had done it, would say it was very foolish not to take things easy and have a good time. "I have had enough of sacrifice, now is the time for a little self-indulgence." And behold the natural order completely upset. But nature is on the watch. She provided the ant with the social instinct; she has just added to it, perhaps in response to a transitory need of instinct, a gleam of intelligence.

However slightly intelligence has thrown instinct out of
gear, it must incontinently set things to rights and undo
what it has done. An act of reasoning will therefore
prove that it is all to the interest of the ant to work for
the ant-hill, and in this way the obligation will apparently find a basis. But the truth is that such a basis would
be very unsafe, and that obligation already existed in
all its force; intelligence has merely hindered its own
hindrance. Our ant-hill philosopher would be none the
less disinclined to admit this; he would doubtless persist
in attributing a positive and not a negative activity to
intelligence. And that is just what most moral philosophers have done, either because they were intellectuals
and afraid of not according enough importance to intelligence, or rather because obligation appeared to them
as an indivisible entity, defying analysis; on the contrary,
if we see in it something approximate to a compulsion
which may be thwarted by a resistance, we realize that
the resistance has come from intelligence, the resistance
to the resistance likewise, and that the compulsion,
which is the essential, has a different origin. In truth,
no philosopher can avoid initially postulating this compulsion; but very often he postulates it implicitly, and
not in words. We have postulated it and said so. We
connect it, moreover, with a principle that it is impossible not to admit. For, to whatever school of philosophy you belong, you are bound to recognize that man
is a living creature, that the evolution of life along its
two main lines has been accomplished in the direction
of social life, that association is the most general form
of living activity, since life is organization, and that, this
being so, we pass by imperceptible transitions from the
relation between cells in an organism to the relation
between individuals in society. We therefore confine
ourselves to noting what is uncontroverted and incon-
trovertible. But, this being admitted, any theorising on
obligation becomes unnecessary as well as futile: unnec-

essary because obligation is a necessity of life; ineffectual because the hypothesis presented can, at the utmost, afford justification in the eyes of intelligence, and very incomplete justification at that, for an obligation anterior to this intellectual reconstruction.

Now, life might have stopped at this point and done nothing more than create closed societies, whose members were bound together by strict obligations. Composed of intelligent beings, these societies would have presented variations not to be found in animal societies, which are governed by instinct; but the variations would not have gone so far as to encourage the dream of a root and branch transformation; society would not have become modified to the extent that a single society, embracing all mankind, could seem possible. In fact, this society does not yet, and perhaps never will, exist; in according to man the requisite moral conformation for living in groups, nature probably did all she could for the species. But, just as there have been men of genius to thrust back the bounds of intelligence, and, thus, far more has been granted to individuals, at certain intervals, than it was possible to grant all at once to the species, so exceptional souls have appeared who sensed their kinship with the soul of Everyman, who thus, instead of remaining within the limits of the group and going no further than the solidarity laid down by nature, were borne on a great surge of love towards humanity in general. The appearance of each one of them was like the creation of a new species, composed of one single individual, the vital impulse culminating at long intervals in one particular man, a result which could not have been obtained at one stroke by humanity as a whole. Each of these souls marked then a certain point attained by the evolution of life; and each of them was a manifestation, in an original form, of a love which seems to be the very essence of the creative effort. The creative emotion which exalted these exceptional souls,

and which was an overflowing of vitality, has spread far
and wide about them; enthusiasts themselves, they radiated enthusiasm which has never been completely
quenched, and which can be readily fanned into flame
again. To-day, when in imagination we call to life these
great moral leaders, when we listen to their words and
see them at work, we feel that they communicate to us
something of their fervour, and draw us in their wake;
this is no longer a more or less attenuated compulsion, it
is a more or less irresistible attraction. But neither does
this second force, any more than the first, call for an
explanation. For you cannot reject these two data: a
compulsion, or something like it, exerted by habits
which correspond, in man, to what you call instinct in
animals, and, beside this, a certain stirring up of the
soul, which you call emotion; in the one case you have
primal obligation, in the other, something which becomes an extension of it; but in both cases you are confronted by forces which are not strictly and exclusively
moral, and whose origin, therefore, it is no special duty
of the moralist to trace. Because they have nevertheless
insisted on doing so, philosophers have misunderstood
the compound nature of obligation in its present-day
form: they have been led to attribute to this or that
mental picture or operation the power of influencing
the will: as if an idea could ever categorically demand
its own realization! as if the idea were anything else, in
this case, than an intellectual extract common to all, or,
better still, the projection on to the intellectual plane of
a whole set of tendencies and aspirations, some above,
some beneath, pure intelligence! Reinstate the duality
of origin, and the difficulties vanish. Nay, the duality
itself merges into a unity, for "social pressure" and "impetus of love" are but two complementary manifestations of life, normally intent on preserving generally the
social form which was characteristic of the human species from the beginning, but, exceptionally, capable of

transfiguring it, thanks to individuals who each represent, as the appearance of a new species would have represented, an effort of creative evolution.

All teachers have not perhaps a full perception of this double origin of morality, but they perceive something of it as soon as they try to inculcate morality into their pupils instead of merely talking about it. We do not deny the utility, the necessity even, of a moral instruction which appeals to reason alone, defining duties and connecting them with a principle of which it follows out in detail the various applications. It is on the plane of intelligence, and on that plane alone, that discussion is possible, and there is no complete morality without reflexion, analysis and argument with others as well as with oneself. But if instruction directed to the intelligence be indispensable to give confidence and delicacy to the moral sense, if it make us fully capable of carrying out our intention where our intention is good, yet the intention must exist in the first place, and intention marks a direction of the will as much as and more than of intelligence. How can we get a hold over the will? Two ways lie open to the teacher. The one is that of training, in the highest meaning of the word; the other the mystic way, the term being taken here, on the contrary, in its most restricted sense. By the first method is inculcated a morality made up of impersonal habits; by the second we obtain the imitation of a person, and even a spiritual union, a more or less complete identification. The primeval training, the training intended by nature, consisted in adopting the habits of the group; it was automatic; it took place spontaneously in those cases where the individual felt himself half merged in the collectivity. As society became differentiated through a division of labour, it delegated to the groups thus formed within itself the task of training the individual, of putting him in harmony with the group and thereby with society itself; but it was still nothing more than a system of habits formed for the sole benefit of society. That a morality of this type may suffice at a pinch, if it be complete, there is no doubt. Thus the man confined strictly within the limits of his calling or profession, wholly absorbed in his daily task, with his life organized so as to turn out the greatest possible quantity, the best possible quality of work, would generally fulfil *ipso facto* many other obligations. Discipline would have made him an honest man. This is the first method: it works in the sphere of the impersonal. The other can supplement it, if need be; it may even take its place. We do not hesitate to call it religious, and even mystic; but we must agree upon the meaning of the words. People are fond of saying that religion is the helpmeet of morality in that it induces a fear of punishment and a hope of reward. This is perhaps true, but they should add that, in this direction, religion does little more than promise an extension and rectification of human justice by divine justice: to the rewards and punishments established by society, whose application is so far from perfect, it adds others, infinitely higher, to be meted out to us in the City of God, when we shall have left the city of men; still it is on the same plane of the city of men that we thus remain; religion is brought in, doubtless, but not in its specifically religious aspect; however high the teaching may rise, it still looks upon moral education as training, and upon morality as discipline; so that it still clings to the first of our two methods, it has not yet sprung over to the second. On the other hand, it is of religious dogmas and the metaphysical theories they imply that we generally think as soon as the word religion is mentioned: so that when religion is said to be the foundation of morality, we picture to ourselves a group of conceptions relating to God and the world, the acceptance of which is supposed to result in the doing of good. But it is quite clear that these conceptions, taken as such, influence our will and our conduct in the same way as theories may do, that is to say, ideas; we are here on the intellectual plane, and, as I hinted above, neither obligation nor the force which extends it can possibly originate in bare ideas, bare ideas affecting our will only to the extent which it pleases us to accept them or put them into practice. Now if you distinguish this metaphysical system from all others by saying that it compels our assent, you may again be right, but then you are not thinking of its content alone, of ideas pure and simple; you introduce something different, which underpins the representation, which imparts to it some undeniable efficacy, and which is the specifically religious element: but then it is this element, and not the metaphysics with which you have associated it, which becomes the religious basis of morality. Here indeed we are concerned with the second method, but then we are dealing with mystic experience. I mean mystic experience taken in its immediacy, apart from all interpretation. True mystics simply open their souls to the oncoming wave. Sure of themselves, because they feel within them something better than themselves, they prove to be great men of action, to the surprise of those for whom mysticism is nothing but visions, and raptures and ecstasies. That which they have allowed to flow into them is a stream flowing down and seeking through them to reach their fellow-men; the necessity to spread around them what they have received affects them like an onslaught of love. A love which each one of them stamps with his own personality. A love which is in each of them an entirely new emotion, capable of transposing human life into another tone. A love which thus causes each of them to be loved for himself, so that through him, and for him, other men will open their souls to the love of humanity. A love which can be just as well passed on through the medium of a person who has attached himself to them or to their evergreen memory and formed his life on that pattern. Let us go further.

If a word of a great mystic, or some one of his imitators, finds an echo in one or another of us, may it not be that there is a mystic dormant within us, merely waiting for an occasion to awake? In the first case a person attaches himself to the impersonal and aims at finding room inside it. Here he responds to the call of a personality, perhaps that of a revealer of moral life or one of his imitators, or even in certain circumstances his own.

Whichever of these two methods be adopted, in both cases the foundations of human nature have been taken into account, whether considered statically in itself or dynamically in its origin. The mistake would be to think that moral pressure and moral aspiration find their final explanation in social life considered merely as a fact. We are fond of saying that society exists, and that hence it inevitably exerts a constraint on its members, and that this constraint is obligation. But in the first place, for society to exist at all the individual must bring into it a whole group of inborn tendencies; society therefore is not self-explanatory; so we must search below the social accretions, get down to Life, of which human societies, as indeed the human species altogether, are but manifestations. But this is not going far enough; we must delve deeper still if we want to understand, not only how society "constrains" individuals, but again how the individual can set up as a judge and wrest from it a moral transformation. If society is self-sufficient, it is the supreme authority. But if it is only one of the aspects of life, we can easily conceive that life, which has had to set down the human species at a certain point of its evolution, imparts a new impetus to exceptional individuals who have immersed themselves anew in it, so that they can help society further along its way. True, we shall have had to push on as far as the very principle of life. Everything is obscure if we confine ourselves to mere manifestations, whether they are all called indiscriminately social, or whether one examines, in social man, more particularly the feature of intelligence. All becomes clear, on the contrary, if we start by a quest beyond these manifestations for Life itself. Let us then give to the word biology the very wide meaning it should have, and will perhaps have one day, and let us say in conclusion that all morality, be it pressure or aspiration, is in essence biological.

The spectacle of what religions have been in the past, of what certain religions still are to-day, is indeed humiliating for human intelligence. What a farrago of error and folly! Experience may indeed say "that is false," and reasoning "that is absurd." Humanity only clings all the more to that absurdity and that error. And if this were all! But religion has been known to enjoin immorality, to prescribe crime. The cruder it is, the more actual space it occupies in the life of a people. What it will have to share later with science, art, philosophy, it demands and obtains at first for itself alone. And that is indeed a matter for surprise, seeing that we began by defining man as an intelligent being.

Our bewilderment increases when we see that the most crass superstition has so long been a universal fact. Indeed it still survives. We find in the past, we could find to-day, human societies with neither science nor art nor philosophy. But there has never been a society without religion.

What should be then our confusion, were we to compare ourselves with animals on this point! It is highly probable that animals are unacquainted with superstition. We know but little of what goes on in minds not our own; but, since religious feeling generally finds expression in attitudes or in acts, we should certainly be made aware by some sign, if animals were capable of a religious sense. But there is nothing for it, facts must be faced. *Homo sapiens*, the only creature endowed with reason, is also the only creature to pin its existence to things unreasonable.

People talk, indeed, of a "primitive mentality," as, for example, to-day that of the inferior races, and in days gone by that of humanity in general, at whose door the responsibility for superstition should be laid. If in speaking thus we mean merely to group certain ways of thinking under one common heading, and note certain connecting links between them, that is indeed useful and unexceptionable work; useful in that it marks off a field of ethnological and psychological studies which are of the greatest interest; unexceptionable since it does no more than establish the existence of certain beliefs and certain practices in a humanity less civilized than our own. It is to this that M. Lévy-Bruhl has apparently confined himself in his remarkable works and particularly in the later ones. But this leaves untouched the question as to how beliefs and practices which are anything but reasonable could have been, and still are, accepted by reasonable beings. We cannot refrain from seeking an answer to this question. Whether he will or no, the reader of M. Lévy-Bruhl's admirable books will draw from them the conclusion that human intelligence has gone through a process of evolution, that natural logic has not always been the same, that "primitive mentality" corresponds to a different fundamental structure, which was supplanted by our own, and which is only found to-day among backward peoples. But this is an admission that habits of mind acquired by individuals in the course of centuries can have become hereditary, modifying nature and giving a new mentality to the species. There is nothing more questionable. Even supposing that a habit formed by parents is ever transmitted to the child, it is a rare occurrence, due to accidental coincidence of a whole concourse of circumstances: it will give rise to no modification of the species. But then, since the structure of the mind remains the same, the experience acquired by successive generations, deposited in the social environment, and given back to each of us by these surroundings, should suffice to explain why we do not think like uncivilized man, why man of bygone days was different from man of to-day. The mind works just the same in both cases, but it may not be working on the same material, because the needs of society are scarcely likely to be the same in the one case as in the other. Our own investigations will indeed lead us to this conclusion. Without anticipating it, let us merely say that the observation of "primitive beings" inevitably raises the question of the psychological origin of superstition, and that the general structure of human thought—the observation therefore of civilized man of the present day—will appear to us to supply sufficient data for the solution of the problem.

We shall have much the same thing to say when we come to "collective" instead of "primitive" mentality. According to Emile Durkheim, there is no need to try and find out why those things which such or such a religion asks us to believe "appear so disconcerting to individual minds. This is simply because the representation of those things by religion is not the work of these minds, but that of the collective mind. Now it is natural that this mentality should see reality differently from our own mind, since it is of another nature. Society has its own mode of existence peculiar to it, and therefore its own mode of thinking." [1] So far as we are concerned, we shall readily admit the existence of collective representations, deposited in institutions, language and customs. Together they constitute a social intelligence which is the complement of individual intelligences. But we fail to see why these two mentalities should clash, and why one should be liable to "disconcert" the other. Experience teaches nothing of the kind, and sociology appears to us to afford no grounds for the supposition. If we held the view that nature stopped short at the individual, that society is the result of an accident or a

[1] *Année sociologique*, Vol. II, pp. 29 *sqq.*

convention, we could push the argument to its conclusion and maintain that this conjunction of individuals, similar to that of primary elements united in a chemical combination, has given rise to a collective intelligence, certain representations of which will be puzzling to the individual mind. But nowadays nobody attributes an accidental or contractual origin to society. If sociology is open to criticism, it would rather be that it leans too much the other way: certain of its exponents tend to regard the individual as an abstraction, and the social body as the only reality. But in that case, how could it be that the collective mentality is not prefigured in the individual mentality? How can we imagine that nature, having made man a "political animal," so disposed human intelligence that it feels out of its element when it thinks "politically"? For our part, we believe that in the study of the individual one can never overestimate the fact that the individual was meant for society. Because it has not sufficiently taken this into account, psychology has made such meagre progress in certain directions. I am not speaking of the benefit to be derived from an intensive study of certain abnormal or morbid states, implying among the members of a community, as among the bees in a hive, an invisible anastomosis: away from the hive, the bee pines away and dies; isolated from society or sharing insufficiently in its activities, man suffers from a similar malady very little studied up to now, called listlessness; when isolation is prolonged, as in solitary confinement, characteristic mental troubles appear. These phenomena would well deserve to have a separate account opened for them in the books of psychology; when closed it would show a handsome profit. But this is not all that there is to be said. The future of a science depends on the way it first dissects its object. If it has had the luck to cut along the lines of the natural joints, like Plato's good cook, the number of "cuts" is of little matter; as the cutting up into pieces will have prepared the way for the analysis into elements, we shall be finally in possession of a simplified representation of the whole. Our psychologists do not sufficiently realize this when they shrink from making subdivisions. For instance, they postulate certain general faculties of perception, interpretation, comprehension, without enquiring whether the mechanisms that come into play are not different, according as the faculties apply to persons or things, or according as the intelligence is immersed or not in the social environment. And yet the mass of mankind has already sketched out this distinction, and has even recorded it in language: alongside of the *senses* which inform us about things it puts *common sense*, which bears on our intercourse with people. We cannot help observing that a man may be a first-rate mathematician, or an expert physicist, or a subtle psychologist, as far as self-analysis goes, and yet completely misunderstand the actions of other men, miscalculate his own and perpetually fail to adapt himself to his surroundings, be, in a word, lacking in common sense. The monomania of persecution, or more precisely of misinterpretation, is there to prove that common sense may become impaired while the reasoning faculties remain intact. The gravity of this malady, its obstinate resistance to all treatment, the fact that the early symptoms are generally to be detected in the remotest past of the sufferer, everything would seem to indicate that we have here a profound congenital psychic insufficiency, and one that is clearly defined. Common sense, then, or as it might be called, social sense, is innate in normal man, like the faculty of speech, which also implies the existence of society and which is none the less prefigured in individual organisms. It is indeed hard to admit that nature, which placed social life at the extremities of the two great lines of evolution ending respectively in the Hymenoptera and in man, while regulating beforehand the detailed activity of every ant in the ant-hill, should have neglected to give man any guiding principles, however general, for the co-ordination of his conduct with that of his fellow-men. Human societies doubtless differ from insect societies in that they leave undetermined the actions of the individual, and indeed those of the collectivity also. But this is equivalent to saying that it is the actions which are preordained in the insect's nature, and that in man it is the faculty alone. The faculty is none the less there, being so organized in the individual that it may function in society. How then should there be a social mentality supervening, as if it were an additional factor, and liable to "disconcert" the individual mentality? How could the first fail to be present in the second? The problem which we stated, and which consists in ascertaining how absurd superstitions have been able and are still able to control the lives of reasonable beings, remains then entirely unsolved. We said that, though we may persist in speaking of primitive mentality, the problem none the less bears on the psychology of the man of to-day. We shall add that, though we may persist in speaking of collective representations, the question none the less concerns the psychology of the individual man.

But does not the difficulty lie precisely in the fact that our psychology is not sufficiently concerned with the subdivision of its subject in accordance with the lines laid down by nature? The representations which produce superstitions possess the common characteristic of being phantasmic. Psychology relates them to a general faculty, imagination. It will also place under the same heading the discoveries and inventions of science and the achievements of art. But why should we group together such different things, give them the same name and thus suggest the idea of a mutual relationship? We do so merely for convenience of speech and for the entirely negative reason that these various activities are neither perception, nor memory, nor logical operations of the mind. Let us then agree to group phantasmic representations separately, and to call "myth-making," or "fiction," the act which produces them. This will be a first step towards the solution of the problem. Let us now remark that psychology, when it splits up the activities of the mind into operations, does not take enough pains to find out the specific purpose of each of them. And this is precisely why the subdivision is all too often inadequate or artificial. Doubtless man can dream and philosophize, but first of all he must live; there is no doubt that our psychical structure originates in the necessity of preserving and developing social and individual life. If psychology does not make this consideration its guiding principle, it will inevitably distort its object. What should we say of a scientist who dealt with the anatomy of organs and the histology of tissues without troubling about their use? He would risk making erroneous divisions and erroneous groupings. If function is comprehensible only from structure, the main lines of a structure are not to be discerned without some idea of its function. We must not therefore consider the mind as being what it is "for no particular reason, just for the fun of the thing." We must not say: its structure being such, it has derived this or that advantage from it. The advantage it derives from its structure is, on the contrary, the factor which must have determined the latter; in any case that is the clue for any research. Let us take, then, in the vaguely and doubtless artificially defined realm of imagination, the natural "cut" which we have called myth-making and see to what use it is naturally put. To this faculty are due the novel, the drama, mythology together with all that preceded it. But then, there have not always been novelists and dramatists, whereas humanity has never subsisted without religion. Very likely, therefore, poetry and fantasy of all kinds appeared as extras, benefiting from the fact that the mind knew how to make myths, but religion is what accounts for the myth-making function: faculty standing to religion in the relationship of effect and not of cause. Some need, individual perhaps, social in any case, must have required from the mind this type of mental activity. Let us ask what this need was. It must be noted that fiction, when it has the power to move us, resembles an incipient hallucination: it can thwart our judgment and reason, which are the strictly intellectual faculties. Now what would nature have done, after creating intelligent beings, if she had wanted to guard against certain dangers of intellectual activity without compromising the future of intelligence? Observation supplies us with the answer. To-day, in the full efflorescence of scientific development, we see the finest arguments in the world come to grief in the face of a single experiment: nothing can resist facts. So that if intelligence was to be kept at the outset from sliding down a slope which was dangerous to the individual and society, it could be only by the statement of apparent facts, by the ghosts of facts; failing real experience, a counterfeit of experience had to be conjured up. A fiction, if its image is vivid and insistent, may indeed masquerade as perception and in that way prevent or modify action. A systematically false experience, confronting the intelligence, may indeed stop it pushing too far the conclusions it deduces from a true experience. It is in some such fashion that nature has proceeded. And that being so, we should not be surprised to find that intelligence was pervaded, as soon as formed, by superstition, that an essentially intelligent being is naturally superstitious, and that intelligent creatures are the only superstitious beings.

It is true that this raises new questions. We must enquire more carefully what is the utility of the myth-making function, and what danger nature had to contend with. Without exploring this point yet, we must note that the human mind may be in the right or in the wrong, but that in either case, whatever direction it has taken, it goes straight ahead: from one conclusion to another, from one analysis to another, it plunges deeper into error, just as it may proceed further and further along the path of truth. We are only acquainted with humanity as already evolved, for the "primitives" we observe to-day are as old as we are, and the documents upon which the history of religion works belong to a relatively recent past. So the immense variety of beliefs with which we have to deal is the result of a lengthy process of proliferation. From their absurdity or strangeness we may doubtless conclude that there is a certain tendency towards the strange or the absurd in the working of a certain function of the mind; but these characteristics are probably thus accentuated simply because the operation has gone so far: if we take into consideration the direction alone, we shall be less surprised at the irrational elements in the tendency, and we may be able to grasp its utility. Who knows indeed if the errors into which this tendency led are not the distortions, at the time beneficial to the species, of a truth destined to be later revealed to certain individuals? But this is not all. A second question arises, which must in fact be answered first: What is the origin of this tendency? Is it connected with other manifestations of life? We spoke of an intention of nature; it was a metaphor, as convenient in psychology as it is in biology; we thus stressed the fact that the contrivance with which we were dealing served the interests either of the individual or the species. But the expression is vague, and for the sake of clarity we should say that the tendency under consideration is an instinct, were it not that it is precisely in the place of an instinct that these phantasmic images arise in the mind. They play a part which *might* have devolved on instinct, and which would actually do so in a being devoid of intelligence. Let us say, for the time being, that it is a *virtual instinct*, meaning that at the extremity of another line of evolution, in insect societies, we find instinct automatically inducing a behaviour comparable, in its utility, to the behaviour which is suggested to man, a being both intelligent and free, by these well-nigh hallucinatory images. But in thus alluding to divergent and complementary developments, which are supposed to have led, on the one hand, to real instincts, on the other to virtual instincts, are we not putting forward a specific view of the evolution of life?

Such is indeed the wider problem raised by our second question. It was implicitly contained in the first. How is it possible to relate to a vital need those fictions which confront and sometimes thwart our intelligence, if we have not ascertained the fundamental demands of life? We shall find later this same problem again in a still more explicit form, when a question arises which we cannot avoid, the question of how religion has survived the danger which brought it into being. How, instead of dying out, has it simply been transformed? Why does it still live on, though science has come to fill the gap, dangerous indeed, left between the form and the matter of intelligence? May it not be that, underlying the need for stability which life reveals in that pause, or rather that turning about on the same spot, which the preservation of the species really is, there is some demand for a forward movement, some remnant of an impulse, a vital impetus? But the two first questions will suffice for the present. They both bring us back to the considerations we have already submitted on the evolution of life. These considerations were by no means hypothetical, as some apparently have thought. In speaking of a "vital impetus" and a creative evolution, we were keeping as close as we could to actual experience. This is what many are beginning to realize, since positive science, merely by abandoning certain theoretical ideas or giving them out as mere hypotheses, is drawing

nearer to our views. In appropriating them, it would
only be entering into its own again.

Let us then go back over a few of the outstanding
features of life, and emphasize the distinctly empirical
character of our conception of the "vital impetus." We
asked whether the phenomena of life could be resolved
into physical and chemical facts. When the physiologist
affirms such a thing, he means, consciously or unconsciously, that the business of physiology is to bring out
whatever is physical and chemical in the vital, that it is
impossible to say when the search will end, and that,
therefore, he must proceed as though the search were
never to have an end; that this is the only way to go
forward. He is thus only laying down the rules of a
method; he is not stating a fact. Let us then keep to
experience: we shall say—and more than one biologist
acknowledges it—that science is as far as ever from a
physico-chemical explanation of life. That is what we
stated, to begin with, when speaking of a vital impetus.
Now, life being given as a fact, how are we to picture its
evolution? Some may maintain that the passage from
one species to another was accomplished by a series of
variations, all of them accidental, being preserved by
selection and fixed by heredity. But if we reflect on the
enormous number of variations, co-ordinate with and
complementary to one another, which must take place
in order that the organism shall benefit by them or even
merely not be injured, we wonder how each one of them,
taken separately, can be preserved by selection and wait
for others which are to complete it. By itself, one of these
variations is more often than not useless; it may even
hamper or paralyse the function. So that in invoking a
combination of chance with chance, in attributing to no
special cause the direction taken by life which is evolv-
ing, biology applies *a priori* the principle of economy
which finds favour with positive science, but it by no
means establishes a fact, and at once comes up against

insurmountable difficulties. This inadequacy of Darwinism is the second point we brought out when we spoke of the vital impetus: to a theory we opposed a fact, we pointed out that the evolution of life occurred in certain definite directions. Now, are these directions imposed on life by the conditions in which it evolves? This would amount to admitting that the modifications undergone by the individual are handed down to his descendants, at least regularly enough to ensure, for instance, the gradual complication of an organ accomplishing the same function with ever greater precision. But the heredity of acquired characteristics is debatable, and, even supposing that it is observed, exceptional; once again it is *a priori*, and in order to meet the needs of the argument, it is taken to be operating regularly. Let us consider this regular transmissibility to be innate: we shall conform to experience and we shall say that it is not the mechanical action of external causes, but an inward impulse that passes from germ to germ through individuals, that carries life in a given direction, towards an ever higher complexity. Such is the third idea to be evoked by the image of the vital impetus.—Let us go further. When one speaks of the progress of an organism or an organ adapting itself to more complex conditions, one means, more often than not, that the complexity of conditions imposes its form on life, as the mould does on the clay: thus alone, one says, is a mechanical, that is a scientific, explanation obtainable. But, after affording oneself the satisfaction of interpreting adaptation in general in this way, one reasons in each particular case as if the adaptation were something quite different—as indeed it is—as if it were the original solution, found by life, of the problem set by external conditions. And this faculty of resolving problems is left unexplained. By introducing at this point "impetus" we did not proffer an explanation either; but, instead of systematically rejecting it in general while resorting to it on the sly in each particular case, we brought out this mysterious character of the operation of life.—But did we do nothing to fathom the mystery? If the marvellous co-ordination of the parts with the whole cannot be explained in terms of mechanics, yet it does not demand, in our opinion, to be treated as finality. The same thing which, seen from outside, can be decomposed into an infinity of parts co-ordinated with one another, may perhaps appear, if realized from inside, an undivided act: just as a movement of the hand, which we feel to be indivisible, is perceived from outside as a curve definable by an equation, that is to say, as a series of points infinite in number, adjacent one to the other, and all obeying one and the same law. In evoking the image of an impetus, we wished to suggest this fifth idea, and even something more: where our analysis, which remains outside, finds positive elements in ever increasing numbers—elements which strike us for that very reason as more and more marvellously co-ordinate with one another—intuition, transferring itself to the inside, would be confronted not with factors that are being combined, but with obstacles that are being circumvented. An invisible hand thrust through a heap of iron filings would merely brush aside the resistance encountered, but the very simplicity of this act, seen from the point of view of the resistance, would appear as an alignment, made in a deliberate order, of the filings themselves.—Now is there nothing to be said concerning this act and the resistance it encounters? If life cannot be resolved into physical and chemical facts, it operates in the manner of a special cause, added on to what we ordinarily call matter, matter in this case being both an instrument and an obstacle. It divides what it defines. We may conjecture that a division of this kind is responsible for the multiplicity of the great lines of vital evolution. But we thereby obtain a suggestion as to the means of preparing and verifying the intuition we would fain have of life. If we see two or three big lines of evolution running freely forward, alongside other paths which come to a dead end, and if along each of these lines an essential characteristic develops more and more, we may conjecture that the vital impulse began by possessing these characteristics in a state of reciprocal implication: instinct and intelligence, which reach their culminating point at the extremities of the two principal lines of animal evolution, must therefore be taken one with the other, before their separation: not combined into one, but one in the beginning, instinct and intelligence being then mere views, taken from two different points, of that simple reality. Such are, since we have begun to number them, the sixth, seventh and eighth ideas which are to be evoked by the idea of a vital impetus.—And even then we have not mentioned, save perhaps by implication, the essential one, namely the impossibility of forecasting the forms which life creates in their entirety, by discontinuous leaps, all along the lines of its evolution. Whether you embrace the doctrine of pure mechanism or that of pure finality, in either case the creations of life are supposed to be predetermined, the future being deducible from the present by a calculation, or designed within it as an idea, time being thus unavailing. Pure experience suggests nothing of the sort. "Neither impulsion nor attraction" seems to be its motto. Now it is just something of this kind that an impetus can suggest, whilst it can also, by the indivisibility of what is felt internally and the divisibility to infinity of what is externally perceived, give the idea of that real and effective duration which is the essential attribute of life.—Such were the ideas we condensed into the image of the "vital impetus." To neglect them, as has been too often done, is to find oneself confronted by an empty concept, like that of the pure "will to live," and by a barren theory of metaphysics. By taking them into account, we have an idea full of matter, obtained empirically, capable of guiding our investigations, which will broadly sum up what we know of the vital process and will also bring out what is still unknown.

From this standpoint, evolution appears as a series of sudden leaps, and the variation constituting the new species as made up of a multitude of differences complementing one another, and emerging all together in the organism formed from the germ. To use again the same comparison, it is like the sudden movement of the hand plunged among the iron filings and causing an instantaneous readjustment of them all. Now, if the transformation takes place in various representatives of the same species, it may not be equally successful in all cases. It may well be that the appearance of the human species was due to several leaps in the same direction, taking place here and there in a previous species and thus resulting in somewhat different types of humanity; each type would then correspond to a successful attempt, in the sense that the multiple variations characterising each one are perfectly co-ordinate with one another; but they might not be equal in quality, the leaps not having covered the same distance in every case. They, none the less, might have all taken place in the same direction. We could say, whilst refraining from fixing any anthropomorphic sense to the word, that they correspond to one and the same intention of life.

Now, whether or not the human species sprang from one stock, whether we have to deal with a single type of humanity, or with several which cannot be reduced to a common denominator, is of little consequence; mankind always presents two essential characteristics, intelligence and sociability. But, from our standpoint, these features take on a special meaning. They are no longer a matter for the psychologist and the sociologist only. They call, first of all, for a biological interpretation. Intelligence and sociability must be given their proper place back in the general evolution of life.

To take sociability first, we find it in its finished form at the two culminating points of evolution, in the hymenopterous insects, such as the ants and bees, and in man. As a mere tendency, it is found everywhere in nature. Some biologists have gone so far as to say that the individual is already a society: the protozoa, formed from a single cell, it is suggested, constituted aggregates which, coming together in their turn, produced aggregates of aggregates; and thus the most widely differentiated organisms originated in the associations of elementary organisms barely differentiated from one another. This is obviously an exaggeration; "polyzoism" is an exceptional and abnormal occurrence. But it is none the less a fact that things take place in a higher organism *as if* the cells had joined together to share the work between them. The bent towards the social form, found in so many species, is therefore evident in the very structure of any of its members. But, once more, this is merely a tendency; and if we wish to deal with fully complete societies, clear-cut organizations of distinct individuals, we must take the two perfect types of association represented by a society of insects and a human society, the one immutable, [2] the other subject to change; the one instinctive, the other intelligent; the first similar to an organism whose elements exist only in the interest of the whole, the second leaving so wide a margin to the individual that we cannot tell whether the organism was made for them or they for the organism. Of the two conditions laid down by Comte, "order" and "progress," the insect chose order only, whereas the aim of at least a section of humanity is progress, sometimes exclusive of order, and always due to individual initiative. These two finished types of social life are then the counterpart of each other and mutually complementary. But the same

[2] It goes without saying that the immutability is not absolute but essential. It exists in principle, but in fact admits of variations on the theme once posited.

could be said of instinct and intelligence, which characterize them respectively. When given their place again in the evolution of life, they appear, as it were, two divergent and complementary activities.

We shall not go over again what we have stated in a former work. Let us merely recall the fact that life is a certain effort to obtain certain things from raw matter, and that instinct and intelligence, taken in their finished state, are two distinct means of utilizing a tool for this object; in the first case, the tool is part of the living creature; in the other, it is an inorganic instrument which man has had to invent, make and learn to handle. Grant the fact of utilization, still more the fact of fabrication, and then, most of all, the fact of invention, and you will find one after the other all the elements of intelligence, for its purpose explains its structure. But we must not forget that there still hangs round the edge of intelligence a fringe of instinct, and that in the depths of instinct there still survive gleams of intelligence. We may conjecture that they were originally involved in one another and that, if we went far enough back into the past, we should find instincts that are nearer to intelligence than those of our insects, and an intelligence closer to instinct than that of our vertebrates. The two activities, which began by mutual interpenetration, had to part company in order to grow; but something of the one has remained attached to the other. Indeed the same thing could be said of all the important manifestations of life. In most cases each reveals, frequently in a rudimentary, latent, or virtual state, the essential characteristics of most of the other manifestations.

If we study, then, at the terminal point of one of the great efforts of nature, these essentially intelligent and partially free groups of beings which constitute human societies, we must not lose sight of the other terminal point of evolution, the societies swayed by pure instinct, in which the individual blindly serves the interests of the community. This comparison will never justify firm conclusions; but it may suggest interpretations. If societies are to be found at the two principal terminal points of the evolutionary movement, and if the individual organism is constructed on a plan which foreshadows that on which societies are organized, this means that life is a co-ordination of disciplined elements among which the work is divided; in fact, that the social underlies the vital. If, in those societies which are already individual organisms in fact, the constituent part must be ready to sacrifice itself for the whole, if this is still so in those societies of societies which form, at the end of one of the two great lines of evolution, the hive and the ant-hill, and lastly, if this result is obtained by instinct which is but an extension of nature's work of organization, this means that nature is more concerned with society than with the individual. If that is no longer the case with man, this means that the inventive efforts manifested throughout the domain of life by the creation of new species has found in humanity alone the means of continuing its activity through individuals, on whom there has devolved, along with intelligence, the faculty of initiative, independence and liberty. If intelligence now threatens to break up social cohesion at certain points—assuming that society is to go on—there must be a counterpoise, at these points, to intelligence. If this counterpoise cannot be instinct itself, for the very reason that its place has been taken by intelligence, the same effect must be produced by a virtuality of instinct, or, if you prefer it, by the residue of instinct which survives on the fringe of intelligence: it cannot exercise direct action, but, since intelligence works on representations, it will call up "imaginary" ones, which will hold their own against the representation of reality and will succeed, through the agency of intelligence itself, in counteracting the work of intelligence. This would be the explanation of the myth-making faculty. Though in-

deed it plays a social rôle, it must also serve the individual, whom as often as not it is to the interest of society
to favour. We may therefore presume that in its original
and elementary form it brings added strength to the individual. But before coming to the second point, let us
consider the first.

Among the facts collected by "psychical research," we
noticed some years ago the following case. A lady was on
the upper floor of an hotel. As she wanted to go down-
stairs, she walked out on to the landing. The gate provided for the lift happened to be open. As the gate was
so contrived as to be open only if the lift were stopped
at that floor, she naturally thought the lift was there and
rushed forward to take it. All of a sudden she felt herself
flung backwards; the man entrusted with the working
of the lift had just appeared and was pushing her back
on to the landing. At this point she emerged from her
fit of abstraction. She was amazed to see that neither
man nor lift were there. The mechanism being out of
order, it was possible for the gate to be open at her
floor, though the lift was still down below. She had been
about to fling herself into the gaping void; a miraculous
hallucination had saved her life. Need we say that the
miracle is easily explained? The lady had reasoned cor-
rectly on a real fact, for the gate was really open and
therefore the lift should have been at that floor. The
mere sight of the empty shaft would have been enough
to show her her mistake; but it would have been too
late, the action consequent upon the correct reasoning
being already under way. It was then that the instinctive or somnambulistic self, which underlies the reasoning personality, came into action. It had seen the
danger, it had to act at once. Instantly it had thrown
her body backwards, at the same time inducing in a
flash the fictitious, hallucinatory perception the best

fitted to evoke and explain the apparently unjustified movement.

Let us imagine then a primitive humanity and rudimentary societies. It would be a simple matter for nature to ensure the requisite cohesion within the groups; she would only have to endow man with the appropriate instincts. This she did for the bee-hive and the ant-hill. And with complete success: here the individual lives for the community alone. Indeed her task was an easy one, since she only had to follow her usual method; instinct is indeed coextensive with life, and social instinct, as found in insects, is nothing more than the spirit of subordination and co-ordination animating the cells and tissues and organs of all living bodies. But it is no longer towards a mere development of instinct, it is towards an expansion of intelligence, that the vital impulse of the vertebrate tends. When the end of the movement is attained in man, instinct is not abolished, it is eclipsed; all that remains of it is a dim penumbra about the centre, now fully illuminated or rather in itself luminous, to wit, intelligence. Henceforth reflexion will enable the individual to invent, and society to progress. But if society is to progress, it must first of all be able to maintain itself. Invention means initiative, and an appeal to individual initiative straightaway involves the risk of endangering social discipline. What if the individual diverts his reflexion from the object for which it was designed, I mean from the task to be performed, the improvement or renovation to be undertaken, and focuses it on himself, on the constraint imposed on him by social life, on the sacrifice he makes to the community? If he were a slave of instinct, like the ant and the bee, he would remain intent on the purely external object to be attained; he would have automatically, somnambulistically, worked for the species. Endowed with intelligence, roused to thought, he will turn to himself and think only of leading a pleasant life. Formal reasoning would doubtless show him that he furthers his own interest by promoting the happiness of others; but it takes centuries of culture to produce a utilitarian such as John Stuart Mill, and Stuart Mill has not convinced all philosophers, let alone the mass of mankind. The truth is that intelligence would counsel egoism first. The intelligent being will rush in that direction if there is nothing to stop him. But nature is on the watch. Just now, before the open gate a guardian appeared, to bar the way and drive back the trespasser. So now some protective deity of the city will be there to forbid, threaten, punish. Intelligence is guided in fact by present perceptions or by that more or less vivid residue of perception called recollection. Since instinct no longer exists except as a mere vestige or virtuality, since it is not strong enough to incite to action or prevent it, it must arouse an illusory perception, or at least a counterfeit of recollection so clear and striking that intelligence will come to a decision accordingly. *Looked at from this first point of view, religion is then a defensive reaction of nature against the dissolvent power of intelligence.*

But this gives us only a figurative symbolization of what actually occurs. For the sake of greater clearness, we have supposed in society a sudden revolt of the individual, and in the individual imagination the sudden apparition of a god to prevent or forbid. Things doubtless take this dramatic form at given times and for a certain period in a humanity already well along the road to civilization. But reality develops towards the precision of drama only by intensification of the essential and elimination of the superfluous. Indeed in human groups, just as they may have come from the hands of nature, the distinction between what does and what does not affect the cohesion of the group is not so clear, the consequences of an act accomplished by the individual do not appear so strictly individual, the force of inhibition which arises at the very instant when the act is on the point of being accomplished is not so completely incarnated in a person. Let us dwell on these three points.

In societies such as ours there are customs and laws. The laws are doubtless often stabilized customs: but a custom becomes a law only when it is of particular, recognizable and definable value; then it stands out from among the others. The distinction is therefore clear between the essential and the accidental: we have, on the one hand, what is merely custom, on the other, what is legal, or even moral, obligation. This cannot be so in less advanced societies where we find only customs, some of them justified by a real need, most of them due to mere accident, or to an irrational extension of the former. Here all customary things are perforce obligatory, since social solidarity, not being condensed into laws, and still less into principles, spreads into an acceptance by all and sundry of these customs. Everything habitual to the members of the group, everything that society expects from individuals, is bound to take on a religious character, if it is true that the observance of custom, and that alone, attaches man to other men, and thus detaches him from himself. Let us note, by the way, that the question of the relation between morality and religion is thus greatly simplified when we consider rudimentary societies. Primitive religions can be called unmoral, or indifferent to morality, only if we take religion as it was in the beginning and compare it with morality such as it became later on. Originally the whole of morality is custom; and as religion forbids any departure from custom, morality is coextensive with religion. It would therefore be vain to raise the objection that religious prohibitions have not always dealt with things that strike us to-day as immoral or antisocial. Primitive religion, taken from our first standpoint, is a precaution against the danger man runs, as soon as he thinks at all, of thinking of himself alone. It is therefore, as we stated above, a defensive reaction of nature against intelligence.

On the other hand, the idea of individual responsibility is by no means so simple as might be supposed. It implies a relatively abstract representation of the activity of the individual, which is taken to be independent because it has been isolated from social activity. But the solidarity between the members of the group is such at first that all are bound to feel that they share to some degree in the lapse of any single one, at least in such cases as they consider serious: moral evil, if we can use the term at this stage, is regarded much the same as a physical evil spreading from one person to another, until it contaminates the whole society. So that, if an avenging power does arise, it will be to castigate society as a whole, without making its weight felt only at the spot from which the evil sprang: the picture of Justice pursuing the criminal is relatively modern, and we have simplified matters too much in showing the individual checked, on the verge of breaking the social bond, by the religious fear of a punishment which would fall on him alone. It is none the less true that things tend to assume this form, and that they assume it more and more distinctly as religion, determining its own features, becomes more frankly mythological. The myth will indeed always bear traces of its origin; it will never clearly distinguish between the physical order and the moral or social order, between intentional orderliness due to the obedience of all to a law and the orderliness manifested in the course of nature. Themis, goddess of human justice, is the mother of the Seasons ("Ωραι) and of Δίχη, who represents the physical law as well as the moral law. Even to-day we have hardly rid ourselves of this confusion; traces of it linger in our language. Mores and morality, regularity and regulation, uniformity *de facto* and uniformity *de jure* are in each case both expressed in much the same way. Does not the word "order" signify both system and command?

Lastly, we spoke of a god arising to prohibit, to prevent, to punish. That means presumably that the moral force, from which the resistance springs, and even, if need be, the vengeance, is incarnated in a person. That it thus tends naturally to assume, in the eyes of man, a human form, there is no doubt. But if mythology is a product of nature, it is a late product, like flower-bearing plants, and the beginnings of religion were more modest. A careful study of what occurs in our consciousness shows us that an intentional resistance, and even a vengeance, at first strike us as self-sufficient entities; for them to be clothed with a definite body, like that of a vigilant and avenging deity, is already a luxury; the myth-making function of the mind doubtless works with artistic pleasure only on conceptions thus arrayed, but it does not form them all at once; it begins by taking them in their nakedness. We shall have to emphasize this point, which has not sufficiently engaged the attention of psychologists. There is no proof that the child who knocks his head against the table and hits back, looks on the table as a person. Indeed this interpretation is far from being accepted by all psychologists to-day. But in this case, after attributing too much to mythological explanation, they now do not go far enough when they suppose that the child simply gives way to an impulse to hit, caused by anger. The truth is that between the identification of the table with a person and the perception of the table as an inanimate object, there lies an intermediate representation which is neither that of a thing nor of a person; it is the image of the act accomplished by the table in striking, or, better still, the image of the act of striking, bringing with it—like luggage borne on its back—the table which stands behind. The act of striking is an element of personality, but not yet a complete personality. The fencer who sees the button of his adversary's foil coming at him knows that it is the movement of the point which has drawn the foil forward, that it is the foil that has drawn the arm forward, that it is the arm that stretched out the body by stretching out itself: he can lunge properly, and give a direct thrust instantaneously, only from the time he feels things in this order. To reverse their order is to reconstruct, and so to philosophize: in any case it is bringing to light the implicit, instead of being content with what action pure and simple requires, with what is directly perceived and really primitive. When we read a signboard "Trespassers will be prosecuted," we begin by perceiving the prohibition; it stands out clearly; it is only behind it, in the shadow, that we have a vision of the constable lying in wait to report us. In the same way, the prohibitions protecting the social order first stand out, just as they are; it is true they are already more than mere words; they resist, and press, and push; but the divinity who forbids, and who was screened by them, will only appear later, as the work of the myth-making function becomes complete. We must not be surprised, therefore, if in uncivilized communities we meet with prohibitions which are semi-physical, semi-moral restraints on certain individual acts; the object occupying the centre of a field of resistance will be called both "sacred" and "dangerous," once these two definite ideas are constituted, and once the distinction is clearly made between a physical force of repulsion and a moral inhibition; up till then, it possesses the two properties fused into one; it is *taboo*, to use the Polynesian term made familiar to us by the science of religions. Did primitive humanity conceive the *taboo* in the same way as the "primitive races" of to-day? Let us first agree on the meaning of the words. There would be no such thing as primitive humanity if the species had been formed by imperceptible transitions; at no given moment would man have emerged from the animal state; but this is an arbitrary hypothesis, which comes up against so many improbabilities and rests on such ambiguities that we believe it to be untenable; [3] by following the clue of facts and analogies, we are far more likely to arrive at a discontinuous evolution which proceeds by bounds, obtaining at each stopping-place a combination, perfect of its kind, like the figures that follow one another in a kaleidoscope; there is then a type of primitive humanity, even though the human species may have been formed by several converging leaps made from various points and not all coming equally near to a realization of the type. On the other hand, the primitive soul would escape us entirely to-day if there had been hereditary transmission of acquired habits. Our moral nature, taken in its raw state, would then differ radically from that of our remotest ancestors. But again it is under the influence of preconceived ideas, and to satisfy the demands of a theory, that one speaks of hereditary habit and, above all, that one believes in a transmission regular enough to bring about a transformation. The truth is that, if civilization has profoundly modified man, it is by accumulating in his social surroundings, as in a reservoir, the habits and knowledge which society pours into the individual at each new generation. Scratch the surface, abolish everything we owe to an education which is perpetual and unceasing, and you find in the depth of our nature primitive humanity, or something very near it. Are the "primitive" peoples we observe to-day the image of that humanity? It is hardly probable, since nature is overlaid, in their case as well, by a layer of habits which the social surroundings have preserved in order to deposit them in each individual. But there is reason to believe that this layer is not so thick as in civilized man, and that it allows nature to show more clearly through it. The multiplication of habits throughout the ages must in their case have occurred in a different way, along the surface,

[3] See *Creative Evolution*, Chaps. I and II.

through a passage from one habit to another analogous habit, and under the influence of adventitious circumstances; whereas the progress of technical skill, of knowledge, in a word of civilization, takes place over fairly considerable periods in one and the same direction, vertically, by superimposed or anastomotic variations, resulting therefore in deep transformations, and not merely in surface complications. Hence, it is easy to see how far we may regard as absolutely primitive the notion of *taboo* which we find among the "primitive" peoples of to-day. Even supposing that it somehow appeared in a humanity fresh from the hands of nature, it did not apply to the same things as now, nor, probably, to so many things. Each *taboo* must have been a prohibition in which society had a well-defined interest. Irrational from the point of view of the individual, since it suddenly checked intelligent activity without resorting to intelligence, it was rational inasmuch as it was in the interests of the society and the species. Hence, sexual intercourse, for example, was satisfactorily regulated by *taboos*. But precisely because no appeal had been made to individual intelligence, because the object was even to thwart it, intelligence, seizing upon the idea of *taboo*, must have extended it arbitrarily in all directions, by chance association of ideas, without troubling about what we might call the original intention of nature. Thus, admitting that *taboo* has always been what it is to-day, it probably did not apply to so many things, nor lead to such absurd consequences. But has it kept its original form? The intelligence of "primitive" peoples is not essentially different from our own; it must have a tendency, like ours, to convert the dynamic into the static, and solidify actions into things. We may presume then that, under its influence, the prohibitions have taken up their abode inside the things to which they applied: they were nothing but resistances opposed to tendencies, but, as a tendency has for the most part an object, it was from the object, and as if dwelling within it, that the resistance appeared to come, having become in this way an attribute of its substance. In stagnant societies this solidification is an accomplished fact. It was perhaps less complete, it was in any case temporary, in what one might call mobile societies, where intelligence was bound in the end to perceive behind the prohibition a person.

We have been dealing with the first function of religion, that which directly concerns social preservation. Now let us come to the other. Once more we shall see it working for the good of society, but indirectly, by stimulating and guiding individual activities. We shall indeed find its work more complex, and we shall be obliged to catalogue the forms it takes. But there is no danger of losing our way in this search, for we have the clue in our hands. We must always remember that the sphere of life is essentially that of instinct; that along a certain line of evolution instinct has to some extent made room for intelligence; that this may lead to a disturbance of life; that nature, in such circumstances, has no other resource than to set up intelligence against intelligence. The intellectual representation which thus restores the balance to nature's advantage is of a *religious* order. Let us take the simplest case first.

Animals do not know that they must die. Doubtless some of them make the distinction between the living and the dead; we mean by this that the sight of a dead creature and of a living one does not produce in them the same reactions, the same movements, the same attitudes; this does not imply that they have a general idea of death, any more than they have of life, or any general idea whatsoever, at least in the sense of a mental picture and not simply a movement of the body. An animal will "sham dead" to escape from an enemy; but it is we who define his attitude thus; so far as he is concerned, he does not stir because he feels that by moving he would excite or again attract attention and invite attack, because movement evokes movement. Cases of animal suicide have been reported, it is true: even admitting this as an actual fact, there is a vast difference between doing what must result in death and knowing that the result is going to be death; to perform an action, even one that is well-contrived and appropriate, is one thing, to forecast the outcome of it is another. But even suppose that an animal has the notion of death. He certainly does not realize that he is bound to die, that he must die a natural death if he does not die a violent one. This would require a series of observations of other animals, then a synthesis, lastly, a process of generalization which already savours of science. Even supposing that the animal could contrive to make any such effort, it would be for something worth while; now nothing could be more useless to him than to know that he must die. It is more to his interest not to know it. But man knows he will die. All other living creatures, clinging to life, are simply carried along by its impetus. Although they do not contemplate themselves *sub specie aeterni*, their confidence, being a perpetual encroachment of the present on the future, is the translation of such contemplation into feeling. But with man reflexion appears, and consequently the faculty of observing with no view to immediate utility, of comparing with one another observations that are temporarily disinterested, in short, of deducing and generalizing. Seeing that every living thing about him ends by dying, he is convinced that he will die too. Nature, in endowing him with intelligence, must inevitably lead him to this conclusion. But this conviction cuts athwart the forward movement of nature. If the impetus of life turns all other living creatures away from the image of death, so the thought of death must slow down in man the movement of life. It may later find its appropriate setting in a philosophy which ends in raising humanity above its own level and increasing its powers of action. But it is at first a depressing thought, and would be more depressing still, if man, while certain that he must die, were not ignorant of the date of his death. Death is indeed bound to come, but as we are constantly becoming aware that it does not come, the continued repetition of the negative experience condenses into a barely conscious doubt, which diminishes the effect of the reasoned certainty. It is none the less true that the certainty of death, arising at the same time as reflexion in a world of living creatures constructed to think only of living, runs counter to nature's intention. Nature, then, looks as if she is going to stumble over the obstacle which she has placed on her own path. But she recovers herself at once. To the idea of inevitable death she opposes the image of a continuation of life after death; this image, flung by her into the field of intelligence, where the idea of death has just become installed, straightens everything out again. [4] This neutralizing of the idea by the image simply expresses the equilibrium of nature, saving herself from slipping. We are therefore again confronted here with that particular interplay of images and ideas which we found characteristic of religion in its beginnings. *Looked at from this second standpoint, religion is a defensive reaction of nature against the representation, by intelligence, of the inevitability of death.*

In this reaction society is as much concerned as the individual. Not only because it profits from the individual effort, and because this effort has a more far-reaching effect when the idea of an ending does not intervene to thwart its impetus, but also and above all

[4] It goes without saying that the image is hallucinatory only in the shape it assumes in the eyes of primitive man. As regards the general question of survival, we have stated our ideas in former works; we shall recur to them in the present book. See Chapter III, pp. 262 *sqq.*, and Chapter IV, pp. 315–17.

because society itself needs stability and duration. A society already civilized is supported by laws, by institutions, even by buildings constructed to defy the ravages of time; but primitive societies are simply "built up of human beings": what would become of their authority if people did not believe in the enduring character of the individualities of which they are composed? It is therefore essential that the dead should remain present. Ancestor-worship will come later. The dead will then be closer to gods. But for this to happen there must be gods, at least in embryo; there must be a definite form of worship; the mind must have deliberately turned towards mythology. In its beginning, intelligence simply sees the dead as mingling with the living in a society to which they can still do good or ill.

In what form does it conceive their survival? We must not forget that we are searching in the depths of the soul, by means of introspection, for the constituent elements of primitive religion. It may be that no single one of these elements has ever manifested itself externally in an unadulterated state, that it would have immediately come up against other simple elements, of the same origin, with which it will have amalgamated, or it may even have been seized upon, either alone or with others, to be used as raw material for the never-ending work of the myth-making function. Thus there are in existence certain themes, some simple, some complex, supplied by nature; and, on the other hand, we have the countless variations played upon them by human fancy. To these themes doubtless may be traced back the fundamental beliefs met with almost everywhere by the science of religions. As to the variations on the themes, they are the myths and even the theoretical conceptions, with their endless diversifications according to time and place. There is no question but that the simple theme we have just indicated combines immediately with others to produce, prior to the myths and the theories, the primitive representation of the soul. But has it any definite shape outside this combination? If the question arises, it is because our present-day idea of a soul living on after the body overlays the image, which presents itself to the immediate consciousness, of the body able to live on after its death. Yet this image does exist, and it takes but a slight effort to recall it. It is nothing more than the visual image of the body detached from the tactile image. We have got into the habit of considering the first as inseparable from the second, as a shadow or effect of the latter. The progress of knowledge is all in that direction. For contemporary science the body is essentially what it is to the touch; it has a definite form and dimension, independent of ourselves; it occupies a given position in space and cannot change it without taking time to occupy successively the intervening positions; the visual image of it would in that case be a phenomenon whose variations we must constantly rectify by recourse to the tactile image; the latter would be the thing itself, the other would merely indicate its presence. But the immediate impression is nothing of the kind. An unwary mind will put the visual image and the tactile image in the same category, will attribute to them the same reality, and will assume them to be relatively independent of one another. The "primitive" man has only to stoop over a pool to see his body just as it really appears, detached from the tactile body. Of course the body he can touch is also a body he can see; this proves that the outer envelope of the body, which constitutes the seen body, can become dual and that one of the two semblances stays with the tactile body. But the fact remains that there is a body which is detachable from the one he can touch, a mere shell of a body, devoid of weight, which has moved in a trice to the place where he sees it. There is doubtless nothing about that body to incline us to believe that it lives on after death. But if we begin by laying down the principle that there must be something that does live on, it will obviously be that body and not the other, for the body we can touch is still present, it lies motionless and speedily decays, whereas the visible envelope may have slipped away somewhere or other and remained alive. The idea that men live on as shades or phantoms is therefore quite natural. It must have preceded, we believe, the more elaborate idea of a principle breathing life into the body; this breath itself has gradually become spiritualized into the soul. It is true that the ghostly envelope of the body seems incapable, by itself, of exerting a pressure on human events, and yet it must exert one, since it is the yearning after continued action that has led to the belief in an after-life. But here a new element supervenes.

We shall not yet define this other elementary tendency. It is as natural as the two preceding ones. It is likewise a defensive reaction of nature. We shall have to seek its origin later. For the present we shall only consider what are its results. It becomes in the end the representation of a force diffused throughout the whole of nature and distributed among individual objects and beings. In the science of religions this emanation is generally reported to be primitive. We hear of the Polynesian *mana*, whose counterpart is found elsewhere under different names: the *wakanda* of the Sioux, the *orenda* of the Iroquois, the *pantang* of the Malays, etc. According to some, the *mana* is a universal principle of life, constituting in particular, to use our own language, the substance of souls. According to others, it is rather a new force supervening, which the soul, or indeed anything else, might well make use of, but which does not belong essentially to the soul. Durkheim, who apparently reasons along the first hypothesis, holds that the *mana* supplies the totemic principle by which the members of the clan commune together; the soul is thus regarded as being a direct individualization of the *totem* and as sharing in the *mana* through this agency. It is not our business to decide between these different interpretations. Speaking generally, we hesitate to consider as primitive, meaning natural, a notion which we should not to-day form naturally. We are of the opinion that what was once primitive has not ceased to be so, even though an effort of self-scrutiny may be necessary to re-discover it. But in whatever shape we take this mental image which we are now considering, we shall have no objection to admitting that the idea of a source of power upon which animate beings, and even a considerable number of inanimate objects, can draw, is one of the first ideas the mind encounters when following a certain tendency, a natural and primary one, which we shall define a little further on. Let us then take this for granted. Man is now provided with what he will call later a soul. Will this soul survive the body? There is no reason to suppose so if we consider the soul alone. There is no reason to believe that a power such as the *mana* should last longer than the body in which it dwells. But if we have started by assuming the principle that the ghostly form of the body persists, there is nothing to prevent our also leaving in it the principle which endowed the body with the strength to act. The result will be an active and effective shade capable of influencing human events. Such seems indeed to be the primitive conception of survival.

The influence thus exerted would not, indeed, be great, if it were not that the soul-idea unites with the spirit-idea. The latter comes from another natural tendency which we shall also have to define. Let us take it also for granted and note that exchanges will occur between the two ideas. The spirits supposed to be present everywhere in nature would not so closely resemble the human form if souls were not already depicted in this shape. On their side, the souls detached from the body would be without influence on natural phenomena if they were not of the same order as the spirits and more or less capable of taking their place among them. The dead are then going to become persons to be reckoned with. They can do harm. They may do good. They have at their disposal, up to a certain point, what we call the forces of nature. In both a literal and figurative sense they cause the rain and the fine weather. People will eschew what might irritate them. They will spare no pains to secure their confidence. They will think of countless ways of winning them over, of buying their favour, even of outwitting them. Once started on this road, there is hardly any absurdity into which intelligence may not stumble. The myth-making function works well enough by itself alone: what will it not do when it is spurred on by fear and necessity! To avert a danger or to secure a favour the living are ready to offer anything they fancy the dead man may want. They will go so far as the cutting off of heads, if that may be pleasing in his sight. Missionary stories are full of detailed accounts of such things. Childish and monstrous deeds compose the interminable list of similar practices indulged in by human stupidity. Looking at them, and at them only, we should be tempted to abominate humanity. But we must not forget that the primitives of to-day or of yesterday have lived as many centuries as we have, have had plenty of time to exaggerate and to aggravate, as it were, the possible irrationalities contained in elementary tendencies, natural enough though they be. The true primitives were probably more reasonable, if they kept to the tendency and its immediate effects. Everything changes, and, as we have said above, the change will take place in breadth if not in depth. There are societies which progress—probably those on whom unfavourable conditions of life have forced a certain effort to live, and which have then consented, at rare intervals, to increase their effort in order to follow a pioneer, an inventor, a man of genius. The change is here an increase of intensity; the direction remains relatively unchanged; the progress is towards an ever higher efficiency. There are, on the other hand, societies that keep to their original level, which is inevitably somewhat low. As, nevertheless, they do change, there takes place within them not that intensification which would be a qualitative progress, but a multiplication or an exaggeration of the primitive state of things: invention, if we can still use the word, no longer requires an effort. From a belief answering to a certain need they have passed to some new belief which resembles the former outwardly, which accentuates one or another of its superficial characteristics, but which no longer serves any purpose. Thenceforth, marking time, they ceaselessly pile up additions and amplifications. Through the double effect of repetition and exaggeration the irrational passes into the realm of the absurd, and the strange into the realm of the monstrous. These successive extensions must also have been due to individuals; but here there was no longer any need for intellectual superiority to invent, or to accept the invention. The logic of absurdity was enough, that logic which leads the mind ever further and further astray towards wilder and wilder consequences, when it starts out from a strange idea without relating it to sources which could explain its strangeness and check its proliferation. We have all come across one of those very united, self-satisfied families, who keep themselves to themselves, because they are shy or supercilious. It is not unusual to notice certain quaint habits among them, aversions or superstitions, which might become serious if they were to go on fermenting in a closed vessel. Each one of these singularities has its particular origin. It was some idea which occurred to one or

another of the family, and which the others have taken
on trust. It may be a walk they took one Sunday and
took again the next Sunday, and which then became a
settled thing every Sunday of the year: if they should
have the misfortune to miss it once, goodness knows
what would happen. In order to repeat, to imitate, to
follow blindly, we have only to relax; it is criticism that
demands an effort. Now take a few hundred centuries
instead of a few years; magnify enormously all the little
foibles of a family living in isolation: you will have no
difficulty in imagining what must have occurred in
primitive societies which have remained self-centred
and self-satisfied, instead of opening windows on to the
outside world, of dispersing the foul vapours as they
gathered about them, and of making a constant effort
to broaden their horizon.

We have just defined above two essential functions
of religion and, in the course of our analysis, we have
met with primary tendencies which appear to provide an
explanation of the general forms assumed by religion.
We now pass to the study of these general forms, of these
primary tendencies. Our method will still remain the
same. We postulate a certain instinctive activity; then,
calling into play intelligence, we try to discover whether
it leads to a dangerous disturbance; if it does, the balance
will probably be restored through representations evoked
by instinct within the disturbing intelligence; if such
representations exist, they are primary religious ideas.
For example, the vital impulse knows nothing of death.
But let intelligence spring to life under pressure from
this impulse, and up comes the idea of the inevitability
of death: to restore to life its impetus, an opposing
representation will start up, and from it will emerge the
primitive beliefs concerning death. But, though death
be the greatest accident of all, yet to how many other
accidents is not life exposed! Does not the very application of intelligence to life open the door to the

unforeseen and let in the feeling of risk? An animal is sure of itself. In its case nothing intervenes between aim and act. If its prey is there, the animal pounces upon it. If it is a matter of lying in wait, its waiting is a forestalling of the act and will form, with the accomplishment of it, an undivided whole. If the ultimate objective is remote, as in the case of the bee building the hive, the animal itself is unaware of the objective; it sees only the immediate object, and the leap it takes is exactly coextensive with the act it has to accomplish. But it is the very essence of intelligence to co-ordinate means with a view to a remote end, and to undertake what it does not feel absolutely sure of carrying out. Between what it does and the result it wants to attain there is more often than not, both in space and in time, an interval which leaves ample room for accident. It begins, and, to enable it to finish, circumstances, as we say, must lend their aid. It may indeed be fully conscious of this margin of the unexpected. The savage, when shooting his arrow, does not know if it will strike the object at which he aimed: we have not here, as in the case of the animal with its prey, continuity between gesture and result; a gap appears, exposed to accident, attracting the unexpected. Doubtless this should not be so in theory. Intelligence is constituted to act mechanically on matter; it thus postulates a universal mechanism and conceives virtually a complete science which would make it possible to foresee, at the very instant when the action is launched, everything it is likely to come up against before reaching its goal. But it is part of the very essence of such an ideal that it is never fulfilled, and that it can at the utmost serve as a stimulus to the work of the intelligence. In fact, human intelligence must confine itself to very limited action on a material about which it knows very little. But the vital impulse is there, brooking no delay, admitting no obstacle. It ignores the accidental, the un-

foreseen, in a word the indeterminate which lies along
its path; it advances by leaps and bounds, seeing only
the end in view, devouring the space between. And
yet it is necessary that intelligence should have cogni-
zance of this anticipation. A representation will accordingly arise, that of favourable powers overriding or
occupying the place of the natural causes and continuing into actions ordained by them, in accordance with
our wishes, the enterprise started on natural lines. We
have set a mechanism going, this is the beginning; we
shall find a mechanism again in the realization of the
desired effect, that is the end: between the two there
must have been inserted a supra-mechanical guarantee
of success. True, if we thus imagine friendly powers
interested in our success, the logic of intelligence will
require that we postulate antagonistic causes, unfriendly
powers, to explain our failure. This last belief will, after
all, have its practical utility; it will indirectly stimulate
our activity by inducing us to be circumspect. But this
is derivation, I might almost say decadence. The representation of a hindering force is scarcely a later development than that of a helping force; if the latter is
natural, the former is its immediate consequence, but
is bound to proliferate above all in stagnant societies
such as those which we now call primitive, where beliefs multiply indefinitely by means of analogies without
any regard for their origin. The vital impulse is optimistic. All the religious representations which here arise
directly from it might then be defined in the same
way: *they are defensive reactions of nature against the
representation, by the intelligence, of a depressing margin of the unexpected between the initiative taken and
the effect desired.*

Any one of us can try the experiment if he pleases;
he will see superstitions start up before his very eyes
from the will to win. Stake a sum of money on a number
at roulette and wait till the ball is near the end of its

gyrations; just as it is perhaps coming, in spite of all its hesitations, to the number you have chosen, your hand goes out to push it, and then to stop it; here it is your own will, projected outside of yourself, which is to fill up the gap between the decision it has taken and the result it expects, thus eliminating chance. Now go regularly to the gaming rooms, and acquire their habits; your hand soon gives up its movement; your will shrinks back into its place, but, as it retires, an entity slips in, emanating from it and delegated by it: this is luck, a transfiguration of the will to win. Luck is not a complete personality; it requires more than this to make a divinity. But it has certain elements of divinity, just enough to make you rely on it.

It is to some such power as this that the savage appeals in order that his arrow may reach its mark. Skip over the stages of a long evolution: you will come to the tutelary gods of the city, whose function is to bring victory to its warriors.

But note that in all cases it is by rational means, it is by complying with mechanical sequences of cause and effect that things are set going. We begin by doing what depends on ourselves: it is only when we feel that it no longer lies with us to help ourselves that we have recourse to extra-mechanical power; even if at the outset, since we believed it present, we invoked its assistance, we in no wise imagined we were thereby excused from taking action. But what might well mislead the psychologist here is the fact that the second causality is the only one we mention. We say nothing about the first, because it is taken for granted. It governs the acts we accomplish with matter as our instrument; we act and live the belief that we have in it; what would be the use of translating it into words and making the idea explicit? This would only have value if we already had a science capable of using it to advantage. But of the second causality it is worth while to think, because we find in it at least an encouragement and an incentive. Were science to supply the uncivilized man with a contrivance ensuring to him the mathematical certainty of hitting the mark, he would abide by that mechanical causality (supposing, of course, that he could instantly do away with inveterate habits of thought). In the absence of that science, his action gets all there is to be got out of mechanical causality, since he draws his bow and takes his aim; but his thought inclines rather towards the extra-mechanical cause which is to direct the arrow where it should go, because, failing the weapon which would make him sure of hitting the mark, his faith in this causality will give him the self-confidence which enables him to take better aim.

Human activity operates among events on which it has a certain influence, but on which it is also dependent. These events are to some extent foreseeable, and, to a greater extent, unforeseeable. Since our science is constantly extending the field of our prevision, we conceive it as ending in a perfect science in which the unforeseeable would cease to exist. This is why, to the reflective thought of a civilized man (we shall see that the case does not apply to his spontaneous representations), the same mechanical concatenation of cause and effect with which he comes in contact when dealing with things must extend to the whole universe. He does not admit that the system of explanation which is appropriate to physical events over which he has some control ought to make room, when he ventures further, for an entirely different system, namely the system he applies in social life when he attributes to good or bad, friendly or hostile intentions the behaviour of other men towards him. If he does so, it is unwittingly; he would not own to it. But the uncivilized man, who has at his disposal nothing but an inelastic science exactly proportionate to the effect he exerts on matter, cannot project into the realm of the unforeseeable a broader science which might embrace it completely and which at once opens up wide vistas to his ambition. Rather than lose heart, he extends to this realm the system of explanation he uses in his intercourse with other men; he will expect to meet there with friendly forces, he will also think himself exposed to malignant influences; in any case he will not be dealing with a world completely alien to him. True, if good and evil genii are to preside over the successive phases of the operation he performs on matter, they will thereby appear to have exerted an influence over that action from the very beginning. So our individual will speak as though he in no way relied, even for that part of the operation which is his own doing, upon the mechanical sequence of cause and effect. But if he did not, in this case, believe in a mechanical sequence, we should not see him, as soon as he acts, do exactly what is necessary to set things going mechanically. Now, whether we are dealing with savages or with civilized people, if we want really to know what is in a man's mind, we must refer to what he does and not to what he says.

In his extremely interesting and instructive books on "primitive mentality," M. Lévy-Bruhl emphasizes the indifference of this mentality to proximate or physical causes, the fact that it immediately turns to "mystic causes." "Our daily activity," he says, "implies unruffled, perfect confidence in the invariability of natural laws. The attitude of mind in primitive man is very different. To him the nature amid which he lives presents itself under an entirely different aspect. All things and all creatures therein are involved in a network of mystic participations and exclusions." [5] And a little further on: "The variable element in collective representations is the occult force to which the illness or the death which has occurred is attributed: now a witch-doctor is the culprit, now the spirit of a dead man, now more or less

[5] *La Mentalité primitive* (Paris, 1922), pp. 17, 18.

definite or individualized forces . . . ; the element
which remains recognizable, we might almost say identical, is the pre-established link between illness and
death, on the one hand, and an invisible power, on the
other." [6] The author brings various confirmatory reports by missionaries and travellers to support this idea,
and quotes the most curious examples.

But one point strikes us at once: namely, that in all
the cases instanced, the effect reported, which is attributed by primitive man to an occult cause, is an event
concerning man, more particularly an accident to a
man, more specifically still a man's death or illness.

There is never any question of action by the inanimate on the inanimate (save in cases of a phenomenon,
meteorological or other, affecting, so to speak, man's
interests). We are not told that the primitive man who
sees a tree bending in the wind or the shingle rolled
up by a wave, or even the dust raised by his foot,
imagines the intervention of anything more than what
we call mechanical causality. The constant relation between the antecedent and the consequent, both of
which he perceives, cannot fail to impress him: it satisfies
him in this case, and, so far as we know, he does not
here superimpose, much less substitute, a "mystic"
causality. Let us go further, leaving aside those physical
facts of which primitive man is an impassive spectator:
can we not say of him also, that his "daily activity implies perfect confidence in the invariability of natural
laws"? Without this confidence, he would not rely on
the current of the river to carry his canoe, nor on the
bending of his bow to shoot his arrow, on his hatchet to
cut into the trunk, on his teeth to bite, on his legs to
walk. It is possible that he does not explicitly picture
this natural causality to himself; he has no interest in
doing so, being neither a physicist nor a philosopher;
but he has faith in it and bases his activity upon it. Let

[6] *Ibid.*, p. 24.

us go further still. When the primitive man turns to a mystic cause for the explanation of death, illness or any other accident, what exactly is the process that he goes through? He sees, for instance, that a man has been killed by a fragment of rock dislodged during a gale. Does he deny that the rock was already split, that the wind loosened the stone, that the blow cracked the skull? Obviously not. He notes, as we do, the operation of these proximate causes. Why then does he bring in a "mystic cause," such as the will of a spirit or witch-doctor, to set it up as the principal cause? Let us look closer: we shall see that what the primitive man explains here by a "supernatural" cause is not the physical effect, it is its *human significance*, it is its importance to man, and more especially to a particular man, the one who was crushed by the stone. There is nothing illogical, consequently nothing "prelogical" or even anything which evinces an "imperviousness to experience," in the belief that a cause should be proportionate to its effect, that, once having admitted the crack in the rock, the direction and force of the wind—purely phsyical things which take no account of humanity—there remains to be explained this fact, so momentous to us, the death of a man. The effect is contained pre-eminently in the cause, as the old philosophers used to put it; and if the effect has a considerable human significance, the cause must have at least an equal significance; it is in any case of the same order: it is an *intention*. That the scientific habit of the mind breaks it of this manner of reasoning is beyond doubt. But it is a natural one; it lingers on in civilized man, and manifests itself every time the opposing force does not intervene. We drew attention to the fact that the gambler, placing his stakes on a number at roulette, will attribute his success or failure to good or bad luck, that is to say to a favourable or unfavourable intention. This will not hinder him from explaining by natural causes

two *Static Religion* 146

everything that occurs between the moment of putting on his money and the moment when the ball stops; but to the mechanical causality he will superadd, at the end of the process, a semi-voluntary choice that may serve as a counterpart to his own: thus the final effect will be of the same importance and the same order as the first cause, which was also a choice. And we grasp the practical origin of this very logical reasoning when we see the gambler make a movement with his hand as though to stop the ball: he is objectifying his will to win, and the resistance to this will, in the form of good or bad luck, in order to feel the presence of a hostile or friendly power, and thus give its full interest to the game. But more striking still is the resemblance between the mentality of the civilized and of the primitive man when dealing with facts such as those we have just had in view: death, illness, serious accident. An officer who took part in the Great War told us he always noticed that the men dreaded the bullets more than the shells, although artillery-fire was far more deadly. The reason is that with bullets we feel we are aimed at; and each of us, in spite of himself, reasons as follows: "To produce the effect, which would mean so much to me, of death or a serious wound, there must be a cause of equal importance, there must be intent." A soldier who, as it happened, had been hit by a splinter from a shell, told us that his first impulse had been to exclaim: "How silly!" That this fragment of shell, projected by a purely mechanical cause, and which might just as well have struck anybody, or nobody, should nevertheless have come and struck him, him and not somebody else, appeared to his natural intelligence illogical. By introducing the idea of "bad luck," he would have demonstrated more clearly still the kinship of this spontaneous intelligence with the primitive mentality. A representation rich in matter, like the idea of a witch-doctor or a spirit, must doubtless relinquish the greater part of its content to become the nation of "bad luck"; yet it subsists, it is not completely emptied; consequently the two mentalities are not so widely different from each other.

The extremely varied examples of "primitive mentality" which M. Lévy-Bruhl has accumulated in his works can be grouped under a certain number of headings. The most numerous are those which show, according to the author, that primitive man obstinately refuses to admit the existence of chance. If a stone falls and crushes a passer-by, it was an evil spirit that dislodged it: there is no chance about it. If a man is dragged out of his canoe by an alligator, it is because he was bewitched: there is no chance about it. If a warrior is killed or wounded by lance-thrust, it is because he was not in a state to parry the blow, a spell has been cast upon him: there is no chance about it.[7] The formula recurs so often in M. Lévy-Bruhl's writings that it may be considered as summing up one of the main characteristics of primitive mentality. But, we shall say to that eminent philosopher, when you reproach primitive man with not believing in chance, or at least when you state it to be a characteristic trait of his mentality that he does not believe in it, are you not admitting the existence of chance? And in admitting it, are you quite sure that you are not relapsing into that primitive mentality you criticize, which at all events you are at great pains to distinguish radically from your own? I don't mean, of course, that you make of chance an active force. But if it were for you a mere nothing, you would not mention it. You would consider the word as non-existent, as well as the thing itself. But the word exists, and you use it, and it stands for something to you, as indeed it does to all of us. Let us ask ourselves what it really represents. A huge tile, wrenched off by the

[7] See in particular *La Mentalité primitive*, pp. 28, 36, 45, etc. Cf. *Les Fonctions mentales dans les sociétés inférieures*, p. 73.

wind, falls and kills a passer-by. We say it was by chance.
Should we say the same if the tile had merely crashed
on to the ground? Perhaps, but it would then be because
we were vaguely thinking of a man who might have
been there, or because, for some reason or other, that
particular spot on the pavement was of special interest
to us, so that the tile seemed to have specially selected
it to fall upon. In both cases chance intervenes only
because some human interest is at stake, and because
things happened as though man had been taken into
account, either with a view of doing him a service, or
more likely with the intention of doing him an injury.[8]
Think only of the wind wrenching off the tile, of the tile
falling on the pavement, of the crash of the tile on the
ground: you see nothing but mechanism, the element
of chance vanishes. For it to intervene it is indispensable that, the effect having a human significance, this
significance should react upon the cause and colour it,
so to speak, with humanity. Chance is then mechanism
behaving as though possessing an intention. It may
perhaps be said that precisely because we use the word
when things occur *as if* there has been intention, we do
not suppose that there has been real intention, we are
recognizing, on the contrary, that everything is capable
of mechanical explanation. And this would be very true
if we were dealing with nothing but reflective, fully
conscious thought. But underlying it is a spontaneous,
semi-conscious thought, which superimposes on the
mechanical sequence of cause and effect something
totally different, not indeed to account for the falling
of the tile, but to explain why its falling should coincide with the passing beneath it of a man, why it should
have chosen just that very moment to fall. The element

[8] We developed this conception of chance in a course of
lectures delivered at the Collège de France in 1898, in connection with the Περὶ εἱμαρμένης of Alexander of Aph-
rodisia.

of choice or intention is as restricted as possible; it re-
cedes as reflexion tries to grasp it; it is elusive, nay,
evanescent, but if it were non-existent we should speak
only of mechanism, there would be no question of
chance. Chance is therefore an intention emptied of
its content. It is nothing more than a mere shadow, but
the shape is there even if the matter is not. Have we
here one of those representations which we call "truly
primitive," formed spontaneously by humanity in obedience to a natural tendency? Not quite. However
spontaneous it may be, the idea of chance reaches our
consciousness only after having first passed through the
layer of accumulated experiences which society deposits
within us from the day it first teaches us to speak. It is
in the course of this passage that it becomes emptied,
since an increasingly mechanistic science drives out of
it what purposefulness it contained. We should therefore have to fill it again, give it a body, if we wanted to
reconstitute the original representation. The phantom
of an intention would then become a living intention.
On the other hand, we should now have to give this
living intention far too much content, over-ballast it
with matter, to obtain the malignant or beneficent entities present in the minds of non-civilized men. It cannot
be said too often: these superstitions usually imply a
magnifying, a thickening, in fine an element of caricature. They denote, more often than not, that the means
has become detached from its end. A belief which begins by being useful, a spur to the will, has been diverted
from the object to which it owed its existence to new
objects where it is no longer of any use, where it might
even become dangerous. Having multiplied lazily
through a superficial imitation of itself, it will now have
the effect of encouraging laziness. Yet we must not go
too far. It is seldom that primitive man feels justified by
that belief in not taking action. The natives of the
Cameroons lay all the blame on the witch-doctor if one

of their tribe is devoured by a crocodile; but M. Lévy-Bruhl, who reports the fact, adds, from the evidence of a traveller, that crocodiles hardly ever attack man in that country.[9] We may rest assured that where crocodiles are habitually dangerous the native avoids going into the water just as we do: there the animal is feared, witchcraft or no. It is none the less true that to pass from the "primitive mentality" to states of mind which might well be our own, we have more often than not to do two things. First we have to make a clean sweep of all our science. Then we must abandon ourselves to a certain laziness, turn aside from an explanation which we surmise to be more reasonable, but which would call for a greater effort of intelligence and, above all, of will. In many cases one of these processes is enough; in others we must combine the two.

Let us take for instance one of the most interesting chapters in M. Lévy-Bruhl's books, the one dealing with the first impressions produced on primitive man by our fire-arms, our writing, our books, in a word everything we have to give him. We find this impression disconcerting at first. We should indeed be tempted to attribute it to a mentality different from our own. But the more we banish from our minds the science we have gradually, almost unconsciously, acquired, the more natural the "primitive" explanation appears. Here we have people before whom a traveller opens a book, and who are told that the book gives information. They conclude that the book speaks, and that by putting it to their ear they will hear a sound. But to look for anything else in a man unacquainted with our civilization would be to expect from him an intelligence far greater than that of most of us, greater even then exceptional intelligence, greater even then genius: it would mean wanting him to re-invent the art of writing. For if he could imagine the possibility of depicting words on a

[9] *La Mentalité primitive*, p. 38.

sheet of paper he would possess the principle of alphabetic, or more generally phonetic, writing; he would straightaway have reached a point which civilized man has reached only by a long accumulation of the efforts of a great number of exceptional men. Let us not then talk of minds different from our own. Let us simply say that they are ignorant of what we have learnt.

There are also, we added, cases where ignorance is coupled with an aversion to effort. Those would be the ones grouped by M. Lévy-Bruhl under the title of "ingratitude of the sick." Primitive men who have been treated by European doctors are not in any way grateful; nay, more, they expect payment from the doctor, as if it were *they* who had done *him* a service. But having no notion of our medical science, no idea that it is a science coupled with an art, seeing moreover that the doctor is far from always curing his patient, and finally considering that he certainly gives his time and his trouble, how can they help thinking that the doctor has some interest, unknown to them, in what he does? And why, instead of striving to shake off their ignorance, should they not adopt quite naturally the interpretation which first occurs to their minds, and from which they can profit? I put this question to the author of *La Mentalité primitive*, and I shall evoke a recollection, a very ancient one, though scarcely older than our old friendship. I was a little boy and I had bad teeth. There was nothing for it but to take me now and again to the dentist, who at once showed no mercy to the offending tooth; he pulled it out relentlessly. Between you and me, it hardly hurt at all, for the teeth in question would have come out of their own accord; but I was no sooner seated in the dentist's chair than I set up a blood-curdling yell for the principle of the thing. My family at last found out a way to make me keep quiet. The dentist, taking care to make a noise about it, would drop a fifty-centime piece into the glass from which I was to

rinse out my mouth (asepticism was unknown in those
far-off days), the purchasing-power of this sum being at
that time ten sticks of barley sugar. I must have been
six or seven, and was no stupider than most boys. I was
certainly capable of guessing that this was a put-up job
between the dentist and my family to bribe me into
silence, and that they conspired together for my particular good. But it would have needed a slight effort to
think, and I preferred not to make it, perhaps from
laziness, perhaps so as not to change my attitude towards
a man against whom my tooth was indeed bared. So I
simply went on not thinking, and the idea I was bound
to form of the dentist then stood out automatically in
my mind in letters of fire. Clearly he was a man who
loved drawing teeth, and he was even ready to pay for
this the sum of half a franc.

But let us close this parenthesis and sum up what we
have said. At the origin of the beliefs we have been
studying we have found a defensive reaction of nature
against a discouragement whose source is to be found
in intelligence. This reaction arouses within intelligence
itself images and ideas which hold in check the depressing representation or prevent it from materializing. Entities then appear which are not necessarily complete
personalities: it suffices that they possess intentions or
even that they coincide with them. Belief then means
essentially confidence; the original source is not fear, but
an assurance against fear. And, on the other hand, the
belief does not necessarily begin by taking a person as its
object; it is content with a partial anthropomorphism.
These are the two points which strike us when we consider the natural attitude of man towards a future about
which he thinks, precisely because he is intelligent, and
at which he would take fright because of the unforeseeable elements he finds in it, were he to confine himself
to the representation of it supplied by intelligence alone.
But such are also the two points we note in cases where

we are dealing not with the future but with the present, and where man is the plaything of forces immeasurably greater than his own strength. Forces like the great catastrophes: earthquakes, floods, tornados. A very old theory attributed the origin of religion to the fear inspired by nature in such cases. *Primus in orbe deos fecit timor.* Science has gone too far in rejecting that entirely; the emotion felt by a man in the presence of nature certainly counts for something in the origin of religions. But, we repeat, religion is less a fear than a reaction against fear, and it is not, in its beginnings, a belief in deities. It will not be out of place to put this statement to a double test, which will not only confirm our preceding analysis, but will enable us to get a more precise notion of those entities of which we have said that they contain an element of personality without being persons. Out of them may grow the gods of mythology, and it will be through a process of enrichment. But these entities could, by a process of impoverishment, as easily yield that impersonal force which primitive man, we are told, sees underlying all things. Let us then follow our usual method. Let us ask our own consciousness, divested of the acquired, restored to its original simplicity, how it reacts to an aggression of nature. The observation of one's own self is a very difficult matter in such a case, owing to the suddenness with which grave events occur; and indeed the occasions are rare when it can be done thoroughly. But certain bygone impressions of which we have only preserved a dim recollection, and which besides were already superficial and vague at the time, will perhaps become more distinct, and assume a clearer shape, if we complete them by the observations made on himself by a master of psychological science. William James happened to be in California during the terrible earthquake of April 1906, which destroyed part of San Francisco. Here is what he wrote on the subject:

"When I departed from Harvard for Stanford University last December, almost the last good-bye I got was that of my old Californian friend B. 'I hope they'll give you a touch of earthquake while you're there, so that you may also become acquainted with *that* Californian institution.'

"Accordingly, when, lying awake at about half-past five on the morning of April 18 in my little 'flat' on the campus of Stanford, I felt the bed begin to waggle, my first consciousness was one of gleeful recognition of the nature of the movement. 'By Jove,' I said to myself, 'here's B.'s old earthquake, after all!' And then, as it went *crescendo*, 'And a jolly good one it is, too!' I said. . . .

"The thing was over, as I understand the Lick Observatory to have declared, in forty-eight seconds. To me it felt as if about that length of time, although I have heard others say that it seemed to them longer. In my case sensation and emotion were so strong that little thought, and no reflexion or volition, were possible in the short time consumed by the phenomenon.

"The emotion consisted wholly of glee and admiration; glee at the vividness which such an abstract idea or verbal term as 'earthquake' could put on when translated into sensible reality and verified concretely; and admiration at the way in which the frail little wooden house could hold itself together in spite of such a shaking. I felt no trace whatever of fear; it was pure delight and welcome.

"'Go it,' I almost cried aloud, 'and go it *stronger!*' . . .

"As soon as I could think, I discerned retrospectively certain peculiar ways in which my consciousness had taken in the phenomenon. These ways were quite spontaneous, and, so to speak, inevitable and irresistible.

"First, I personified the earthquake as a permanent individual entity. It was *the* earthquake of my friend

B.'s augury, which had been lying low and holding itself back during all the intervening months in order, on that lustrous April morning, to invade my room and energize the more intensely and triumphantly. It came, moreover, directly to *me*. It stole in behind my back, and once inside the room had me all to itself, and could manifest itself convincingly. Animus and intent were never more present in any human action, nor did any human activity ever more definitely point back to a living agent as its source and origin.

"All whom I consulted on the point agreed as to this feature in their experience. 'It expressed intention,' 'It was vicious,' 'It was bent on destruction,' 'It wanted to show its power,' or what not. To me it wanted simply to manifest the full meaning of its *name*. But what was this 'It'? To some, apparently, a vague demoniac power; to me an individualized being, B.'s earthquake, namely.

"One informant interpreted it as the end of the world and the beginning of the final judgment. This was a lady in San Francisco Hotel, who did not think of its being an earthquake till after she had got into the street and someone had explained it to her. She told me that the theological interpretation had kept fear from her mind, and made her take the shaking calmly. For 'science,' when the tensions in the earth's crusts reach the breaking-point and strata fall into an altered equilibrium, earthquake is simply the collective *name* of all the cracks and shakings and disturbances that happen. They *are* the earthquake. But for *me* the earthquake was the *cause* of the disturbances, and the perception of it as a living agent was irresistible. It had an overpowering dramatic convincingness.

"I realize now better than ever how inevitable were men's earlier mythological versions of such catastrophes, and how artificial and against the grain of our spontaneous perceiving are the later habits into which science educates us. It was simply impossible for untutored men

to take earthquakes into their minds as anything but
supernatural warnings or retributions." [10]

The first thing we notice is that William James speaks of
the earthquake as an "individual being"; he notes that
he personified the earthquake "as a permanent individual entity." But he does not say that there was—be it
god or demon—an integral personality, capable of a variety of actions, of which the earthquake was one
particular manifestation. On the contrary, the entity in
question is the phenomenon itself, regarded as permanent; its manifestation conveys its whole essence; its
unique function is to be an earthquake; there is a soul,
but that soul is simply the intention pervading the act. [11]
If the author tells us that "never did human activity
more definitely point back to a living agent as its source
and origin" he means by this that the intent and the
animus seemed to belong to the earthquake in the same
way as the acts performed by a living agent seem to
belong to the agent while he remains, so to speak, behind them. But that the living agent is in this case the
earthquake itself, that it possesses no other activity, no
other property, that consequently what it is coincides
with what it does, is borne out by the whole account.
An entity of this kind, whose being and appearance are
one, which is indistinguishable from a given act and
whose intention is immanent in that act itself, being
but the design and the conscious meaning of it, is precisely what we have been calling an element of personality.

There is now another point which cannot fail to strike
us. The San Francisco earthquake was a terrible catas-

10 William James, *Memories and Studies*, pp. 209–214.
Quoted by H. M. Kallen in *Why Religion?* (New York),
1927.

11 "Animus and intent were never more present in any human action."

trophe. But to William James, finding himself suddenly face to face with the danger, it appears rather as something mischievous which invites familiarity. "By Jove, here's the old earthquake!" And other people present had the same impression. The earthquake was "wicked"; it had a mind of its own, "it was bent on destruction." That is just the way we speak of a young scapegrace with whom we may not have broken entirely. But the fear that paralyses is the fear born of the thought that blind and overwhelming forces are about to crush us to pulp unconsciously. Thus does the material world appear to intelligence pure and simple. The scientific conception of the earthquake, alluded to by William James in the last lines, is likely to be the most dangerous of all, so long as science, which gives us a clear perception of the peril, has not supplied us with means of escaping it. To counteract this scientific conception, and more generally the mental picture which it has endowed with greater precision, there comes a defensive reaction in the presence of a grave and sudden peril. The disturbances with which we have to deal, each of them entirely mechanical, combine into an Event, which resembles a human being, possibly a "bad lot" but none the less one of us. He is not an outsider. A certain comradeship is possible between us. This suffices to dispel fright, or rather to prevent its arising. Generally speaking, fright has its uses, like all other feelings. An animal to whom fear is unknown might have no idea of flying or resisting; it would soon succumb in the struggle for life. This explains the existence of a feeling such as fear. It is intelligible too that fear should be in proportion to danger. But it is a feeling which pulls us up, turns us aside or pushes us back: it is essentially inhibitive. When the peril is great, when the fear is nearing its paroxysm and almost paralysing, a defensive reaction of nature occurs to counteract the emotion, which was also natural. Our faculty of feeling could certainly not be changed, it remains what it was; but intelligence, impelled by instinct, transforming the situation, evokes the reassuring image. It lends to the Event a unity and an individuality which make of it a mischievous, maybe a malignant, being, but still one of ourselves, with something sociable and human about it.

I ask the reader to search his memory. Unless I am much mistaken, he will find a confirmation of William James's analysis. I shall at any rate take the liberty of mentioning one or two recollections of my own. The first goes back to the far-off days, since I was very young at the time and went in for sports, particularly riding. Now one fine day, having just encountered on the road that most fantastic of apparitions, a cyclist perched on a tall velocipede, my horse took fright and bolted. That this might happen, that in such cases there were certain things I should do, or at least try to do, I knew as well as any pupil in the riding school. But I had never thought of the possibility otherwise than in an abstract form. That the accident should actually occur, at a given point in time and space, that it should happen to me rather than to someone else, struck me as implying a preference for me personally. Who then had chosen me? It was not the horse. It was no complete being, whatever it was, good or evil genius. It was the occurrence itself, an individual with no body of its own, for it was nothing but a combination of circumstances, but it had a soul, a very elementary one, hardly distinguishable from the intention apparently manifested by circumstances. It followed me in my wild gallop, mischievously watching to see how I should manage. And my one idea was to show it what I could do. If I felt no fear, it was precisely because my whole mind was centred on this one idea; and also, perhaps, because the malice of my strange companion did not preclude a certain good fellowship. I have often thought of this little incident, and said to myself that nature could not have conceived any better psychical mechanism than this, if she intended, while endowing us with fear as a salutary emotion, to preserve us from it in cases where we had best not give way to it.

I have just cited a case where the "good fellowship" nature of the Accident is the most striking thing about it. Here is another case, which perhaps brings out more distinctly still its unity, its individuality, the clearness with which it carves itself out a place in the continuity of the real. While still a boy, in 1871, on the morrow of the Franco-Prussian War, I had, like all people of my generation, considered another war to be imminent during the twelve or fifteen years that followed. Later on that war appeared as at once probable and impossible: a complex and contradictory idea, which lasted right down to the fatal day. Indeed it called up no image to our minds, beyond its verbal expression. It kept its abstract character right down to those terrible hours when the conflict became obviously inevitable, down to the very last minute, while we were still hoping against hope. But when, on August 4, 1914, I opened the *Matin* newspaper and read in great headlines: "Germany Declares War on France," I suddenly felt an invisible *presence* which all the past had prepared and foretold, as a shadow may precede the body that casts it. It was as though some creature of legend, having escaped from the book in which its story was told, had quietly taken possession of the room. True, I was not dealing with a complete personality. There was only enough of it to produce a certain effect. It had bided its time; and now unceremoniously it took its seat like one of the family. It was to intervene just at this moment, in this place, that it had been vaguely interlinked with my life-history. To the staging of this scene, the room with its furniture, the paper upon the table, myself standing in front of it, the event pervading every nook and cranny, forty-three years of vague foreboding had all been leading up. Horror-struck as I was, and though I felt a war, even a victo-

rious war, to be a catastrophe, I experienced what
William James expresses, a feeling of admiration for the
smoothness of the transition from the abstract to the
concrete: who would have thought that so terrible an
eventuality could make its entrance into reality with so
little disturbance? The impression of this facility was
predominant above all else. On reflexion, one realizes
that, if nature intended to oppose a defensive reaction
against fear, and prevent a paralysis of the will brought
about by an over-intelligent representation of a cata-
clysm entailing endless consequences, she would create
between us and the event simplified, transmuted into a
rudimentary personality, just this very familiarity which
puts us at our ease, relieves the strain, and disposes us
quite simply to do our duty.

We must search for these fleeting impressions, which
are immediately blotted out by reflexion, if we want to
find some vestige of what may have been felt by our
remotest ancestors. We should not hesitate to do so, if
we were not imbued with the preconceived idea that
the moral and intellectual acquisitions of humanity, incorporated in the substance of individual organisms,
have come down to us through heredity. In that case
we should be born totally different from what our ancestors were. But heredity does not possess this virtue. It
cannot make natural tendencies out of habits contracted
from generation to generation. If it had any hold on
habit, it would have a very slight one, accidentally and
exceptionally; it has probably none at all. The natural,
then, is to-day what it has always been. True, things
happen as if it had been transformed, since all that society has acquired overlays it, since society moulds individuals by means of an education that goes on without
a break from the hour of their birth. But let a sudden
shock paralyse these superficial activities, let the light in
which they work be extinguished for a moment: at once
the natural reappears, like the changeless star in the

night. The psychologist who wants to go back to what is primitive must seek after these out-of-the-way experiences. For all that, he will not let go his guiding thread, he will not forget that nature is utilitarian, and that every instinct has its function; those instincts which we might call intellectual are defensive reactions against the exaggeratedly and above all the prematurely intelligent elements in intelligence. But the two methods will help each other: the one serving rather for research, the other for verification. It is our pride, a twofold pride, which generally makes us shy at them. We want man to be born superior to what he used to be, as if true merit did not lie in effort, as though a species in which each individual has to rise above himself by a laborious assimilation of all the past were not, to say the least, on a par with a species in which each generation would be raised in its entirety to a higher level than the preceding ones by the automatic play of heredity! But there is yet another pride, that of intelligence, which will not admit its original subordination to biological necessities. No one would study a cell, a tissue, an organ, without caring about its function; in the field of psychology itself, no one would consider he had fully accounted for an instinct unless he had connected it with some need of the species; but once you come to intelligence, farewell nature! farewell life! Intelligence is assumed to be what it is "for no particular reason, for the fun of the thing." As if it also did not primarily correspond to vital needs! Its original business is to resolve problems similar to those resolved by instinct, though indeed by a very different method which ensures progress and which cannot be applied unless it be, in theory, completely independent of nature. But this independence is limited in fact: it ceases at the exact moment when intelligence would defeat its own object by injuring some vital interest. Intelligence is then inevitably kept under observation by instinct, or rather by life, the common origin of instinct and intelligence. This is just what we mean when we speak of intellectual instincts; we are then dealing with representations formed naturally by intelligence, by way of safeguarding itself, through certain beliefs, against certain dangers of knowledge. Such are then the tendencies, such are the experiences psychology must bear in mind, if it wants to get back to the fountainhead.

The study of the uncivilized will be none the less valuable. We have said, and we cannot repeat it too often: they are as far from the beginning of things as we are, but they have invented less. So they have had to apply the same knowledge in countless different ways; theirs has perforce been a process of exaggeration, caricature, in a word, distortion, rather than radical transformation. But whether it be a matter of transformation or one of distortion, the original form subsists, merely covered over by the acquired; in both cases, therefore, the psychologist in search of origins will have the same kind of effort to make, but the road may be shorter in the second case than in the first. This is what will occur especially when we come to find similar beliefs among peoples between whom there can have been no possible communication. These beliefs are not necessarily primitive, but they have very likely come straight from one of those fundamental tendencies which an effort of introspection would enable us to discover within ourselves. They may then put us in the way of this discovery, and guide that introspection which will later serve to explain them.

We have always to go back to these questions of method if we do not wish to go astray in our search. At the turning-point which we have reached we stand particularly in need of them. For we are dealing with nothing less than the reactions of man to his perception of things, of events, of the universe in general. That intelligence is made to utilize matter, to dominate things, to master events, there is no doubt. That its power is in direct proportion to its knowledge is no less certain. But this science is in the beginning very limited; very small indeed is the portion of the universal mechanism that it embraces, of the space and time over which it has control. What about the rest? Left to itself, intelligence would simply realize its ignorance; man would feel himself lost in immensity. But instinct is on the watch. To the strictly scientific knowledge which goes with technical progress, or is implied in it, instinct adds, for all those things which are beyond our scope, the belief in powers that are supposed to take man into account. The universe is thus peopled with intentions which are, it is true, fleeting and variable; the only purely mechanical area is supposed to be that within which we act mechanically. This area expands with the advance of civilization: the whole universe ends by appearing as a mechanism to an intelligence which conceives the ideal vision of a complete science. We have reached this stage, and it takes, to-day, a vigorous effort of introspection to rediscover the original beliefs which our science covers over with all it knows and hopes to know. But, as soon as we get at them, we see how they are to be explained by the joint working of intelligence and instinct, how they must have corresponded to a vital interest. Turning then to uncivilized man, we verify what we have observed in ourselves: but in his case the belief is swollen, exaggerated, multiplied: instead of receding, as it does with civilized man, in the face of the progress of science, it overflows into the area reserved to mechanical action, and overlays activities which ought to preclude it. This brings us to an essential point. It has been asserted that religion began as magic. Magic has also been considered as a forerunner of science. If we confine ourselves to psychology, as we have done, if we reconstitute, by an effort of introspection, the natural reaction of man to his perception of things, we find that, while magic and religion are akin, there is nothing in common between magic and science.

We have indeed just seen that primitive intelligence divides its experience into two separate parts. There is, on the one side, that which obeys the action of the hand or the tool, that which can be foreseen and relied on: this part of the universe is conceived physically, until such time as it is conceived mathematically; it appears as a concatenation of causes and effects, in any case it is treated as such; no matter if this conception be indistinct, or barely conscious; it may never be expressed, but we need only look at what intelligence does in order to know what it implicitly thinks. Then, on the other hand, there is that part of experience upon which *homo faber* feels he has entirely lost his grip. This part is treated no longer physically, but morally. Since we can exert no power over it, we hope it will exert some power in our behoof. Thus nature becomes in such a case impregnated with humanity. But she will acquire this human quality only as far as is necessary. In default of power, we must have confidence. For us to feel comfortable, the event which singles itself out before our eyes from the mass of reality must appear animated with a purpose. That will be indeed our natural and original conviction. But we shall not stop there. It is not enough for us to have nothing to fear, we would fain have something to hope for as well. If the event is not utterly devoid of feeling, can we not manage to influence it? Will it not allow itself to be convinced or constrained? This will be difficult if it remains what it is, a transient intention, a rudimentary soul; it would not have personality enough to hearken to our prayers, it would have too much to be at our beck and call. But our mind can easily impel it in one direction or the other. For the pressure of instinct has given rise, within intelligence, to that form of imagination which is the myth-making function. Myth-making has but to follow its own course in order to fashion, out of the elementary personalities looming up at the outset, gods that assume more and more exalted form like those of mythology, or deities ever more degraded, such as mere spirits, or even forces which retain only one property from their psychological origin, that of not being purely mechanical, and of complying with our wishes, of bending to our will. The first and second directions are those of religion, the third that of magic. Let us begin with the latter.

There has been a great deal of discussion about the notion of *mana* which was brought out some years ago by Codrington in his famous book on the Melanesians, and about its equivalent, or rather something analogous to it, supposed to exist among other primitives: such as the *orenda* of the Iroquois, the *wakanda* of the Sioux, etc. All these words seem to connote a force present throughout nature, a force of which some if not all things are said to partake in different degrees. From this to the hypothesis of a primitive philosophy taking form in the human mind at the very dawn of thought there is but a step. Some authorities have indeed supposed that the minds of the non-civilized were obsessed by a vague kind of pantheism. But it is very unlikely that humanity starts from such general and abstract notions. Before any man can philosophize he must live. Scholars and philosophers are too much inclined to believe that the mind works in all men as with them, for the sheer love of thinking. The truth is that the mind aims at action, and that, if there really is any philosophy to be found in the uncivilized man, it is certainly in action rather than in thought; it is implied in a whole group of operations which are useful or considered as such; it emerges from them, it expresses itself in words—and they are inevitably very vague—only for the convenience of action. MM. Hubert and Mauss, in their very interesting *Théorie générale de la magie*, have made out a strong case for the belief in magic being inseparable from the conception of the *mana*. According to them it would appear that this belief derives from that conception. Is it not just the other way round? It does not strike us as probable that the representation corresponding to such terms as *mana*, *orenda*, etc., was formed first and that magic originated thence. Quite the contrary, it is because man believed in magic, because he practised it, that he must have represented things to himself in this way: his magic apparently worked, and he did but explain, or rather express, its success. Now, that he should have begun at once to practise magic is easy to understand; he realized at once that the limits of his normal influence over the outside world were soon reached, and he could not resign himself to going no further. So he carried on the movement, and, since the movement could not by itself secure the desired result, nature must needs take the task in hand. It could be so only if matter were, so to speak, magnetized, if it turned of its own accord towards man, to undertake his errands and carry out his orders. Matter remained none the less amenable, as we should say to-day, to physical laws; this had to be so, for the sake of the mechanical hold upon it. But it was, besides, impregnated with humanity, I mean charged with a force capable of entering into human designs. Man could turn this tendency to advantage so as to extend his action further than physical laws permitted. We can easily convince ourselves of this if we consider the nature of the magical recipes, and of the conceptions of matter which made it possible to imagine confusedly that magic could succeed.

The operations have often been described, but as the applications of certain theoretical principles such as "like acts on like," "the part stands for the whole," etc. That these formulae can serve to classify magical processes there is no doubt. But it in no wise follows that magical operations are derived from them. If primitive intelligence had begun by conceiving principles, it would very soon have capitulated before the evidence of experience, which would have proved them erroneous. But here again it merely translates into a conception what was suggested by an instinct. To put it more clearly, there is a logic of the body, an extension of desire, which comes into play long before intelligence has found a conceptual form for it. Take, for instance, a "primitive" man who wants to kill his enemy: that enemy, however, is far away; it is impossible to get at him. No matter! Our man is in a rage; he goes through the motions of pouncing on the absent man. Once started he goes on to the bitter end; he squeezes his fingers round the neck of the victim he thinks he has hold of, or wants to have hold of, and throttles him. But he knows very well that the result is not complete. He has done everything that he himself could do: he demands that things should do the rest. They will not do it mechanically. They will not yield to a physical necessity, as when our man stamped on the earth, moved his arms or legs, in a word, obtained from matter reactions corresponding to his actions. Therefore he wants matter, not only to be obliged to give back mechanically what it receives, but also to possess the faculty of fulfilling desires and obeying orders. There will be nothing impossible in this if nature already tends of her own accord to take man into account. It will suffice that the same compliance shown by certain *events* should also be found in *things*. The latter will then be more or less charged with submissiveness and potency: they will hold at man's disposal a power which yields to the desires of man, and of which man may avail himself. Words such as *mana*, *wakanda*, etc., express this force, and at the same time the prestige surrounding it. You will not find the same precise meaning for all of them, if you are looking for precise meanings; but they all correspond to the same vague idea. They express that which causes things to lend themselves to the operations of magic. As to these operations themselves, we have just determined their nature. They begin the act which man cannot finish. They go through the motions which alone could not produce the desired effect, but which will achieve it, if the man concerned knows how to prevail upon the goodwill of things.

Magic is then innate in man, being but the outward projection of a desire which fills the heart. If it has appeared artificial, if it has been connected with superficial associations of ideas, it is because it has been studied in processes which were especially devised to relieve the magician from putting his heart and soul into them, and to enable him to obtain the same result without the same effort. An actor studying his part really and truly lives the emotion he has to express; he notes the gestures and inflections to which it gives rise; later, when facing the public, he will produce only the inflection and the gesture, he can afford to dispense with the emotion. It is the same with magic. The "laws" which have been found for it tell us nothing of the natural impulse from which it sprang. They are only a formula for the expedients which laziness has suggested to the original magic in order that it might be perpetuated.

It arises first of all, we are told, from the fact that "like begets like." There is no apparent reason why humanity should begin by positing so abstract and arbitrary a law. But it is understandable that after having gone instinctively through the motions of flinging himself on his absent enemy, after having convinced himself that his anger, projected into space and conveyed forward by some obliging matter, will proceed to accomplish the act begun, a man should want to obtain the same effect without having to work himself up into the same state. He will therefore go through the process again in cold blood. That very action, described in his wrath, which he performed when he thought he was locking his fingers about his enemy's throat, he will reproduce by means of a ready-made model, a dummy whose outlines he will merely have to go over. It is thus that he will practise hoodoo. The puppet he uses need not even resemble his enemy, since its only function is to ensure that the act is repeated exactly as before. Such seems to be the psychological origin of a principle to be expressed in some such formula as "like is equivalent to like" or, better still, in more precise terms, "the static can replace the dynamic if it traces the pattern of the latter." In this ultimate form, reminiscent of its origin, the principle would not lend itself to indefinite extension. But in the first form it permits of the belief that it is possible to affect a distant object through the intermediary of a near object bearing the merest superficial resemblance to it. It need not even be explicitly stated or formulated. Merely implied in an almost instinctive process, it enables this natural magic to proliferate indefinitely.

Magic practices are referred to yet other laws: "it is possible to influence a being or a thing by acting on something it has touched," "the part is valid for the whole," etc. But the psychological origin remains the same. The essential is always to repeat in tranquillity, with the conviction that it is efficacious, the act which has given a quasi-hallucinatory impression of its efficacy when performed in a moment of excitement. In time of drought, the sorcerer is asked to produce the rain. If he were actually to put his whole soul into the task, he would, by an effort of imagination, raise himself up to the cloud, he would believe that he felt himself cleaving it asunder, and scattering it in rain-drops. But he will find it simpler to suppose he has nearly come back to earth again, and then to pour out a little water; this minute fraction of the event will produce it in its entirety, if the effort which would have had to be launched from earth to heaven finds something to take its place, and if the intermediary matter is more or less charged—as it were with positive or negative electricity—with a readiness, half physical and half moral, to serve or to thwart man. This amounts to saying that there exists a very simple natural magic, reducible to a small number of practices. It is reflexion upon these practices, or perhaps the mere translation into words, which has made it possible for them to multiply in every direction and to absorb all superstitions as well, because the formula always goes beyond the fact which it expresses.

Magic then seems to us to resolve itself into two elements: the desire to act on a thing, even on that which is out of reach, and the idea that things are charged, or can be charged, with what we should call human fluid. We must revert to the first point to draw the comparison between magic and science, and to the second to show the connexion of magic with religion.

That there have been cases where magic has accidentally been of service to science is not impossible: matter cannot be manipulated without some benefit accruing. But even then, to utilize an observation or simply to note it, there must be some propensity for scientific research. Now the moment such is the case you are turning your back on magic. It is indeed easy to define science, since it has always worked in the same direction. It measures and calculates with a view to anticipation and action. It first supposes, then verifies, that the universe is governed by mathematical laws. In a word, all progress in science consists in a wider knowledge and a richer utilization of the universal mechanism. This progress, moreover, is accomplished by an effort of our intelligence, which is designed to guide our action upon things, and whose structure must therefore be modelled on the mathematical framework of the universe. Although we are called upon to act only on the things about us, and though such was the original intention of the function of intelligence, yet, since the mechanism of the universe is present in each of its parts, it was absolutely necessary that man should be born with an intelligence virtually capable of embracing the whole material world. It is the same with the working of the mind as with the faculty of sight: the eye too was only meant to reveal to us objects on which we can act; but just as nature could obtain the requisite degree of vision only with an apparatus whose effect goes beyond its object (since we can see the stars, while we have no control over them), in the same way she necessarily had to give us, along with the faculty of understanding the matter we have to deal with, a virtual knowledge of the rest, and the no less virtual power of utilizing it. True, it is a far cry, in this case, from the virtual to the actual. All effective progress, in the realm of knowledge as in that of action, has demanded the persistent effort of one or several superior men. There was, each time, creation, which nature had doubtless made possible in that she endowed us with an intelligence whose form exceeds its content, but a creation which went, so to speak, beyond what nature had intended. Man's structure seemed indeed to destine him for a more humble existence. His instinctive resistance to innovations is a proof. The inertia of humanity has never yielded, save under the impulsion of genius. In a word, science demands a twofold effort, that of a few men to find some new thing and that of all the others to adopt it and adapt themselves to it. A society may be called civilized when you find in it such a power to lead and willingness to be led. The second condition is indeed more difficult of fulfilment than the first. What was lacking among the uncivilized was probably not the exceptional man (there seems to be no reason why nature should not have had always and everywhere such fits of abstraction) but the chance for such a man to show his superiority, and the readiness of other men to follow him. Once a society is already on the road to civilization, the prospect of a mere increase of well-being will doubtless suffice to overcome its ingrained habits. But to get it on to this road, to start it into motion the first time, requires a great deal more:

perhaps the menace of extermination, such as that created by the discovery of a new weapon by an enemy
tribe. Those societies which have remained more or less
"primitive" are probably those that have had no neigh-
bours, more generally still those for whom life has been
too easy. They were not called upon to make the initial
effort. Subsequently, it was too late; the society could
not advance, even if it wanted to, because it was con-
taminated by the products of its own laziness. These
products are precisely the practices of magic, at least
inasmuch as they are excessive and all-encroaching. For
magic is the reverse of science. So long as the inertia of
the environment does not cause it to proliferate, it has
its function to perform. It temporarily calms the un-
easiness of an intelligence whose form exceeds its content, which is vaguely aware of its ignorance and realizes
the danger of it, which divines, outside the very small
circle in which action is sure of its effect, where the
immediate future is predictable and within which therefore science already prevails, a vast area of the unpredict-
able such as may well discourage action. And yet act it
must. Magic then steps in, as an immediate effect of the
vital impulse. As man widens his knowledge through effort, magic will gradually recoil. Meanwhile, as it is
apparently successful (for the failure of a magical process can always be attributed to the success of some
counter-magic) it produces the same moral effect as
science. But this is its only feature in common with
science, from which it is separated by the whole distance
between wishing and willing. Far from paving the way
for science, as some have maintained, it has been the
great obstacle against which methodical knowledge has
had to contend. Civilized man is a being in whom incipient science, implicit in the daily round, has been
able to encroach, thanks to an ever-active will, on that
magic which was occupying the rest of the field. Non-
civilized man is, on the contrary, one who, disdaining

effort, has allowed magic to invade the realm of incipient science, to overlay it, and conceal it, even to the point of making us believe in a primitive mentality devoid of all real science. Moreover, once in possession, it plays thousands of variations upon its own themes, being more prolific than science, since its inventions are pure fantasy and cost no effort. Let there be no talk, then, of an era of magic followed by an era of science. Let us say that science and magic are both natural, that they have always co-existed, that our science is very much more extensive than that of our remote ancestors, but that these ancestors must have been much less given to magic than non-civilized men to-day. We have remained, at bottom, what they were. Driven back by science, the inclination towards magic still survives, and bides its time. Let our attention to science relax for one instant, and magic will at once come rushing back into our civilized society, just as a desire, repressed in our waking hours, takes advantage of the lightest sleep to find satisfaction in a dream.

There remains then the problem of the relationship between magic and religion. Everything depends, obviously, on the meaning of this last term. The philosopher studies for the most part a thing to which common sense has already given a name. Man may have got only a glimpse of it and that glimpse may have been deceptive; the thing may have been jumbled up with other things, from which it must be isolated. It may even have been segregated from reality as a whole merely for convenience of speech, and so not effectively constitute an entity, lending itself to independent study. Herein lies the great inferiority of philosophy compared to mathematics and even to natural sciences. Its starting-point must be the cutting up of reality by speech—a division and distribution which is perhaps entirely relative to the needs of the city: philosophy too often ignores this origin, and proceeds like a geographer who, in order to

discriminate between the different regions of the globe
and indicate the physical connections between them,
should take it into his head to go by the frontiers established by treaties. In the study we have undertaken,
we have guarded against this danger by passing directly
from the word "religion" and everything it embraces in
virtue of a possibly artificial disgregation of things, to a
certain function of the mind which can be directly observed, without considering the separation of the real
into concepts corresponding to words. In our analysis
of the operations of this function we have successively
rediscovered several of the meanings given to the word
religion. Continuing our study, we shall find other
shades of meaning, and we may add one or two new
ones. It will then be plainly demonstrated that this time
the word embraces a reality: a reality which, it is true,
will somewhat overstep, upwards and downwards, the
limits of the usual significance of the word. But we shall
then grasp it in itself, in its structure and in its principle,
as happens whenever we relate to a physiological function, such as digestion, a great number of facts observed
in different parts of the organism, and even discover
thereby new facts. If we look at the matter from this
angle, magic is evidently part of religion. I mean, of
course, the lower type of religion, the one with which
we have been dealing up to now. But magic, in common
with this religion, generally speaking, represents a precaution of nature to meet certain dangers encountered
by the intelligent being.—Now, it is possible to follow
another line, to start from the various ordinary interpretations of the word religion, compare them, and extract
therefrom an average meaning: in this way we shall have
solved a dictionary question rather than a philosophical
problem; but no matter, so long as we realize what we
are about, and do not imagine (a constant illusion of
philosophers) that we have obtained the essence of a
thing when we have agreed upon the conventional

meaning of the word. Let us then set out all the accep-
tations of the word, like the colours of the spectrum or
the notes in a scale: we shall find, somewhere about the
middle, at an equal distance from the two extremities,
the adoration of gods to whom men pray. It goes without saying that religion thus conceived is the opposite of
magic. The latter is essentially selfish, the former admits
of and often even demands disinterestedness. The one
claims to force the compliance of nature, the other im-
plores the favour of the god. Above all, magic works in
an environment which is semi-physical and semi-moral
—the magician, at all events, is not dealing with a person; whereas on the contrary it is from the god's personality that religion draws its greatest efficacy. Granted
that primitive intelligence thinks it perceives around it,
in phenomena and in events, elements of personality
rather than complete personalities, religion, as we have
just understood it, will ultimately reinforce these elements to the extent of completely personifying them;
whereas magic looks upon them as debased, dissolved,
as it were, in a material world in which their efficacy can
be tapped. Magic and religion, then, go their separate
ways, having started from a common origin, and there
can be no question of deriving religion from magic: they
are contemporaneous. It is understandable, however,
that there should be something of the one hovering
round the other, that some magic lingers in religion, and
still more, some religion in magic. We know that the
magician sometimes works through the medium of spirits, that is to say of beings relatively individualized, but
which do not possess the complete personality nor the
eminent dignity of gods. On the other hand, incanta-
tion may partake of both command and prayer.

The history of religions has long regarded the belief
in spirits as primitive and explanatory of all the rest. As
each one of us has his soul, a subtler essence than that
of the body, so, in nature, everything is said to have been

animated, to be accompanied by a vaguely spiritual entity. Spirits once having been posited, humanity passed, so it is said, from belief to adoration: hence a natural philosophy, animism, from which religion sprang. To this hypothesis another theory is apparently preferred to-day. In a "pre-animist" or "animatist" phase, humanity is supposed to have imagined an impersonal force, such as the Polynesian *mana*, present in the whole, unequally distributed between the parts; the spirits were conceived later. If our analyses are correct, what was first conceived was neither an impersonal force nor spirits already individualized: man simply attributed purpose to things and events, as if nature had eyes everywhere which she focused on man. That this is an original tendency, we can all verify when a sudden shock arouses the primitive man dormant within us all. What we feel in these cases is the sensation of an *efficient presence*; the nature of this presence is of little consequence, the essential point is its efficiency: the moment there is any regard for us, even if the intention is not good, we begin to count for something in the universe. That is what experience tells us. But, even before we consult experience, it would seem highly unlikely that humanity should have begun by theoretical views of any sort or kind. We shall say it over and over again: before man can philosophize man must live; it is from a vital necessity that the primeval tendencies and convictions must have originated. To connect religion with a system of ideas, with a logic or a "pre-logic," is to turn our remote ancestors into intellectuals, and intellectuals such as we ought to be in greater numbers ourselves, for we often see the finest theories succumbing to passion and interest and holding good only in our hours of speculative thought, whereas ancient religions pervaded the whole of life. The truth is that religion, being coextensive with our species, must pertain to our structure. We have just now connected it with a fundamental experience; but that experience was such that we had foreseen it before encountering it; in any case it is quite easily explained when it has been encountered; all we have to do is to consider man again in his place among living things, and psychology as a part of biology. For, look at any other animal. It avails itself of everything it finds useful. Does it actually believe itself to be the centre of the world? Probably not, for it has no conception of the world as such, and, besides, it has not the slightest inclination to speculate. But since it only sees, or at least only takes note of what can satisfy its needs, since things exist for it only in so far as it makes use of them, it obviously behaves as though everything in nature were combined solely with a view to its well-being and in the interest of its species. Such is its conviction, not intellectualized, but lived, a conviction which sustains the animal and is indistinguishable from its effort to live. You bring reflexion into play, however, and this conviction will vanish; man will perceive himself, will think of himself as a speck in the immensity of the universe. He would feel lost, if the effort to live did not at once project into his intelligence, into the very place that this perception and this reflexion were about to occupy, the opposing image of things and events turning towards man; whether well or ill disposed, a certain intention of his environment follows him then everywhere, just as the moon seems to run with him when he runs. If it be good, he will rely on it. If it bodes harm, he will try to avert its effects. In any case, it means that he has been taken into account. Here is no theory, no room for the arbitrary. This conviction is forced upon him, there being no philosophy about it, but a vital impulsion.

In like manner, if indeed it splits and evolves into two divergent directions, on the one hand towards belief in spirits already individualized, and on the other towards the idea of an impersonal essence, that is not on account of any theory: such reasoning leads to controversy, permits of doubt, gives rise to doctrines which may exert an influence on conduct, but which do not impinge upon all the incidents of existence, and could not possibly become the guiding forces of life as a whole. The truth is that once the conviction is firmly implanted in the will, the latter impels it in the directions which are open already, or which open out before it at the points of least resistance all along the path of its effort. It will utilize in every possible way the intention which it feels to be present, either by taking the physical effectiveness which the intention possesses, exaggerating its materiality and then trying to master it by force, or by approaching it from the moral side, by impelling it, on the contrary, in the direction of a personality to be won over by prayer. It is, then, from the demands of an efficient magic that there arose a conception such as *mana*, an impoverishment or a materialization of the original belief: and it is the desire to obtain favours that drew from the same belief, in the opposite direction, spirits and gods. Neither has the impersonal evolved towards the personal, nor have pure personalities been posited at the outset: but, out of some intermediate thing, intended rather to sustain the will than to inform the intelligence, there have emerged through dissociation, downwards and upwards, the forces that lie beneath the weight of magic, and the gods towards whom the voice of human prayer is raised.

On the first point we have made our opinion clear. We should have a heavy task if we had to deal at length with the second. The gradual evolution of religion towards gods of increasingly marked personality, who are more and more definitely interrelated or who tend to become merged into a single deity, corresponds to the first of the two great advances of humanity towards civilization. It went on until the day when the religious spirit turned from the outer to the inner, from the static to the dynamic, by a change of front similar to that performed by pure intelligence when it passed over from the study of finite magnitudes to the differential calculus. This last change was doubtless the decisive one: transformations of the individual became possible, like those that have produced the successive species in the organized world; progress could thenceforth consist in the creation of new qualities, and not as previously in a mere increase in size; instead of merely taking what life had to give, motionless, at whatever point had been reached, humanity could now continue the vital movement. We shall deal with this religion, an entirely inward one, in the next chapter. We shall see that it sustains man by the very movement it imparts to him putting him again in the stream of the creative impetus, and not as hitherto by imaginative representations intended to reconcile in him the activity of the parts with the immobility of the whole. But we shall also see that religious dynamism needs static religion for its expression and diffusion. It is therefore comprehensible that the latter should hold first place in the history of religions. It is not our business, we repeat, to follow static religion through the immense variety of its manifestations. It will suffice to indicate the principal ones and bring out the connexion between them.

Let us start then from the idea that there are intentions inherent in things: this brings us at once to the representation of spirits. They are the vague entities dwelling, for instance, in springs, rivers and fountains. Each spirit is bound to the spot where it manifests itself. This feature already distinguishes it from a divinity proper, which will be able, while remaining indivisible, to apportion itself between various places, and to hold sway over everything belonging to one and the same genus. This divinity will bear a name; it will have its own particular shape, its clearly defined personality, whereas the countless spirits of the woods and fountains are copies of one model and could, at most, say with Horace: *nos numerus sumus*. Later on, when religion has attained to the height of those exalted personages, the gods, it may well conceive of spirits in their image: such spirits will be minor deities; and they will then appear to have always been so. But this is merely a retroactive effect. It probably took a long time, in Greece, for the spirit of a spring to become a graceful nymph, and the spirit of the wood a hamadryad. In the beginning, the spirit of the spring must have been the spring itself, as possessing a beneficent virtue for man. To put it more clearly, that beneficent action, in its ever-present aspect, *was* the spirit. It would be an error in such a case to regard as an abstract idea—I mean an idea extracted from things by an intellectual effort—the representation of the act and of its continuation. It is a datum provided directly by the senses. Our philosophy and our language posit first the substance and surround it with attributes, and then make such and such acts arise therefrom like emanations. But we cannot too often repeat that the action may be forthcoming first and be self-sufficient, especially in cases where man is particularly concerned. Such is the act of supplying us with drink: it can be localized in a thing, and then in a person; but it has its own independent existence; and if the process goes on indefinitely, its very persistence will set it up as the animating spirit of the spring at which we drink, whilst the spring, detached from the function which it performs, will relapse the more completely into the state of a thing pure and simple. It is true that the souls of the dead naturally enough join with the spirits; though detached from their bodies, they have not yet renounced their personality. In mingling with the spirits they inevitably colour them and, by the hues with which they tinge them, pave the way for them to become persons. Thus, by different but converging paths, the spirits will be advancing towards a complete personality. But in the elemental form which they first possess, they fulfil so natural a need that we must not be surprised to find the belief in spirits underlying all ancient religions. We spoke of the part it played among the Greeks: after being their primitive religion, so far as we can judge by the Mycenean civilization, it remained the popular religion. It was the basis of the Roman religion even after the most generous provision had been made for the greater divinities imported from Greece or elsewhere: the *lar familiaris*, who was the spirit of the house, was always to retain its importance. With the Romans as with the Greeks, the goddess called Hestia or Vesta must have begun as nothing more than the flame on the hearth, considered in its function, I mean in its beneficent intention. Suppose we leave classical antiquity and turn to India and China and Japan: everywhere we shall find this belief in spirits; we are told that even to-day it constitutes (with ancestor-worship, which is very closely akin to it) the essential element of Chinese religion. Because it is universal, it was easy to believe that it was original. Let us at least note that it is not very far removed from the original state, and that the human mind naturally passes through this belief before attaining to the adoration of the gods.

It might well stop at an intermediate stage. We are alluding to the cult of animals, so widespread among past humanity that some people have considered it as still more natural than the adoration of the gods in human shape. We find it, full of life and tenacity, holding its own even in countries where man already represents the gods in his own image. It survived thus right up to the end in ancient Egypt. Sometimes the god that has emerged from the animal form refuses to cast it off entirely; his human body is crowned by an animal's head. Such things appear to-day very surprising. This is mainly because man has become endowed in our eyes with an outstanding dignity. We regard intelligence as his main characteristic, and we know that there is no superiority which intelligence cannot confer on us, no inferiority for which it cannot compensate. It was not so in the days before intelligence had proved its worth. Its actual inventions were too few for its boundless potentialities of invention to be apparent; the weapons and tools with which it supplied man could hardly stand comparison with those the animal inherited from nature. Even reflexion itself, the secret of man's strength, might look like weakness, for it is the source of indecision, whereas the reaction of an animal, when it is truly instinctive, is instantaneous and unfailing. Even the fact that it lacks the power of speech has served the animal by surrounding it with a halo of mystery. Its silence, moreover, can pass for contempt, as though it had something better to do than to converse with us. All this explains why humanity should have felt no aversion to animal worship. But how did it come about? We must note that it is for some specific quality that the animal is adored. In ancient Egypt the bull represented strength in battle; the lioness, destruction; the vulture, so careful of her young, motherhood. Now it would be incomprehensible that animals should become the object of a cult if man had begun by believing in spirits. But if man did not first have recourse to beings, but to beneficent or malevolent actions regarded as permanent, it is natural that after having gained control of actions, he should have wanted to get hold of qualities; these qualities seemed to be present, unalloyed, in animals, whose activity is simple, invariably consistent and apparently set in one direction. The adoration of animals was not, then, the primitive phase of religion; but on emerging from that phase, man had the choice between the cult of spirits and that of animals.

Just as the nature of an animal seems to be concentrated in one single quality, so it would seem that its individuality merges into a type. To recognize a man

is to distinguish him from other men; but to recognize
an animal is usually to identify the species to which it
belongs: such is the particular character of our interest
in each case; consequently in the first case our perception seizes on the individual characteristics, whereas in
the latter it nearly always ignores them. An animal, for
all it is something concrete and individual, nevertheless
stands forth as essentially a quality, essentially also a
species. Of these two striking features the first, as we
have just seen, largely explains the cult of animals. The
second would account to a certain extent, we believe,
for that strange thing, totemism. This is not the place
to study the question: we cannot, however, refrain from
saying a word about the subject, for if totemism is not
animal worship, it nevertheless implies that man treats
an animal, or even a vegetable species, sometimes a mere
inanimate object, with a deference which is not without
some resemblance to religion. Let us take the common-
est case, that of an animal, a rat or a kangaroo, for example, which serves as a "totem," that is to say a patron,
for a whole clan. The most striking thing is that the
members of the clan assert they are one with it; they *are*
rats, they *are* kangaroos. True, it remains to be seen in
what sense they use the word. To conclude straightaway
that there is a specific logic, peculiar to "primitive man"
and exempt from the principle of contradiction, would
be somewhat over-hasty. Our verb "to be" carries meanings that we have difficulty in defining for all our civilization: how can we reconstitute the meaning given by a
primitive man in such and such a case to a similar word,
even when he supplies us with explanations? These explanations would possess an element of precision only
if he were a philosopher, and even then we should have
to know all the fine shades of his language to understand
them. Think of the opinion he, on his side, would have
of us and our powers of observation and reasoning, of
our common sense, if he knew that the greatest of our

moralists has said "man is a reed that thinks." [12] And besides, does he converse with his totem? Does he treat it as a man? Note that we are always being brought back to the same point: to know what is going on in the mind of a primitive man, or even of a civilized man, we must study what he does at least as closely as what he says. Now, if the primitive man does not identify himself with his totem, does he simply take it as an emblem? This would be going too far the other way: even if totemism is not at the basis of the political organization of non-civilized people, as Durkheim would have it, it occupies too large a place in their existence for us to see in it merely a means of designating the clan. The truth must lie somewhere half-way between these two extreme explanations. Let us offer, simply as a hypothesis, the interpretation to which we might be led by our principles. That a clan is said to be such or such an animal, offers no ground for deduction; but that two clans within the same tribe must necessarily be two different animals is far more enlightening. Let us suppose, indeed, that it is desired to indicate these two clans as constituting two species, in the biological sense of the word: how is this to be managed in cases where the language is not yet impregnated by science and philosophy? The individual characteristics of an animal do not catch our attention; the animal is perceived, we said, as a species. To express the fact that two clans constitute two different species, the name of one animal will be given to one, that of another to the other. Each of these designations, taken singly, is no more than a label: taken together they are equivalent to an affirmation. They indicate in fact that the two clans are of *different blood*. Why is this? If totemism is to be found, as we are assured it is, in various parts of the globe among communities which can have held no possible communication

[12] "L'homme n'est qu'un roseau, le plus faible de la nature, mais c'est un roseau pensant" (PASCAL).

with one another, it must correspond to a common need
of these communities, a vital necessity. In fact we know
that the clans into which the tribe is divided are often
exogamous: in other words, marriages are contracted between members of different clans, but not within one
clan. It was even believed for a long time that this was a
general law, and that totemism always implied exogamy.
Let us suppose that this was so at the beginning, and
that in many cases exogamy fell out of use later on. It is
easy to understand that it is in the interests of nature
to prevent the members of a tribe from habitually inter-
marrying, for the result in a closed society such as this
would be unions between near relations: the race would
very soon degenerate. An instinct, overlaid by quite different habits as soon as it ceases to be useful, will
predispose the tribe to split up into clans, within which
marriage will be forbidden. This instinct, as a matter of
fact, will attain its object by at once causing a feeling
of relationship between members of the same clan, and
between clan and clan a feeling of being as foreign as
possible to each other, for its *modus operandi*, which we
can see working in our societies as well, is to diminish
the sexual attraction between men and women who live
together or who know they are related. [13] How then will
the members of two different clans convince themselves,
and express the fact, that they are not of the same blood?
They will get into the habit of saying that they are not
of the same species. So then, when they declare that they
constitute two animal species, it is not on the animality,
but on the duality that they lay the stress. At least it must
have been so in the beginning. [14] We must indeed admit

[13] See, on this subject, Westermarck, *History of Human
Marriage* (London, 1901), pp. 290 *sqq*.

[14] The idea that the class takes its descent from the totem
animal—an idea which M. Van Gennep emphasizes in his
interesting work on *L'Etat actuel du problème totémique*
(Paris, 1920)—may quite well be grafted on to the representation we have indicated.

that we are dealing here merely with the probable, not to say with the purely possible. We only want to apply, to a very controversial problem, the method which appears to us as the surest generally. Starting from a biological necessity, we search for the corresponding need in the living creature. If this need does not actually create a real and active instinct, it conjures up, by means of what we call a virtual or latent instinct, an imaginative representation which determines conduct in the same way as instinct would have done. At the basis of totemism there may well be a representation of this sort.

But let us close this parenthesis, opened for an object, of which it may be said that it deserved better treatment. We were dealing with spirits. We believe that, to get at the very essence of religion and understand the history of mankind, one must needs pass at once from the static and outer religion, with which we have been dealing up to now, to that dynamic, inner religion which we shall discuss in the next chapter. The first was designed to ward off the dangers to which intelligence might expose man; it was infra-intellectual. Let us add that it was natural, for the human species marks a certain stage in the vital evolution: it was here that at a given moment the forward movement stopped; man was then posited as a whole, with, therefore, his intelligence, with the dangers this intelligence might involve, with the myth-making function designed to cope with them; magic and elementary animism, it all appeared as an unbroken whole, it all corresponded exactly to the needs of the individual and of society, the one and the other limited in their ambitions, such as nature intended them. Later, and by an effort which might easily never have been made, man wrenched himself free from this motion of his on his own axis. He plunged anew into the current of evolution, at the same time carrying it forward. Here was dynamic religion, coupled doubtless with higher intellectuality, but distinct from it. The first form of religion had been infra-intellectual; we know why. The second, for reasons which we shall indicate, was supra-intellectual. By contrasting them from the outset, we shall best understand them. For these two extreme religions are alone essential and pure. The intermediate forms, which developed in antique civilizations, could only lead the philosophy of religion astray, if they induced the belief that man passed from one extremity to the other by the road of gradual perfection: doubtless a natural error, explained by the fact that static religion has to some extent lingered on into dynamic religion. But these intermediate forms have occupied so large a place in the known history of humanity that we cannot but dwell on them. For our part we see in them nothing absolutely new, nothing comparable to dynamic religion, nothing but variations on the twofold theme of elementary animism and of magic; a belief in spirits, after all, has always remained the basis of popular religion. But from the myth-making faculty, which had elaborated it, there issued, through a later development, a mythology round which there grew up a literature, an art, institutions, in a word, the essential elements of antique civilization. Let us discuss, then, that mythology without ever losing sight of that which was its starting-point, and which is still visible through it.

The transition from spirits to gods may be gradual, the difference is none the less striking. The god is a person. He has his qualities, his defects, his character. He bears a name. He stands in definite relationship to other gods. He fulfils important functions, and, above all, he is alone in fulfilling them. On the contrary, there are thousands of different spirits, scattered far and wide over the country, all doing the same work; they are described by a common name, and this name may, in certain cases, not even possess a singular form: *manes* and *penates*, to take only these examples, are Latin words only found in the plural. If the true original religious representation is that of an "effective presence," of an act rather than of a person or a thing, belief in spirits lies very close indeed to those origins; the gods appear only later, when the pure and simple substantiality of the spirits rises, in this or that one of them, to the level of a personality. These gods are superadded to the spirits, but do not replace them. The cult of spirits remains, as we have said, the basis of popular religion. The more enlightened part of the nation will none the less prefer the gods, and it may be said that progress towards polytheism is an advance towards civilization.

It is useless to seek for a rhythm or a law in this advance. It is essentially capricious. From among the countless spirits we see some local deity spring up, modest at first, growing with the city, and finally adopted by the whole nation. But other evolutions are also possible. It is indeed rare for the evolution to end in anything like finality. However exalted the god may be, his divinity by no means implies immutability. On the contrary, it is the principal gods of antique religions that have undergone the greatest changes, enriching themselves with new attributes by the absorption of other gods, and thus increasing their own substance. In Egypt, for example, the sun god Re, at first an object of supreme adoration, absorbs other divinities, assimilates them or couples himself to them, amalgamates with the great Theban god, Amon, forming in this case Amon-Re. Thus Marduk, the god of Babylon, appropriates the attributes of Bel, the high god of Nippur. Thus several Assyrian gods are merged into the mighty goddess Ishtar. But no evolution is richer than that of Zeus, the sovereign god of Greece. After having begun probably as the god worshipped on the mountaintops, holding sway over the clouds, and the rain, and the thunder, he added to what we might call his meteorological functions certain social attributes which became more and more complex; and he ended by being the tutelary god of all social groups, from the family to the state. It became necessary to place after his name the most varied epithets to distinguish all the lines of his activity: Xenios, when he watched over the observances of hospitality; Horkios, when he presided over the swearing of oaths; Hikesios, when he protected the supplicants; Genethlios, when he was invoked for a marriage, etc. The evolution is generally slow and natural; but it can be rapid also, and be effected artificially under the very eyes of the worshippers. The divinities of Olympus date from the Homeric poems, which did not perhaps create them, but in which they were given the forms and the attributes under which we know them, and which co-ordinated and grouped them under Zeus, the process this time being rather one of simplification than of complication. They were none the less accepted by the Greeks, though the latter knew the circumstances and almost the date of their birth. But there was no need to call in the genius of the poets; a prince's decree sufficed to make and unmake gods. Without going into the details of such interventions, let us merely recall the most radical of them all, that of the Pharaoh who took the name of Iknaton: he abolished the gods of Egypt in favour of one among them, and succeeded in getting this sort of monotheism accepted until the time of his death. We know, moreover, that the Pharaohs themselves shared in the divinity. From the most remote antiquity they styled themselves "sons of Re." And the Egyptian tradition of treating the sovereign as a god was continued under the Ptolemies. It was not confined to Egypt. We meet with it in Syria under the Seleucides, in China, in Japan, where the Emperor receives divine honours during his lifetime and becomes a god after his death, and lastly in Rome, where the Senate deified Julius Caesar, before Augustus, Claudius, Vespasian, Titus, Nerva, and finally all the emperors rose to the rank of gods. Doubtless the adoration of the sovereign is not taken equally seriously everywhere.

There is a great distance, for example, between the divinity of a Roman emperor and that of a Pharaoh. The latter is closely related to the divinity of the chief in primitive societies; it is perhaps connected with the idea of a special fluid, or a magic power, supposed to reside in the sovereign, whereas the divinity conferred on Caesar was a case of mere toadyism, being utilized later by Augustus as an *instrumentum regni*. And yet the half-sceptical attitude mingled with the adoration of the emperors remained, in Rome, a prerogative of cultivated minds; it did not extend to the people; it certainly did not spread to the provinces. This means that the gods of antiquity could be born, die, be transformed at the whim of man or by circumstances, and that pagan faith was limitless in its compliance.

Precisely because men's fancy and fortuitous circumstances have played so large a part in their genesis, the gods cannot be fitted into a hard and fast classification. The most we can do is to bring out a few main trends of mythological fantasy; and even so, no single one has been by any means regularly followed. As gods were for the most part set up to serve a useful purpose, it is natural that functions should be generally attributed to them, and that in many cases the idea of a particular function should have predominated. This is what occurred in Rome, and it has made it possible to say that the specialization of gods was characteristic of Roman religion. For the sowing there was Saturn; for the flowering of fruit trees, Flora; for the ripening of fruit, Pomona. The guardianship of the door was attributed to Janus, that of the hearth to Vesta. Rather than attribute to the same god a multiplicity of interrelated functions, it preferred to set up distinct gods, content to give them the same name with varying epithets. There was Venus Victrix, Venus Felix, Venus Genetrix. Jupiter himself was Fulgur, Feretrius, Stator, Victor, Optimus Maximus; and these were, up to a certain point, distinct; they were milestones along the road from Jupiter, dispenser of rain or sunshine, to Jupiter, protector of the state in peace as in war. But the same tendency is exhibited everywhere in varying degrees. Ever since man began to cultivate the soil, there have been gods to watch over the harvest, to dispense heat, to ensure the regularity of the seasons. These agricultural functions must have been characteristic of some of the most ancient deities, even though they have been lost sight of, as the evolution of the god made him a complex personality, overlaid with a long history. Thus Osiris, the richest figure in the Egyptian pantheon, seems to have been at first the god of vegetation. This was the primitive function vested in the Adonis of the Greeks. It was also that of Nisaba, in Babylonia, who held sway over the corn crops before she became the goddess of Science. In the first rank of the divinities of India figure Indra and Agni. To Indra man owed the rain and the storms beneficent for the soil; to Agni, fire, and the protection of the domestic hearth; and here again the diversity of functions goes with a difference of character, Indra being distinguished by his strength, Agni by his wisdom. The most exalted function is indeed that of Varuna, who presides over the universal order of things. We find in the Shinto religion, in Japan, the earth-goddess, the goddess of harvests, the gods that watch over the mountains, the trees, etc. But no divinity of this type has so marked and complete a personality as the Demeter of the Greeks; she too is a goddess of the soil and harvests, but she also cares for the dead, to whom she gives a place of abode, besides presiding, under the name of Thesmophoros, over family and social life. There you have the most conspicuous development of the god-making fantasy.

By endowing them with functions, however, it attributes to them a sovereignty which quite naturally assumes a territorial form. The gods are supposed to share the universe between them. According to the Vedic po-

ems their various spheres of influence are heaven, earth
and the middle air. In the Babylonian cosmology the
sky is the realm of Anu, the earth that of Bel; in the
depths of the sea dwells Ea. The Greeks divided
the world between Zeus, god of heaven and earth,
Poseidon, god of the seas, and Hades, to whom belonged
the infernal regions. These realms are marked out by nature herself. Now the sun, moon and stars are no less distinct in outline; they are individualized by their shape
as well as by their movements, which appear to depend
on themselves; one of them is the dispenser of life here
below, and the others, even though they be not equally
powerful, must none the less be of the same nature; so
in them also we find the stuff of gods. It is in Assyria
that the belief in the divinity of the heavenly bodies
assumed the most systematic form. But the worship of
the sun and also of the sky is to be found more or less
everywhere: in the Shinto religion of Japan, where the
goddess of the sun is set up as sovereign, with, under
her, a moon-god and a star-god; in the primitive Egyptian religion, where the moon and the sky are considered
as gods alongside the sun, who is their lord; in the Vedic
religion, where Mitra (identical with the Iranian
Mithra, who is a sun-deity) has attributes which would
be appropriate to a god of sun or light; in the ancient
Chinese religion, where the sun is a personal god; lastly,
among the Greeks themselves, where Helios is one of
the most ancient gods. Among the Indo-Germanic peoples, in general, the sky has been the object of a special
cult. Under the name of Dyaus, Zeus, Jupiter, Ziu, such
a god is common to Vedic India, the Greeks and Romans and the Teutons, though only in Greece and
Rome is he king of the gods, like the celestial deity of
the Mongols in China. Here especially we note the tendencies of the very ancient gods, entrusted in the beginning with entirely material tasks, to enrich themselves,
as they grow older, with moral attributes. In Southern

Babylonia the sun, who is all-seeing, has become the guardian of right and justice; he receives the title of "judge." The Vedic Mitra is the champion of truth and right; he gives victory to the righteous cause. And the Egyptian Osiris, who has become one with the sun-god after having been the god of vegetation, has ended by being the great judge, merciful and just, who reigns over the land of the dead.

All these gods are closely connected with things. But there are others—often the same ones seen from a different angle—that are defined by their connexion with persons or groups. Are we to consider as a god the personal genius or daemon of a particular individual? The Roman genius was *numen*, not *deus*; it had neither shape nor name; it was very near to that mere "effective presence" which we have seen to be the primitive and essential element of divinity. The personality of the *lar familiaris*, who watched over the family, was scarcely more marked. But the bigger the group, the stronger its right to a real god. In Egypt, for example, each of the primitive cities had its divine guardian. And these gods were distinguished one from the other precisely by their connexion with this or that community; to call them "He of Edfu," "He of Nekkeb," was clear enough. But in most cases they were deities who existed before the group, and whom the latter had adopted. This was the case, in Egypt itself, with Amon-Re, god of Thebes. It was the same in Babylonia, where the city of Ur had as its goddess the moon, the city of Uruk the planet Venus. It was the same in Greece, where Demeter was particularly at home in Eleusis, Athene on the Acropolis, Artemis in Arcadia. Often protectors and protected stood or fell together; the gods of a city gained by the aggrandisement of that city. War thus became a struggle between rival deities. The latter might indeed come to terms, and the gods of the conquered people then entered the pantheon of the victor. But the truth is that

the city or the empire on the one hand, and its tutelary
gods on the other, formed an undefined partnership,
which must have varied indefinitely in character.

Nevertheless, it is for our own convenience that we
thus define and classify the gods of fable. No law governed their birth, any more than their development; in
this case humanity has given free play to its instinct for
myth-making. Doubtless this instinct does not go very
far when left to itself, but it progresses unceasingly if
one is pleased to exercise it. The differences are very
great, on this point, between the mythologies of different peoples. Classical antiquity shows us an example of
this contrast: Roman mythology is poor, that of the
Greeks superabundant. The gods of ancient Rome coincide with the functions with which they are clothed
and are thus, so to speak, immobilized in them. They
barely possess a body, I mean an imaginable shape. They
are barely gods. On the contrary each god of ancient
Greece has his physiognomy, his character, his history.
He moves about, does things quite outside the mere
performance of his functions. His adventures are told,
his intervention in our affairs described. He lends himself to every fancy of the artist and the poet. He would
be, more accurately, a character in a novel, if it were not
that he had a power greater than that of mortal man
and the privilege, at least in certain cases, of interfering
with the regular working of the laws of nature. In a
word, the myth-making function of the mind has in the
first case stopped short, in the second it has continued
its work. But it remains the same function. It will resume, if need be, the interrupted work. This is what
happened with the introduction of Greek literature, and
more generally of Greek ideas, into Rome. We know
how the Romans identified some of their gods with those
of Hellas, thus endowing them with a more marked personality, and changing them from immobility to movement.

We have said of this myth-making function that it would be inaccurate to define it as a variant of imagination. This last word has a somewhat negative meaning. We call imaginative any concrete representation which is neither perception nor memory. Since such representations depict neither a present object nor a past thing, they are all considered in the same light by common sense and given the same name in ordinary speech. But the psychologist must not for that reason group them in the same category, or connect them with the same function. Let us then leave aside imagination, which is but a word, and consider a very clearly defined faculty of the mind, that of creating personalities whose stories we relate to ourselves. It is singularly vivid in novelists and dramatists. There are some among them who become really obsessed by their hero; it is he who controls them, not they who control him; they even have difficulty in getting rid of him when they have finished their play or their novel. These writers are not necessarily those whose work is of the highest quality; but, better than others, they enable us to put our finger on the existence, at least in some of us, of a special faculty of voluntary hallucination. In truth, it is found, to some degree, in everyone. It is very vivid in children. We find a child keeping up a daily intercourse with some imaginary person, whose name he can give, whose impressions about every incident of the day he can repeat to you. But the same faculty comes into play in those who, without creating fictitious beings for themselves, are as interested in fictions as in real things. What sight is there more amazing than that of a theatre audience in tears? We shall be told that the play is being performed by actors and that human beings of flesh and blood are on the stage. Agreed, but we can be almost as completely "gripped" by the novel we are reading, and sympathize just as keenly with the people whose story is being told us. How is it that psychologists have not been struck by

the mysterious element in such a faculty as this? The
answer will be that all our faculties are mysterious, inasmuch as we are ignorant of the inner mechanism of
them. True, but this is no question of mechanical reconstruction, we are entitled to ask for a psychological explanation. And the explanation is the same in
psychology as in biology: the existence of a function
is accounted for, when we have shown how and why it is
necessary to life. Now novelists and dramatists are certainly not necessities; the myth-making faculty in general does not correspond to a vital need. But let us
suppose that on one particular point, when utilized for
a given object, this function be indispensable to the existence of individuals as well as of societies: we can easily
understand that, while designed for this work, for which
it is indispensable, it should be further employed, since
it is still there, for mere amusement. As a matter of fact,
we pass quite easily from the novel of to-day to more or
less ancient tales, to legends, to folklore, and from folklore to mythology, which is not the same thing, but
which was developed in the same way; mythology, in
its turn, merely develops the personalities of the gods
into a story, and this last creation is but the extension
of another and simpler one, that of the "semi-personal
powers" or "efficient presences" which are, we believe,
at the origin of religion. Here we get at what we have
shown to be a fundamental demand of life: this demand
has called into being the myth-making faculty; the myth-
making function is thus to be deduced from the conditions of existence of the human species. Without going
back over what we have already stated at great length,
let us recall that, in the realm of life, what appears under analysis to be infinitely complex presents itself to
intuition as an undivided act. The act might quite well
not have been performed; but, if it *is* performed, then
it has, in one stride, got across all the obstacles. These
obstacles, each one of which raised up another, consti-

tute an endless multiplicity, and it is precisely with the removal, one after the other, of all these obstacles that our analysis has to deal. To try and explain each of these processes of elimination by the preceding one would be going the wrong way to work; they are all to be explained by one single operation, which is the act itself in its simplicity. Thus the undivided movement of the arrow triumphs at one sweep over the innumerable obstacles which our perception, assisted by Zeno's reasoning, thinks it detects in the immobility of the points making up the line of flight. Thus, too, the undivided act of vision, by the mere fact of succeeding, overcomes at a stroke thousands and thousands of obstacles; it is these obstacles, surmounted, which appear to our perception and to our science in the multiplicity of cells constituting the eye, the intricateness of our visual apparatus, in short, the endless series of mechanisms which are at work in the process of seeing. Posit in the same way the human species, that is to say the sudden leap by which life in its evolution came to man, both individual and social, you will then be positing a tool-contriving intelligence and consequently an effort which is bound to go on, of its own momentum, beyond the mere tool-making operation for which it was intended; and this creates a danger. If the human species does exist, it is because the very act which posited man with his tool-contriving intelligence, with the necessary continuation of his intellectual effort, and the danger arising from such a continuation, begot the myth-making function. The latter was not, then, purposed by nature; and yet it sprang up naturally. If, indeed, we add it to all the other psychical functions, we find that the sum total expresses in a multiple form the indivisible act by which life leapt onwards to man, from that rung of the ladder at which it had stopped.

But let us look more closely into the reason why the myth-making function imposes its inventions with ex-

ceptional force when working in the realm of religion.
There, without any doubt, it is at home; it is made for
the creation of spirits and gods; but since it continues
its myth-making work elsewhere, we must ask why,
though operating in the same way, it no longer commands the same credence. We may find two reasons for
this.

The first is that, where religion is concerned, the ad-
herence of each individual is reinforced by the adher-
ence of all. Even in the theatre, the spectator's ready
acceptance of the dramatist's suggestions is singularly
increased by the attention and the interest of the society
in which he finds himself. But in this case we have a
society just the size of the hall, and enduring only just
as long as the play lasts: what if the individual belief is
supported, confirmed by a whole people, and if it rests
both on the past and on the present? What if the god
is sung by poets, if he dwells in temples, if he is portrayed
by art? So long as experimental science is not firmly established, there will be no surer guarantee of the truth
than universal assent. Nay, truth will as a rule *be* this
very assent. We may note, by the way, that this is one of
the causes of intolerance. The man who does not accept
the common belief prevents it, while he dissents, from
being utterly true. Truth will regain its entirety only if
he retracts or disappears.

We do not mean to say that religious belief can never
have been, even in polytheism, an individual belief.
Each Roman had a genius attached to his person; but he
believed so firmly in his genius only because every other
Roman had *his* own genius, and because his faith, personal on this point, was guaranteed to him by a universal faith. We do not mean to say either that religion
has ever been social in essence rather than individual:
we have, indeed, seen that the myth-making function,
innate in the individual, has as its first object the consolidation of society; but we know that it is also in-

tended to support the individual himself, and that, moreover, such is the interest of society. As a matter of fact, the individual and society are implied in each other: individuals make up society by their grouping together; society shapes an entire side of individuals by being prefigured in each one of them. The individual and society thus condition each other, circle-wise. The circle, intended by nature, was broken by man the day he became able to get back into the creative impetus, and impel human nature forward instead of letting it revolve on one spot. From that day there dates an essentially individual religion, one that has become thereby, it is true, more profoundly social. But we shall revert to this point. Let us only say that the guarantee brought by society to individual belief, in the matter of religion, would suffice in itself to put these inventions of the myth-making function in a unique position.

But we must bear yet another thing in mind. We have seen how the ancients witnessed, unconcerned, the birth of this or that god. Thenceforth they would believe in him as they did in all the others. This would be incredible, if we supposed that the existence of their gods was of the same nature to them as the objects they saw and touched. It was real, but with a reality that yet hinged in some degree on the human will.

The gods of pagan civilization are indeed distinguishable from older entities, elves, gnomes, spirits, which popular belief never actually abandoned. The latter were the almost direct product of that myth-making faculty which is natural to us; and they were naturally adopted, just as they had been naturally produced. They conformed exactly to the need from which they sprang. But mythology, which is an amplification of primitive activity, extends beyond this need in all directions. The interval it leaves between this need and itself is filled with a matter in the choice of which human fancy has a large share, and this affects the assent accorded to it.

It is always the same faculty intervening, and it obtains
for its inventions, as a whole, the same credence. But
each invention, taken separately, is accepted with the
reservation that another would have been possible. The
pantheon exists independent of man, but on man depends the placing of a god in it, and the bestowal of
existence on that deity. Such an attitude of mind does
indeed surprise us to-day. Yet we lapse into it ourselves
in certain dreams, where we can introduce, at a certain
moment, the incident we desire: thus a part comes into
being through us, whilst the whole has its own existence
independent of us. In just the same way it could be said
that each distinct god is contingent, whereas the gods
as a whole, or rather the godhead in general, is necessary.
If we were to delve into this point, by pushing logic
further than did the ancients, we should find that there
has never been any absolute pluralism other than the belief in spirits, and that polytheism, strictly speaking,
along with its mythology, implies a latent monotheism,
in which the multiple deities exist only secondarily, as
representatives of the divine.

But the ancients would have held such considerations
to be unessential: they would be of importance only if
religion belonged to the realm of knowledge or contemplation. In that case a mythological tale could be treated
like a historical narrative, and in the one case as in the
other the question of authenticity might arise. But the
truth is that there is no possible comparison between
them, because they are not of the same order. History
is knowledge, religion is mainly action: it concerns
knowledge, as we have repeated over and over again,
only in so far as an intellectual representation is needed
to ward off the dangers of a certain intellectuality. To
consider this representation apart, to criticize it *as* a representation, would be to forget that it forms an amalgam
with the accompanying action. We commit just such an
error when we ask ourselves how it is that great minds

can have accepted the tissue of childish imaginings, nay, absurdities, which made up their religion. The movements of a swimmer would appear just as silly and ridiculous to anyone forgetting that the water is there, that this water sustains the swimmer, and that the man's movements, the resistance of the liquid, the current of the river, must be taken all together as an undivided whole.

Religion supplies strength and discipline. For that reason regularly repeated exercises are necessary, like those whose automatism ends by instilling into the body of the soldier the confidence he will need in the hour of danger. This means that there is no religion without rites and ceremonies. The religious representation is above all an occasion for these religious acts. They doubtless emanate from belief, but they at once react on it and strengthen it: if gods exist, they must have their worship; but since there is worship, then there must be gods. This solidarity of the god with the homage paid him makes of religious truth a thing apart, having no common measure with speculative truth, and depending, up to a certain point, on man.

It is precisely towards the tightening up of this solidarity that rites and ceremonies tend. One might dilate on them at length. We shall merely touch on the two principal ones, sacrifice and prayer.

In the religion which we shall call dynamic, prayer is independent of its verbal expression; it is an elevation of the soul that can dispense with speech. In its lowest form, on the other hand, it was not unlike the incantations of magic; it then aimed, if not at compelling the will of the gods and above all of the spirits, at least at capturing their goodwill. Prayer, as understood in polytheism, generally finds its place half-way between these two extremities. No doubt antiquity hit upon admirable forms of prayer, in which there was manifested an aspiration of the soul to improvement. But these were exceptions and, as it were, anticipations of a purer religious belief. Polytheism more generally imposes on prayer a stereotyped form, with the latent idea that it is not only the meaning of the phrase, but also the sequence of the words, together with all the accompanying gestures, which impart to prayer its efficacy. We may even say that the more polytheism evolves, the more particular it becomes on this point; the agency of a priest becomes more and more indispensable to ensure the schooling of the believer. How can we fail to see that this habit of extending the idea of the god, once evoked, through prescribed words and set attitudes, endows his image with a greater objectivity? We have shown elsewhere that what constitutes the reality of a perception, what distinguishes it from a figment of the imagination, is, above all, the whole group of incipient movements which it communicates to the body, and which complete this perception by the automatic beginnings of an action. Movements of this kind may develop owing to some other cause: but their actuality will flow back just the same towards the representation that produced them, and will practically convert it into a thing.

As to sacrifice, it was, doubtless, to begin with, an offering made with a view to buying the favour of the god, or turning aside his wrath. If so, the greater the cost and the more valuable the thing sacrificed, the more acceptable it was likely to be. This is probably the explanation, at least in part, of the custom of human sacrifice, a custom to be found in most ancient religions, perhaps in all, could we trace them back far enough. There is no limit to the extent of error, or of horror, to which logic may lead, when it is applied to matters not pertaining to pure intelligence. But there is something else in sacrifice: otherwise there would be no explaining why the offering had to be animal or vegetable, nearly always animal. To begin with, it is generally agreed that sacrifice originated in a repast of which the god and his worshippers were supposed to partake in common. Next, above all, there was a special virtue in blood. As the principle of life, it gave the god strength, and enabled him the better to help man, and perhaps also (but this was a barely conscious idea) it ensured to him a more substantial existence. It was, like prayer, a link between man and the deity.

Thus polytheism with its mythology had the twofold effect of exalting more and more the invisible powers with which man is surrounded, and of putting man in ever closer contact with them. Being co-extensive with the ancient civilizations, it battened on everything they produced, having inspired literature and art, whence it received still more than it gave. This means that religious feeling, in antiquity, was made up of many elements, varying from people to people, but which have all grouped themselves round an original nucleus. We have concentrated on this nucleus, because we wished to bring out the specifically religious element in antique religions. To some of them, those of India and Persia, a philosophy has been superadded. But philosophy and religion always remain distinct. More often than not, indeed, philosophy only comes into existence to satisfy more cultivated minds; religion lives on, among the people, in the way we have described. Even in those cases where the two are mingled, the elements keep their individuality: religion will have moments when it is inclined to speculate, philosophy will not shun all idea of action; but the first will none the less remain essentially action, the second, above all, thought. In those cases where religion really became philosophy among the ancients, it rather discouraged action, and renounced what it had come into the world to accomplish. Was it still religion? We may attribute what meaning we like to words, so long as we define their meaning first; but it would be a mistake to do so when we happen to be dealing with a word which corresponds to a *natural* cutting-

up of continuous reality: we should then at most reject
the extension of the term to such or such a thing which
had become accidentally included in it. Such is the
case with religion. We have shown how this name is
ordinarily applied to representations directed towards
action, and called forth by nature for a clearly defined
purpose; it may be that exceptionally, and for obvious
reasons, the meaning of the word has been extended so
as to include some other object; religion must none the
less be defined in conformity with what we have called
the intention of nature.

We have explained more than once what is meant in
this case by intention. We have also dwelt at length in
this chapter on the function that nature has assigned to
religion. Magic, animal or spirit worship, worship of
gods, mythology, superstitions of all kinds, seem very
complex, if we take them one at a time. But, taken all
together, they make up a whole which is extremely simple.

Man is the only animal whose actions are uncertain,
who hesitates, gropes about and lays plans in the hope
of success and the fear of failure. He is alone in realizing
that he is subject to illness, alone in knowing that he
must die. The rest of nature goes on its expanding
course in absolute tranquillity. Although plants and animals are the sport of chance, they rely on the passing
hour as they would on eternity. We drink in something
of this unshakable confidence during a country walk,
from which we return quieted and soothed. But this is
not saying enough. Of all the creatures that live in society, man alone can swerve from the social line by giving way to selfish preoccupations when the common
good is at stake; in all other societies the interests of
the individual are inexorably co-ordinate with and subordinate to the general interest. This twofold shortcom-
ing in man is the price paid for intelligence. Man cannot
exert his faculty of thought without imagining an un-

certain future, which rouses his fears and his hopes. He cannot think about what nature demands of him, in so far as she has made a social being of him, without saying to himself that he might often find it more profitable to ignore others and to think of himself alone. In both cases there would be a break of the normal, natural order of things. And yet it was nature who ordained intelligence, who placed it at the end of one of the two great lines of evolution as a counterpart to the highest form of instinct, which is the terminal point of the other. It is impossible that she should not have taken the precaution to see that a condition of order, which had been even slightly disturbed by intelligence, should tend to re-establish itself automatically. As a matter of fact, the myth-making function, which belongs to intelligence, and which yet is not pure intelligence, has precisely this object. Its rôle is to elaborate that religion we have been dealing with up to now, that which we call static, and of which we should say that it was natural religion, if the term were not used in another sense. We have then only to sum up what we have said to define this religion in clear terms. *It is a defensive reaction of nature against what might be depressing for the individual, and dissolvent for society, in the exercise of intelligence.*

Let us conclude with two remarks, to forestall two misunderstandings. When we say that one of the functions of religion, as it was ordained by nature, is to maintain social life, we do not at all mean by this that there is solidarity between such a religion and morality. History is witness to the contrary. To sin has always been to offend the deity; but the deity has by no means always been offended by immorality or even crime; there have been cases where he has prescribed them. True, humanity seems in general to have wished its gods to be good; it has often placed the different virtues under their patronage; it may even be that the coincidence we pointed out between original morality and primitive religion, both alike rudimentary, has left in the depths of the human soul the vague ideal of a more developed morality and an organized religion dependent the one on the other. It is none the less true that morality has taken definite shape along its own lines, that religions have evolved along theirs, and that men have always accepted their gods from tradition without asking them for a certificate of good conduct, nor expecting them to guarantee the moral order. But a distinction must be drawn between social obligations of a very general character, without which no life in common would be possible, and the particular concrete social tie which causes the members of a particular social community to be intent on its preservation. The first have little by little emerged from the confused background of customs which we have found at the outset; they have emerged through purification and simplification, through abstraction and generalization, to form a social morality. But what binds together the members of a given society is tradition, the need and the determination to defend the group against other groups and to set it above everything. To preserve, to tighten this bond is incontestably the aim of the religion we have found to be natural; it is common to the members of a group, it associates them intimately with each other in rites and ceremonies, it distinguishes the group from other groups, it guarantees the success of the common enterprise and is an assurance against the common danger. The fact that religion, such as it issued from the hands of nature, has simultaneously fulfilled, to use the language of the day, the two functions, moral and national, appears to us unquestionable: these two functions were in fact inevitably confounded in rudimentary societies where only custom existed. But that societies, as they developed, should have carried religion with them in the second direction, will be easily understood by reference to what we have just explained. Indeed, the conclusion might have been reached immediately in view of the fact that human societies, at the end of one of the great lines of biological evolution, form the counterpart to the most perfectly developed animal societies, placed at the extremity of the other great line, and that the myth-making function, though not an instinct, plays in human societies a part exactly corresponding to that of instinct in these animal societies.

Our second remark, which we might well refrain from making after all we have so often repeated, concerns the meaning we give to the "intention of nature," an expression we have used in speaking of "natural religion." As a matter of fact, we were dealing less with this religion itself than with the effect it produced. There is an impetus of life which rushes through matter and wrests from it what it can, though it necessarily divides itself in the process. At the extremity of the two main lines of evolution thus established lie intelligence and instinct. Precisely because intelligence is a success, as indeed instinct is too, it cannot be posited without the accompaniment of a tendency to eliminate any obstacle to the production of its full effect. This tendency forms with intelligence, as with all presupposed by intelligence, an undivided whole, which becomes divisible when coming within the scope of our faculty—which is entirely relative to the intelligence itself—of perception and analysis. Let us revert to what has been said about the eye and sight. We have the act of seeing, which is simple, and we have an infinity of elements, and of reciprocal actions of these elements on each other, by means of which the anatomist and the physiologist reconstitute that simple act. Elements and actions express, analytically and so to speak negatively, being resistances opposed to resistances, the indivisible act, alone positive, which nature has effectively obtained. In the same way the anxieties of man, cast upon this earth, and the temptations the individual may have to put his interests before those of the community—anxieties and temptations which are peculiar to an intelligent being—could lend themselves to endless enumeration. Indefinite in number also are the forms of superstition, or rather of static religion, which resist these resistances. But the complexity vanishes if we place man back in nature as a whole, if we consider that intelligence is apt to be an obstacle to the serenity we find everywhere else, and that the obstacle must be surmounted, the balance restored. Regarded from this point of view, which is that of a genesis and no longer that of an analysis, all the elements of disquiet and weakness entailed in the application of intelligence to life, with all the peace brought by religions, become a perfectly simple thing. Unrest and myth-making counteract and nullify each other. In the eyes of a god, looking down from above, the whole would appear indivisible, like the perfect confidence of flowers unfolding to the spring.

Let us cast a glance backward at Life, this life which we had previously followed in its development up to the point where religion was destined to emerge from it. A great current of creative energy is precipitated into matter, to wrest from it what it can. At most points, remember, it came to a stop; these stops are equivalent, in our eyes, to the phenomena of so many living species, that is to say, of organisms in which our perception, being essentially analytical and synthetic, distinguishes a multitude of elements combining to fulfil a multitude of functions; yet the work of organization was but the step itself, a simple act, like the making of a footprint, which instantly causes a myriad grains of sand to cohere and form a pattern. We might have thought that along one of these lines where it had succeeded in going furthest, this vital energy would carry the best of itself with it and would go straight on; but it swerved inward, and the whole circle reformed: certain creatures emerged whose activity ran indefinitely in the same circle, whose organs were ready-made instruments and left no room for the ceaselessly renewed invention of tools, whose consciousness lapsed into the somnambulism of instinct instead of bracing itself and revitalizing itself into reflective thought. Such is the condition of the individual in those insect societies where organization is highly perfected, but the effect of it is sheer automatism.

The creative effort progressed successfully only along that line of evolution which ended in man. In its passage through matter, consciousness assumed in that case, as it were from a mould, the shape of tool-making intelligence. And invention, which carries reflexion with it, was at liberty to develop.

But intelligence was not without its dangers. Up to that point, all living creatures had drunk greedily of the cup of life. They lapped up with relish the honey which nature had smeared on the rim; they were prepared to gulp down the rest blindly. Not so intelligence, which peered into the bottom of the cup. For the intelligent being was not living in the present alone; there can be no reflexion without foreknowledge, no foreknowledge without inquietude, no inquietude without a momentary slackening of the attachment to life. Above all, there is no humanity without society, and society demands of the individual an abnegation which the insect, in its automatism, carries to the point of an utter obliviousness of self. Reflexion cannot be relied upon to keep up this selflessness. Intelligence, except it be that of a subtle utilitarian philosopher, would more likely counsel egoism. Thus, from two directions it called for a counterpoise. Or rather it was already provided with one, for nature, we repeat, does not make her creatures piecemeal; what is multiple in its manifestation may well be simple in its genesis. A new species coming on to the scene brings with it, in the indivisibility of the act creating it, all the elements that impart life to it. The very check of the creative impetus which has expressed itself in the creation of our species has provided, along with intelligence, within human intelligence, the myth-making function that contrives the pattern of religions. That then is the office, that is the significance of the religion we have called static or natural. Religion is that element which, in beings endowed with reason, is called upon to make good any deficiency of attachment to life.

It is true that the possibility of another solution at once occurs to the mind. Static religion, such as we find it when it stands alone, attaches man to life, and consequently the individual to society, by telling him tales on a par with those with which we lull children to sleep. Of course they are not like other stories. Being produced by the myth-making function in response to an actual need and not for mere pleasure, they counterfeit reality as actually perceived, to the point of making us act accordingly: other creations of the imagination have this same tendency, but they do not demand our compliance; they can remain just ideas; whereas the former are ideo-motory. They are none the less myths, which critical minds, as we have seen, often accept in fact, but which they should, by rights, reject. The active, moving principle, whose mere stopping at an extreme point has expressed itself in mankind, doubtless requires of all created species that they cling to life. But, as we have previously shown, if this principle produces all species in their entirety, as a tree thrusts out on every side branches which end in buds, it is the act of placing in matter a freely creative energy, it is man, or some other being of like significance—we do not say of like form—which is the purpose of the entire process of evolution. The whole might have been vastly superior to what it is, and this is probably what happens in worlds where the current rushes through matter less refractory than ours: just as the current might never have found a free outlet—even to this inadequate extent—in which case the quality and quantity of creative energy represented by the human species would never have been released at all on our planet. But whichever way we look at it, life is a thing at least as desirable, even more desirable, to man than to the other species, since the latter receive it as the effect, produced in passing, by the creative energy, whereas in man life is that successful effort itself, however precarious and incomplete this success may be. This being so, why should man not recover the confidence he lacks, or which has perhaps been undermined by reflexion, by turning back for fresh impetus, in the direction whence that impetus came? Not through intelligence, at least not through intelligence alone, could he do so: intelligence would be more likely to proceed in the opposite direction; it was provided for a definite object, and when it attempts speculation on a higher plane, it enables us, at the most, to conceive possibilities, it does not attain any reality. But we know that all around intelligence there lingers still a fringe of intuition, vague and evanescent. Can we not fasten upon it, intensify it, and above all, consummate it in action, for it has become pure contemplation only through a weakening in its principle, and, if we may put it so, by an abstraction practised on itself?

A soul strong enough, noble enough to make this effort would not stop to ask whether the principle with which it is now in touch is the transcendant cause of all things or merely its earthly delegate. It would be content to feel itself pervaded, though retaining its own personality, by a being immeasurably mightier than itself, just as an iron is pervaded by the fire which makes it glow. Its attachment to life would henceforth be its inseparability from this principle, joy in joy, love of that which is all love. In addition it would give itself to society, but to a society comprising all humanity, loved in the love of the principle underlying it. The confidence which static religion brought to man would thus be transfigured: no more thought for the morrow, no more anxious heart-searching; materially the object would no longer be worth while, and morally would take on too high a significance. Now detachment from each particular thing would become attachment to life in general. But should we, in such a case, still speak of religion? Or were we right to have used the word before for all the preceding argument? Are not the two things so different as to exclude each other, and to make it impossible to call them by the same name?

Yet there are many reasons for using the word religion in both cases. In the first place mysticism—for that is what we have in mind—may, it is true, lift the soul to another plane: it none the less ensures for the soul, to a pre-eminent degree, the security and the serenity which it is the function of static religion to provide. But we must above all bear in mind that pure mysticism is a rare essence, that it is generally found in a diluted form, that even then it still gives to the substance with which it mingles its colour and fragrance, and that it must be taken together with the substance, to be regarded as practically inseparable from it, if it is to be observed in its active state—since it was in this state that it finally imposed its sway upon the world. Looking at it from this angle, we should perceive a series of transitions, and, as it were, differences of degree, whereas really there is a radical difference of nature. Let us go back briefly over each of these points.

In defining mysticism by its relation to the vital impetus, we have implicitly admitted that true mysticism is rare. We shall deal presently with its significance and its value. Let us confine ourselves for the moment to noting that it lies, according to the above, at a point which the spiritual current, in its passage through matter, probably desired to reach but could not. For it makes light of obstacles with which nature has had to come to terms, and, on the other hand, we can understand the evolution of life, setting aside any bypaths it has been compelled to follow, only if we view it as seeking for something beyond its reach, something to which the great mystic attains. If all men, if any large number of men, could have soared as high as this privileged man, nature would not have stopped at the human species, for such a one is in fact more than a man. The same can be said of other forms of genius: they are all equally rare. It is not by chance, then, it is by reason of its very essence that true mysticism is exceptional.

But when it does call, there is in the innermost being of most men the whisper of an echo. Mysticism reveals, or rather would reveal to us, if we actually willed it, a marvellous prospect: we do not, and in most cases we could not, will it; we should collapse under the strain. Yet the spell has worked; and just as when an artist of genius has produced a work which is beyond us, the spirit of which we cannot grasp, but which makes us feel how commonplace were the things we used to admire, in the same way static religion, though it may still be there, is no longer what it was, above all it no longer dares to assert itself, when truly great mysticism comes on the scene. To static religion, mainly at any rate, humanity will still turn for the support of which it is in need; it will leave the myth-making function, remoulding it as best it can, to go on with its work; in a word, man's confidence in life will remain much the same as was ordained by nature. But he will sincerely believe that he has sought and even to some extent found that contact with the very principle of nature which expresses itself in quite a different attachment to life, in a transfigured confidence. Incapable of rising to these heights, he will go through the motions, assume the appropriate attitudes and in his speech reserve the foremost place for certain formulae which he can never see filled with their whole meaning, the whole operation being reminiscent of some ceremony where certain chairs, reserved for high dignitaries, are standing empty. Thus may arise a mixed religion, implying a new direction given to the old, a more or less marked aspiration for the ancient god who emanated from the myth-making function to be merged into the God Who effectively reveals Himself, Who illuminates and warms privileged souls with His presence. Thus do we find interposed, as we were suggesting, transitions and differences, ostensibly of degree, between two things which are as a matter of fact radically different in nature and which, at first sight, we can hardly believe deserve the same name. The contrast is striking in many cases, as for instance when nations at war each declare that they have God on their side, the deity in question thus becoming the national god of paganism, whereas the God they imagine they are evoking is a God common to all mankind, the mere vision of Whom, could all men but attain it, would mean the immediate abolition of war. And yet we should not, on the strength of this contrast, disparage religions born of mysticism, which have generalized the use of its formulae and yet have been unable to pervade all humanity with the full measure of its spirit. It sometimes happens that well-nigh empty formulae, the veriest magical incantations, contrive to summon up here and there the spirit capable of imparting substance to them. An indifferent schoolmaster, mechanically teaching a science created by men of genius, may awaken in one of his pupils the vocation he himself has never possessed, and change him unconsciously into an emulator of those great men, who are invisible and present in the message he is handing on.

Yet there is a difference between the two cases, and if we take it into account, we shall notice, in the matter of religion, a gradual disappearance of the contrast between the static and the dynamic, on which we have just insisted in order to bring out the characteristics of the two religions. The great majority of men may very well know practically nothing about mathematics and yet admire the genius of a Descartes or a Newton. But those who have, from afar off, bowed their heads to the mystic word, because they heard a faint echo of it within themselves, will not remain indifferent to its message. If they already have their different faiths, from which they will not or cannot break away, they will persuade themselves that they are effecting a transformation of them, as indeed they are: the same elements will subsist, but they will be magnetized and by this very magnetizing process be diverted into another direction. A religious historian will have no difficulty in discovering in the material form of a vaguely mystic belief, which has spread far and wide among mankind, some mythical and even magic elements. He will prove thereby that there exists a static religion, natural to man, and that human nature is unchanging. But, if he stops at that, he will have overlooked something, and perhaps the essential. At any rate he will, unwittingly perhaps, have bridged the gulf between the static and the dynamic, and justified the use of the same word in such widely different instances. One will indeed be still dealing with a religion, but with a new one.

We shall be still more convinced of this, we shall see from another angle how these two religions are antagonistic and yet come together, if we take into consideration the attempts of the second to lodge within the first, preparatory to supplanting it. As a matter of fact, it is we who convert them into attempts by an act of retrospection. They were, when they occurred, complete and self-sufficient actions, and they have assumed the guise of initial preparatory efforts only since the day when ultimate success transformed them into partial failures, by virtue of the mysterious power which the present exerts over the past. They will none the less serve us to mark the intervening stages, to analyse into its virtual elements the indivisible act by which dynamic religion is posited, and at the same time to show, by the manifest unity of direction of all those efforts which now prove to have been unsuccessful, that the sudden leap which marked final achievement was in no way fortuitous.

Among the tentative efforts leading to the mysticism which was to come, certain aspects of the pagan mysteries occupy a foremost position. We must not allow ourselves to be led astray by the term: there was nothing mystic about most of the mysteries. They were connected with the established religion, which considered it perfectly natural that they should exist along with it. They glorified the same gods, or gods originating from the same myth-making function. They merely strengthened the religious spirit among the initiate by adding to it that satisfaction which men have always had in forming little societies within the larger one, and setting themselves up as privileged beings on the strength of an initiation kept jealously secret. The members of these closed societies felt as if they were nearer to the god upon whom they called, if only because the performance of mythological scenes played a greater part here than in the public ceremonies. In a certain sense the god was present; the initiates shared to some extent in his divinity. They could therefore hope for more and better things in another life than the national religion held out to them. But these were, most probably, nothing but ready-made ideas imported from foreign lands: we know how deeply the ancient Egyptians had always been preoccupied with the fate of man after death, and we must remember the evidence of Herodotus, according to which the Demeter of the Eleusian mysteries and the Dionysos of Orphism were transformations of Isis and Osiris; so that the celebration of the mysteries, or at least what we know of it, discloses no striking divergence from the public cult. At first sight, then, there would seem to be no more mysticism about this religion than the other. But we must not confine ourselves to that aspect which was probably the only one to interest most of the initiates. We must ask ourselves if some at least of these mysteries did not bear the stamp of this or that great personality whose spirit they claimed to recall to life. We must also note the importance most of the authors give to scenes of religious enthusiasm, where the soul was thought to become really possessed by the god it invoked. In fact the most conspicuously alive of them, those which ended by attracting into their orbit the mysteries of Eleusis themselves, were those of Dionysos and his continuator, Orpheus. As a foreign god from Thrace, Dionysos was by his violence a sharp contrast to the serenity of the gods upon Olympus. He was not originally the god of wine, but he easily became so, because the intoxication of the soul he produced was not unlike that of wine. We know how William James was treated for having described as mystical, or at least having regarded as such for purposes of study, the condition induced by inhaling protoxide of nitrogen. People took this to be a profanation. And they would have been right, if the philosopher had made the protoxide a psychical equivalent of the "interior revelation," the protoxide then being, as the metaphysicians say, the efficient and sufficient cause of the result produced. But in his eyes the intoxication was presumably the occasion rather than the cause. The psychic disposition was there, potentially, along with the others, only awaiting a signal to express itself in action. It might have been evoked spiritually by an effort made on its own spiritual level. But it could just as well be brought about materially, by an inhibition of what inhibited it, by the removing of an obstacle, and this effect was the wholly negative one produced by the drug; the psychologist preferred making use of the latter, which enabled him to obtain his result whenever he wished. It is possible that no more important rôle attached to wine, when its effect was compared to the Dionysiac frenzy. But that is not the main point. What we want to find out is whether this frenzy can be considered, in retrospect, and once mysticism has come on the scene, as heralding certain mystic states. In order to answer this question, we need but glance at the evolution of Greek philosophy.

This evolution was purely rational. It carried human thought to its highest level of abstraction and generalization. It gave such strength and flexibility to the dialectic function of the mind that even to-day for such training we go to school with the Greeks. Yet two points must be noted. The first is that at the origin of this great movement there was an impulsion or a shock which was not of a philosophic nature. The second is that the doctrine in which the movement culminated, and which brought Greek thought to a climax, claimed to transcend pure reason. There is no doubt that the Dionysiac frenzy was continued into Orphism, and that Orphism went on into Pythagoreanism: well, it is to this latter, perhaps even to the former, that the primary inspiration of Platonism goes back. We know in what an atmosphere of mystery, in the Orphic sense of the word, the Platonic myths were wrapped, and how the theory of Ideas itself was inclined, by a covert sense of affinity, towards the Pythagorean theory of numbers. True, no influence of this kind is noticeable in Aristotle and his immediate successors; but the philosophy of Plotinus, in which the development culminates, and which owes as much to Aristotle as it does to Plato, is unquestionably mystic. If it has undergone the influence of Eastern thought, so very much alive in the Alexandrine world, this occurred without the knowledge of Plotinus himself, who thought he was merely condensing all Greek philosophy, with the whole object of opposing it to foreign doctrines. Thus, to sum up, there was in the beginning a leaven of Orphism, and at the end a metamorphosis of dialectics into mysticism. From this the conclusion might be drawn that it was an extra-rational force which had caused this rational development and carried it to its culmination at a point beyond reason. In the same way the slow, steady phenomena of sedimentation, which alone are visible to us, are the outcome of invisible seismic forces which, by heaving up at certain times the earth's crust, start the sedimentary activity in a given direction. But another interpretation is possible; and we are inclined to think it more probable. We may suppose that the development of Greek thought was solely the work of reason, and that, alongside and independent of it, there occurred at rare intervals in certain predisposed souls an effort to strike out, beyond the limits of intelligence, in search of a vision, a contact, the revelation of a transcendant reality. This effort may never have attained its object, but each time, just as it was nearly spent, it handed on to dialectics what remained of itself, instead of disappearing entirely; and thus, with the same expenditure of energy, a fresh attempt could not fail to reach a more distant goal, intelligence being caught up again at a more advanced point of philosophic development, the latter having in the interval acquired greater elasticity and revealing a greater degree of mysticism. We do, as a matter of fact, see a first wave, purely Dionysiac, merging into Orphism, which was of a higher intellectual character; a second wave, which we might call Orphic, led to Pythagoreanism, that is to say, to a distinct philosophy; in its turn Pythagoreanism transmitted something of its spirit to Platonism, and the latter, having adopted it, in time expanded naturally into Alexandrine mysticism. But in whatever form we imagine the relation between the two currents, the one intellectual, the other extraintellectual, it is only by placing ourselves at the terminal point that we can call the latter supra-intellectual or mystic, and regard as mystic an impulsion which originated in the mysteries.

It remains to be seen, in this case, whether the final stage of the movement was complete mysticism. One may give words whatever connotation one likes, provided one begins by defining that meaning. In our eyes, the ultimate end of mysticism is the establishment of a contact, consequently of a partial coincidence, with the creative effort which life itself manifests. This effort is of God, if it is not God himself. The great mystic is to be conceived as an individual being, capable of transcending the limitations imposed on the species by its material nature, thus continuing and extending the divine action. Such is our definition. We are free to posit it, provided we ask ourselves whether it ever finds its application, and then whether it fits such and such a particular case. As regards Plotinus, there is no doubt about the answer. It was granted to him to look upon the promised land, but not to set foot upon its soil. He went as far as ecstasy, a state in which the soul feels itself, or thinks it feels itself, in the presence of God, being irradiated with His light; he did not get beyond this last stage, he did not reach the point where, as contemplation is engulfed in action, the human will becomes one with the divine will. He thought he had reached the summit: in his eyes, to go further would have meant to go downhill. This is what he expressed in language of rare beauty, yet which is not the language of thoroughgoing mysticism. "Action," he said, "is a weakening of contemplation." [1] Therein he remains faithful to Greek intellectualism, he even sums it up in a striking formula; and at any rate he did contrive to impregnate it with mysticism. In short, mysticism, in the absolute sense in which we have agreed to take the word, was never attained by Greek thought. No doubt it would like to have come into being; as a mere virtuality, it knocked more than once at the door. The door opened wider and wider, but never wide enough for mysticism wholly to enter.

There is a radical distinction, in this case, between the mystical and the dialectical; they only come together at long intervals. Elsewhere, on the contrary, they have been constantly intermingled, in appearance helping each other, perhaps in actual fact mutually preventing each other from attaining full maturity. This is what

[1] Ἐπεὶ καὶ ἄνθρωποι, ὅταν ἀσθενήσωσιν εἰς τὸ θεωρεῖν, σκιὰν θεωρίας καὶ λόγον τὴν πρᾶξιν ποιοῦνται (Enn. III. viii. 4).

appears to have happened in Hindu thought. We shall not engage in any profound study of it nor sum it up in its essentials. Its development extends over a considerable period of time. Being both a philosophy and a religion, it has varied with time and place. It is expressed in a language some of whose many shades of meaning probably escape even those who know it best. Moreover, the words of this language have by no means always retained the same sense, even supposing that sense to have been always a precise one, or to have ever been so. But, for our purpose, a glance at the doctrine as a whole will suffice. And since, to obtain this bird's-eye view, we must inevitably content ourselves with piling up and trying to blend together views which have been held by experts, we shall, by picking out these lines which coincide, stand a fair chance of not going far wrong.

Let us first remark that India has always practised a religion similar to that of ancient Greece. Gods and spirits played the same parts as they did elsewhere. Rites and ceremonies were similar. Sacrifice was an extremely important element. These cults persisted through Brahmanism, Jainism, and Buddhism. How were they compatible with a teaching such as that of the Buddha? We must note that Buddhism, which came to deliver man, believed that the gods too needed to be delivered. It therefore treated men and gods as creatures of the same species, subject to the same laws of fate. This is easily conceivable in a hypothesis such as ours: man lives naturally in societies, and, as the result of a natural function, which we have called myth-making, he surrounds himself with phantasmic beings of his own creation, who live a life akin to his own, on a higher plane, but bound up with his own; such is the religion we regard as natural. Did the thinkers of India ever see things in this light? It is hardly likely. But any mind that sets out on the mystic way, beyond the city gates, feels more or less distinctly that he is leaving men and gods behind him. And this very fact makes him see them intermingled.

Now, just how far did Hindu thought progress in this direction? We are considering, of course, ancient India only, alone with herself, untouched by the influences which have since been brought to bear on her by Western civilization, or by the impulse to resist them. For, be it static or dynamic, we take religion at its origins. We have found that the first was foreshadowed in nature; we see now that the second is a leap beyond nature, and we study the leap in those cases where the impetus was insufficient or thwarted. The Hindu soul seems to have striven for this impetus in two different ways.

One of them is at the same time of a physiological and psychological character. Its remotest origin is to be found in a practice common to Hindus and Iranians, previous, therefore, to their separation: the recourse to an intoxicating drink which they both call *soma*. It produced a divine rapture, somewhat like that which the devotees of Dionysos sought in wine. Later came a set of practices designed to inhibit all sensation, to dull mental activity, in a word to induce states similar to hypnosis; these became systematized into the *yoga*. Should this be called mysticism in our sense of the word? There is nothing mystical in hypnotic states as such, but they may become so, or at least herald true mysticism and pave the way for it, through the suggestions which creep into them. And they will become so very easily, their form will be predisposed to fill out with this matter, if they already entail visions, ecstasies, which suspend the critical functions of intelligence. Such must have been, in one aspect at least, the significance of the practices which culminated in *yoga*. Here mysticism was no more than outlined; but a more marked mysticism, a purely spiritual concentration, could utilize the *yoga* in its material elements, and by that very operation spiritualize it. In fact, the *yoga* seems to have been, according to the time and place, a more popular form of mystic contemplation or else a complete system which included this contemplation.

We must ascertain then what this contemplation was, as also what connexion there can have been between it and mysticism as we understand it. From the most remote times, the Hindu speculated on being in general, on nature, on life. But his effort, sustained through many centuries, has not led, like the effort of the Greek philosophers, to a knowledge susceptible, as was Greek science, of unlimited development. The reason lies in the fact that to him knowledge was always rather a means than an end. The problem for him was to escape from life, which he felt to be unremitting cruelty. And suicide would not have provided this escape, for the soul has to pass into another body after death, and this would have meant a perpetual round of living and suffering. But from the very beginnings of Brahmanism, he drifted into the belief that deliverance could be won by renunciation. This renunciation was absorption in the Whole as well as in self. Buddhism, which gave a new turn to Brahmanism, did not modify it in essentials. It made it, above all, into something much more elaborate. Till then human experience had shown indeed that life meant suffering; the Buddha worked back to the cause of this suffering; he found it in desire of every kind, in the craving for life. Thus the road to deliverance could be more accurately traced. Brahmanism, Buddhism, even Jainism, therefore preached with increasing vehemence the extinction of the will to live, and this preaching strikes us at first as a call on intelligence, the three doctrines differing only in a greater or lesser degree of intellectuality. But on looking closer, we perceive that the conviction they aimed at implanting was far from being a purely intellectual state. Already in antique Brahmanism it was neither by reasoning nor by study that the ultimate conviction was obtained; it consisted in a vision, passed on by him who *had* seen. Buddhism, more philosophical on the one hand, is still more mystical on the other. The state towards which it guides the soul is beyond joy and pain, beyond consciousness. It is by a series of stages, and by a whole system of mystical discipline, that it leads to Nirvana, to the abolition of desire during life and of Karma after death. We must not forget that the origin of the Buddha's mission lies in the illumination that came to him in his early youth. Everything in Buddhism which can be put into words can doubtless be considered as a philosophy; but the essential is the final revelation, transcending both reason and speech. It is the conviction, gradually neared and suddenly attained, that the goal is reached: man's sufferings, the only certainty, and consequently the only living thing in life, are over. If we consider that we are here dealing, not with a theoretical view, but with an experience closely resembling ecstasy, that in an effort at oneness with the creative impetus a soul might indeed take the path thus described and only fail because it stopped half-way, dangling all dizzy in the void between two activities, between the human life it has left behind and the divine life it has not reached, then we shall not hesitate to see mysticism in the Buddhist faith. But we shall understand why it is not complete mysticism. This would be action, creation, love.

Not that Buddhism ignored charity. On the contrary it recommended it in the most exalted terms. And it joined example to precept. But it lacked warmth and glow. As a religious historian very justly puts it, it knew nothing "of the complete and mysterious gift of self." Let us add—and it comes perhaps to the same thing—that it did not believe in the efficacy of human action. It had no faith in such action. And faith alone can grow to power and move mountains. A complete mysticism would have reached this point. It is perhaps to be met with in India, but much later. That enthusiastic charity, that mysticism comparable to the mysticism of Christianity, we find in a Ramakrishna or a Vivekananda, to take only the most recent examples. But Christianity, and this is just the point, had come into the world in the interval. Its influence on India—gone over meanwhile to Islamism—was superficial enough, but to the soul that is predisposed a mere hint, the slightest token, is enough. But let us suppose even that the direct action of Christianity, as a dogma, has been practically nil in India. Since it has impregnated the whole of Western civilization, one breathes it, like a perfume, in everything which this civilization brings in its wake. Industrialism itself, as we shall try to prove, springs indirectly from it. And it was industrialism, it was our Western civilization, which unloosed the mysticism of a Ramakrishna or a Vivekananda. This burning, active mysticism could never have been kindled in the days when the Hindu felt he was crushed by nature and when no human intervention was of any avail. What could be done when inevitable famine doomed millions of wretches to die of starvation? The principal origin of Hindu pessimism lay in this helplessness. And it was pessimism which prevented India from carrying her mysticism to its full conclusion, since complete mysticism is action. But then, with the advent of machines which increased the yield of the land, and above all moved the products from place to place, with the advent also of political and social organizations which proved experimentally that the mass of the people was not doomed, as though by some inexorable necessity, to a life of grinding labour and bitter poverty, deliverance became possible in an entirely new sense; the mystical impulse, if operating anywhere with sufficient power, was no longer going to be stopped short by the impossibility of acting; it was no longer to be driven back into doctrines of renunciation or the systematic practice of ecstasy; instead of turning inwards and closing, the soul could open wide its gates to a universal love. Now these inventions and organization are essentially Western; it is they who, in this case, have enabled mysticism to develop to its fullest extent and reach its goal. We may therefore conclude that neither in Greece nor in ancient India was there complete mysticism, in the one case because the impetus was not strong enough, in the other case because it was thwarted by material conditions or by too narrow an intellectual frame. It is its appearance at a given moment that enables us to follow in retrospect its preparatory phases, just as the volcano, bursting into activity, explains a long series of earthquakes in the past.[2]

For the complete mysticism is that of the great Christian mystics. Let us leave aside, for the moment, their Christianity, and study in them the form apart from the matter. There is no doubt that most of them passed through states resembling the various culminating phases of the mysticism of the ancients.[3] But they merely passed through them: bracing themselves up for an entirely new effort, they burst a dam; they were then swept back into a vast current of life; from their increased

[2] We are perfectly aware of the fact that there existed other mysticisms in antiquity besides Neo-Platonism and Buddhism. But, for the object we have in view, we need only take those that advanced furthest.

[3] M. Henri Delacroix, in a book which deserves to become a classic (Études d'histoire et de psychologie du mysticisme, Paris, 1908), has called attention to the essentially active element of the great mystics. Similar ideas will be found in the remarkable works of Evelyn Underhill (Mysticism, London, 1911; and The Mystic Way, London, 1913). The latter author connects certain of her views with those we expressed in L'Evolution Créatrice, and which we have taken up again, to carry them further, in the present chapter. See, in particular, on this point, The Mystic Way.

vitality there radiated an extraordinary energy, daring, power of conception and realization. Just think of what was accomplished in the field of action by a St. Paul, a St. Teresa, a St. Catherine of Siena, a St. Francis, a Joan of Arc, and how many others besides! Nearly all this superabundant activity was devoted to spreading the Christian faith. Yet there are exceptions, and the case of Joan of Arc will suffice to show that the form can be separated from the matter.

When we grasp that such is the culminating point of the inner evolution of the great mystics, we can but wonder how they could ever have been classed with the mentally diseased. True, we live in a condition of unstable equilibrium; normal health of mind, as, indeed, of body, is not easily defined. Yet there is an exceptional, deep-rooted mental healthiness, which is readily recognizable. It is expressed in the bent for action, the faculty of adapting and re-adapting oneself to circumstances, in firmness combined with suppleness, in the prophetic discernment of what is possible and what is not, in the spirit of simplicity which triumphs over complications, in a word, supreme good sense. Is not this exactly what we find in the above-named mystics? And might they not provide us with the very definition of intellectual vigour?

If they have been judged otherwise, it is because of the abnormal states which are, with them, the prelude to the ultimate transformation. They talk of their visions, their ecstasies, their raptures. These are phenomena which also occur in sick people and which are part of their malady. An important work has lately appeared on ecstasy regarded as a psycho-asthenic manifestation. [4] But there exist morbid states which are imitations of healthy states; the latter are none the less healthy, and the former morbid. A lunatic may think he is an emperor; he will systematically introduce a Napoleonic

[4] Pierre Janet, *De l'angoisse à l'extase.*

touch into his gestures, his words, his acts, and therein lies his madness: does it in any way reflect upon Napoleon? In just the same way it is possible to parody mysticism, and the result will be mystic insanity: does it follow that mysticism is insanity? Yet there is no denying that ecstasies, visions, raptures, are abnormal states, and that it is difficult to distinguish between the abnormal and the morbid. And such indeed has been the opinion of the great mystics themselves. They have been the first to warn their disciples against visions which were quite likely to be pure hallucinations. And they generally regarded their own visions, when they had any, as of secondary importance, as wayside incidents; they had had to go beyond them, leaving raptures and ecstasies far behind, to reach the goal, which was identification of the human will with the divine will. The truth is that these abnormal states, resembling morbid states, and sometimes doubtless very much akin to them, are easily comprehensible, if we only stop to think what a shock to the soul is the passing from the static to the dynamic, from the closed to the open, from everyday life to mystic life. When the darkest depths of the soul are stirred, what rises to the surface and attains consciousness takes on there, if it be intense enough, the form of an image or an emotion. The image is often pure hallucination, just as the emotion may be meaningless agitation. But they both may express the fact that the disturbance is a systematic readjustment with a view to equilibrium on a higher level: the image then becomes symbolic of what is about to happen, and the emotion is a concentration of the soul awaiting transformation. The latter is the case of mysticism, but it may partake of the other; what is only abnormal may be accompanied by what is distinctly morbid; we cannot upset the regular relation of the conscious to the unconscious without running a risk. So we must not be surprised if nervous disturbances and mysticism sometimes go together; we find the same disturbances in other forms of genius, notably in musicians. They have to be regarded as merely accidental. The former have no more to do with mystical inspiration than the latter with musical.

Shaken to its depths by the current which is about to sweep it forward, the soul ceases to revolve round itself and escapes for a moment from the law which demands that the species and the individual should condition one another. It stops, as though to listen to a voice calling. Then it lets itself go, straight onward. It does not directly perceive the force that moves it, but it feels an indefinable presence, or divines it through a symbolic vision. Then comes a boundless joy, an all-absorbing ecstasy or an enthralling rapture: God is there, and the soul is in God. Mystery is no more. Problems vanish, darkness is dispelled; everything is flooded with light. But for how long? An imperceptible anxiety, hovering above the ecstasy, descends and clings to it like its shadow. This anxiety alone would suffice, even without the phases which are to come, to distinguish true and complete mysticism from what was in bygone days its anticipated imitation or preparation. For it shows that the soul of the great mystic does not stop at ecstasy, as at the end of a journey. The ecstasy is indeed rest, if you like, but as though at a station, where the engine is still under steam, the onward movement becoming a vibration on one spot, until it is time to race forward again. Let us put it more clearly: however close the union with God may be, it could be final only if it were total. Gone, doubtless, is the distance between the thought and the object of the thought, since the problems which measured and indeed constituted the gap have disappeared. Gone the radical separation between him who loves and him who is beloved: God is there, and joy is boundless. But though the soul becomes, in thought and feeling, absorbed in God, something of it remains outside; that something is the will, whence the soul's action, if it acted, would quite naturally proceed. Its life, then, is not yet divine. The soul is aware of this, hence its vague disquietude, hence the agitation in repose which is the striking feature of what we call complete mysticism: it means that the impetus has acquired the momentum to go further, that ecstasy affects indeed the ability to see and to feel, but that there is, besides, the will, which itself has to find its way back to God. When this agitation has grown to the extent of displacing everything else, the ecstasy has died out, the soul finds itself alone again, and sometimes desolate. Accustomed for a time to a dazzling light, it is now left blindly groping in the gloom. It does not realize the profound metamorphosis which is going on obscurely within it. It feels that it has lost much; it does not yet know that this was in order to gain all. Such is the "darkest night" of which the great mystics have spoken, and which is perhaps the most significant thing, in any case the most instructive, in Christian mysticism. The final phase, characteristic of great mysticism, is imminent. To analyse this ultimate preparation is impossible, for the mystics themselves have barely had a glimpse of its mechanism. Let us confine ourselves to suggesting that a machine of wonderfully tempered steel, built for some extraordinary feat, might be in a somewhat similar state if it became conscious of itself as it was being put together. Its parts being one by one subjected to the severest tests, some of them rejected and replaced by others, it would have a feeling of something lacking here and there, and of pain all over. But this entirely superficial distress would only have to be intensified in order to pass into the hope and expectation of a marvellous instrument. The mystic soul yearns to become this instrument. It throws off anything in its substance that is not pure enough, not flexible and strong enough, to be turned to some use by God. Already it had sensed the presence of God, it had thought it beheld God in a symbolic vision, it had even been united to Him in its ecstasy; but none of this rapture was lasting, because it was mere contemplation; action threw the soul back upon itself and thus divorced it from God. *Now* it is God who is acting through the soul, in the soul; the union is total, therefore final. At this point words such as mechanism and instrument evoke images which are better left alone. They could be used to give us an idea of the preliminary work. They will teach us nothing of the final result. Let us say that henceforth for the soul there is a superabundance of life. There is a boundless impetus. There is an irresistible impulse which hurls it into vast enterprises. A calm exaltation of all its faculties makes it see things on a vast scale only, and, in spite of its own weakness, produce only what can be mightily wrought. Above all, it sees things simply, and this simplicity, which is equally striking in the words it uses and the conduct it follows, guides it through complications which it apparently does not even perceive. An innate knowledge, or rather an acquired ignorance, suggests to it straightaway the step to be taken, the decisive act, the unanswerable word. Yet effort remains indispensable, endurance and perseverance likewise. But they come of themselves, they develop of their own accord, in a soul acting and acted upon, whose liberty coincides with the divine activity. They represent a vast expenditure of energy, but this energy is supplied as it is required, for the superabundance of vitality which it demands flows from a spring which is the very source of life. And now the visions are left far behind: the divinity could not manifest itself from without to a soul henceforth replete with its essence. Nothing remains to distinguish such a man outwardly from the men about him. He alone realizes the change which has raised him to the rank of *adjutores Dei*, "patients" in respect to God, agents in respect to man. In this elevation he feels no pride. On the contrary, great is his humility. How could he be aught but humble, when there has been made manifest to him, in mute colloquy, alone with The Alone, through an emotion in which his whole soul seemed to be absorbed, what we may call the divine humility?

Even in the mysticism which went only as far as ecstasy, that is to say contemplation, a certain line of action was foreshadowed. Hardly had these mystics come back from Heaven to earth, when they felt it incumbent on them to teach mankind. They had to tell all men that the world perceived by the eyes of the body is doubtless real, but that there is something else, and that this something is no mere possibility or probability, like the conclusion of an argument, but the certainty of a thing experienced: here is one who has seen, who has touched, one who knows. And yet these were but the tentative beginnings of an apostolate. The enterprise was indeed discouraging: how could the conviction derived from an experience be handed down by speech? And, above all, how could the inexpressible be expressed? But these questions do not even present themselves to the great mystic. He has felt truth flowing into his soul from its fountainhead like an active force. He can no more help spreading it abroad than the sun can help diffusing its light. Only, it is not by mere words that he will spread it.

For the love which consumes him is no longer simply the love of man for God, it is the love of God for all men. Through God, in the strength of God, he loves all mankind with a divine love. This is not the fraternity enjoined on us by the philosophers in the name of reason, on the principle that all men share by birth in one rational essence: so noble an ideal cannot but command our respect; we may strive to the best of our ability to put it into practice, if it be not too irksome for the individual and the community; we shall never attach ourselves to it passionately. Or, if we do, it will be because we have breathed in some nook or corner of our civilization the intoxicating fragrance left there by mysticism. Would the philosophers themselves have laid down so confidently the principle, so little in keeping with everyday experience, of an equal participation of all men in a higher essence, if there had not been mystics to embrace all humanity in one simple indivisible love? This is not, then, that fraternity which started as an idea, whence an ideal has been erected. Neither is it the intensification of an innate sympathy of man for man. Indeed we may ask ourselves whether such an instinct ever existed elsewhere than in the imagination of philosophers, where it was devised for reasons of symmetry. With family, country, humanity appearing as wider and wider circles, they thought that man must naturally love humanity as he loves his country and his family, whereas in reality the family group and the social group are the only ones ordained by nature, the only ones corresponding to instincts, and the social instinct would be far more likely to prompt societies to struggle against one another than to unite to make up humanity. The utmost we can say is that family and social feeling may chance to overflow and to operate beyond its natural frontiers, with a kind of luxury value; it will never go very far. The mystic love of humanity is a very different thing. It is not the extension of an instinct, it does not originate in an idea. It is neither of the senses nor of the mind. It is of both, implicitly, and is effectively much more. For such a love lies at the very root of feeling and reason, as of all other things. Coinciding with God's love for His handiwork, a love which has been the source of everything, it would yield up, to anyone who knew how to question it, the secret of creation. It is still more metaphysical than moral in its essence. What it wants to do, with God's help, is to complete the creation of the human species and make of humanity what it would have straightaway become, had it been able to assume its final shape without the assistance of man himself. Or to use words which mean, as we shall see, the same thing in different terms: its direction is exactly that of the vital impetus; it *is* this impetus itself, communicated in its entirety to exceptional men who in their turn would fain impart it to all humanity and by a living contradiction change into creative effort that created thing which is a species, and turn into movement what was, by definition, a stop.

Can it succeed? If mysticism is to transform humanity, it can do so only by passing on, from one man to another, slowly, a part of itself. The mystics are well aware of this. The great obstacle in their way is the same which prevented the creation of a divine humanity. Man has to earn his bread with the sweat of his brow; in other words, humanity is an animal species, and, as such, subject to the law which governs the animal world and condemns the living to batten upon the living. Since he has to contend for his food both with nature and with his own kind, he necessarily expends his energies procuring it; his intelligence is designed for the very object of supplying him with weapons and tools, with a view to that struggle and that toil. How then, in these conditions, could humanity turn heavenwards an attention which is essentially concentrated on earth? If possible at all, it can only be by using simultaneously or successively two very different methods. The first would consist presumably in intensifying the intellectual work to such an extent, in carrying intelligence so far beyond what nature intended, that the simple tool would give place to a vast system of machinery such as might set human activity at liberty, this liberation being, moreover, stabilized by a political and social organization which would ensure the application of the mechanism to its true object. A dangerous method, for mechanization, as it developed, might turn against mysticism: nay more, it is by an apparent reaction against the latter that mechanization would reach its highest pitch of development. But there

are certain risks which must be taken: an activity of a
superior kind, which to be operative requires one of a
lower order, must call forth this activity, or at least permit it to function, if necessary, even at the cost of having
to defend itself against it; experience shows that if, in
the case of two contrary but complementary tendencies,
we find one to have grown until it tries to monopolize
all the room, the other will profit by this, provided it has
been able to survive; its turn will come again, and it will
then benefit by everything which has been done without
its aid, which has even been energetically developed in
specific opposition to it. However that may be, this
means could only be utilized much later; in the mean-
time an entirely different method had to be followed.
This consisted, not in contemplating a general and immediate spreading of the mystic impetus, which was
obviously impossible, but in imparting it, already weakened though it was, to a tiny handful of privileged souls
which together would form a spiritual society; societies
of this kind might multiply; each one, through such of
its members as might be exceptionally gifted, would give
birth to one or several others; thus the impetus would
be preserved and continued until such time as a profound change in the material conditions imposed on
humanity by nature should permit, in spiritual matters,
of a radical transformation. Such is the method followed
by the great mystics. It was of necessity, and because
they could do no more, that they were particularly prone
to spend their superabundant energy in founding con-
vents or religious orders. For the time being they had no
need to look further. The impetus of love which drove
them to lift humanity up to God and complete the divine creation could reach its end, in their eyes, only with
the help of God Whose instruments they were. Therefore all their efforts must be concentrated on a very
great, a very difficult, but a limited task. Other efforts
would be forthcoming, indeed others had already been;

they would all be convergent, since God imparted to them their unity.

We have, indeed, simplified a great deal. To make things clearer, and, above all, to take the difficulties one by one, we have reasoned as though the Christian mystic, the bearer of an inner revelation, had made his appearance in a humanity utterly ignorant of such a thing. As a matter of fact, the men to whom he spoke already had their religion, the same, moreover, as his own. If he had visions, these visions showed him, in the form of images, what his religion had impressed on him in the form of ideas. His ecstasies, when they occurred, united him to a God probably greater than anything he had ever conceived, but who did nevertheless correspond to the abstract descriptions with which religion had supplied him. The question may even be asked if these abstract teachings are not at the root of mysticism, and if the latter has ever done more than go over the letter of the dogma, in order to retrace it in characters of flame. The business of the mystics would in this case be nothing but bringing to religion, in order to restore its vital heat, something of the ardour with which they were fired. Now, the man who professes such an opinion will certainly have no difficulty in getting it accepted. For the teaching of religion, like all teaching, is meant for the intelligence, and anything of a purely intellectual order can be brought within the reach of all men. Whether or no we subscribe to religion, it is always possible to assimilate it intellectually, even if we must admit its mysteries to be mysterious. On the contrary, mysticism means nothing, absolutely nothing, to the man who has no experience of it, however slight. Therefore everyone will appreciate that mysticism may assert itself, original and ineffable, now and then, in a pre-existing religion which is formulated in terms of intelligence, whereas it is difficult to obtain acceptance for the idea of a religion which exists only through mysticism, and

which is a mere extract of it—an extract capable of being
formulated by the intellect and therefore grasped by all.
It is not for us to decide which of these interpretations
conforms to religious orthodoxy. Let us only say that
from the psychologist's point of view the second is much
more likely than the first. A doctrine which is but a doctrine has a poor chance indeed of giving birth to the
glowing enthusiasm, the illumination, the faith that
moves mountains. But grant this fierce glow, and the
molten matter will easily run into the mould of a doctrine, or even become that doctrine as it solidifies. We
represent religion, then, as the crystallization, brought
about by a scientific process of cooling, of what mysticism had poured, while hot, into the soul of man.
Through religion all men get a little of what a few privileged souls possessed in full. True, religion had to accept a great deal to get itself accepted. Humanity really
understands the new only when it inherits much of the
old. Now the old was, on the one hand, what had been
built up by the Greek philosophers, and, on the other
hand, what had been imagined by ancient religions.
That Christianity received or derived a great deal from
both there is no doubt. It is permeated with Greek philosophy, and has preserved many rites, many ceremonies,
many beliefs even, from the religion we called static or
natural. It was in its interest to do so, for its partial
adoption of the Aristotelian Neo-Platonism enabled it
to win over philosophic thought, and its borrowings
from ancient religions were bound to help this new religion—with its marked tendency in the opposite direction, having hardly anything in common with past
religions but the name—to become popular. But none of
all that was essential; the essence of the new religion
was to be the diffusion of mysticism. There is such a
thing as high-level popularization, which respects the
broad outlines of scientific truth, and enables ordinary
cultivated minds to get a general grasp of it until the

time comes when a greater effort reveals it to them in detail, and, above all, allows them to penetrate deeply into its significance. The propagation of the mystical through religion seems to us something of the kind. In this sense, religion is to mysticism what popularization is to science.

What the mystic finds waiting for him, then, is a humanity which has been prepared to listen to his message by other mystics invisible and present in the religion which is actually taught. Indeed his mysticism itself is imbued with this religion, for such was its starting-point. His theology will generally conform to that of the theologians. His intelligence and his imagination will use the teachings of the theologians to express in words what he experiences, and in material images what he sees spiritually. And this he can do easily, since theology has tapped that very current whose source is the mystical. Thus his mysticism is served by religion, against the day when religion becomes enriched by his mysticism. This explains the primary mission which he feels to be entrusted to him, that of an intensifier of religious faith. He takes the most crying needs first. In reality, the task of the great mystic is to effect a radical transformation of humanity by setting an example. The object could be attained only if there existed in the end what should theoretically have existed in the beginning, a divine humanity.

So then mysticism and religion are mutually cause and effect, and continue to interact on one another indefinitely. Yet there must have been a beginning. And indeed at the origin of Christianity there is Christ. From our standpoint, which shows us the divinity of all men, it matters little whether or no Christ be called a man. It does not even matter that he be called Christ. Those who have gone so far as to deny the existence of Jesus cannot prevent the Sermon on the Mount from being in the Gospels, with other divine sayings. Bestow what name you like on their author, there is no denying that there was one. The raising of such problems does not concern us here. Let us merely say that, if the great mystics are indeed such as we have described them, they are the imitators, and original but incomplete continuators, of what the Christ of the Gospels was completely.

He Himself may be considered as the continuator of the prophets of Israel. There is no doubt but that Christianity was a profound transformation of Judaism. It has been said over and over again: a religion which was still essentially national was replaced by a religion that could be made universal. A God who was doubtless a contrast to all other gods by His justice as well as by His power, but Whose power was used for His people, and Whose justice was applied, above all, to His own subjects, was succeeded by a God of love, a God Who loved all mankind. This is precisely why we hesitate to classify the Jewish prophets among the mystics of antiquity: Jehovah was too stern a judge, Israel and its God were not close enough together for Judaism to be the mysticism which we are defining. And yet no current of thought or feeling has contributed so much as the thought and feeling of Jewish prophets to arouse the mysticism which we call complete, that of the Christian mystics. The reason is that, if other currents carried certain souls towards a contemplative mysticism and thereby deserved to be regarded as mystic, pure contemplation they remained, and nothing more. To cover the interval between thought and action an impetus was needed—and it was not forthcoming. We find this impetus in the prophets: they longed passionately for justice, demanded it in the name of the God of Israel; and Christianity, which succeeded Judaism, owed largely to the Jewish prophets its active mysticism, capable of marching on to the conquest of the world.

If mysticism is really what we have just said it is, it must

furnish us with the means of approaching, as it were
experimentally, the problem of the existence and the
nature of God. Indeed we fail to see how philosophy
could approach the problem in any other way. Generally
speaking, we look upon an object as existing if it is perceived, or might be perceived. Such an object is therefore presented in actual or possible experience. No
doubt you may construct the idea of an object or of a
being, as the geometrician does for a geometrical figure;
but experience alone will decide whether it actually exists outside the idea thus constructed. Now, you may
assert that this is just the question, and that the problem
precisely is to know whether a certain Being is not distinctive from all other beings in that He stands beyond
the reach of our experience, and yet is as real as they
are. Granted, for this once; although an assertion of this
kind, with its attendant arguments, appears to me to
imply a fundamental illusion. But then you must prove
that the Being thus defined, thus demonstrated, is indeed God. You may argue that He is so by definition,
and that one is at liberty to confer any meaning one
likes on words, provided one defines them first. Granted
again; but if you attribute to a word a radically different
meaning from that which it usually bears, it will apply
to a new object; your reasoning no longer refers to the
former one; it is therefore understood that you are speaking to us of something else. This is precisely what occurs
in most cases when the philosopher speaks of God. So
remote is this conception from the God most men have
in mind that if, by some miracle, and contrary to the
opinion of philosophers, God as thus defined should
step down into the field of experience, none would recognize Him. For religion, be it static or dynamic, regards Him, above all, as a Being who can hold
communication with us: now this is just what the God
of Aristotle, adopted with a few modifications by most
of his successors, is incapable of doing. Without going

deeply here into an examination of the Aristotelian notion of the divinity, we shall simply say that it seems to us to raise a double question: (1) Why did Aristotle posit as first principle a motionless Mover, a Thought thinking itself, self-enclosed, operative only by the appeal of its perfection? (2) Why, having posited this principle, did he call it God? But in the one case as in the other the answer is easy: the Platonic theory of Ideas ruled over the thought of Greece and Rome ere ever it penetrated into modern philosophy; and the relation of the first principle of Aristotle to the world is the very same as that which Plato establishes between the Idea and the thing. For anyone who sees in ideas nothing but the product of social and individual intelligence, it is in no way surprising that a limited number of immutable ideas should correspond to the infinitely varied and changing things of our experience; for we contrive to find resemblances between things in spite of their diversity, and to take a stable view of them in spite of their instability; in this way we obtain ideas which we can control, whereas the actual things may elude our grasp. All this is the work of man. But he who starts philosophizing when society is already well advanced with its work, and finds the results stored up in language, may be struck with admiration for this system of ideas, which now seem to set the standard for all things. Are they not, in their immutability, models which things, changing and shifting as they are, merely imitate? May they not be true reality, and do not change and motion express the unceasing and unsuccessful attempts of well-nigh non-existent things, running, as it were, after themselves, to coincide with the immutability of the Ideas? It is therefore understandable that, having placed above the world of the senses a hierarchy of Ideas with the Idea of Ideas, that is, the Idea of Good at its apex, Plato should have judged that the Ideas in general, and still more so the Good, acted through the attractive power of their perfection. Now this is exactly the sort of action that Aristotle ascribes to the Thought of Thoughts, which seems indeed akin to the Idea of Ideas. True, Plato did not identify this idea with God. The Demiurge of the *Timaeus*, who organizes the world, is distinct from the Idea of Good. But the *Timaeus* is a mythical dialogue; the Demiurge has therefore only a semi-existence; and Aristotle, who abandons myths, surmises as coincident with the Divinity a Thought which, so it would seem, is barely a thinking Being, and which we should call rather Idea than Thought. Thus the God of Aristotle has nothing in common with the gods worshipped by the Greeks; nor has he much more in common with the God of the Bible, of the Gospels. Religion, whether static or dynamic, confronts the philosopher with a God who raises totally different problems. Yet it is to Aristotle's God that metaphysical thought has generally attached itself, even at the price of investing him with attributes incompatible with his essence. Why not have gone back to his origin? It would have seen him develop by the concentration of all ideas into one. Why not have gone on to consider each of these ideas? It would have realized that they served to prepare the way for the action of society and of the individual on things, that society supplied them for this purpose to the individual, and that to set up their quintessence as a divinity is merely to deify the social. Why not, lastly, have analysed the social conditions of this individual action, and the nature of the work done by the individual with the help of society? It would have seen that if, in order to simplify the work and also to facilitate co-operation, things are first reduced to a few categories, or ideas, translatable into words, each of these ideas stands for a stable property or condition culled from some stage or other in the process of becoming; the real is mobile, or rather movement itself, and we perceive only continuities of change; but to have any action on the real, and especially to perform the constructive task which is the natural object of human intelligence, we must contrive to have halts here and there, just as we wait for a momentary slowing down or standing still before firing at a moving target. But these halts, each of which is really the simultaneousness of two or more movements and not, as it seems to be, a suppression of movement, these qualities which are but snapshots of change, become in our eyes the real and essential, precisely because they are what concerns our action on things. Rest then becomes for us something anterior and superior to movement, motion being regarded only as agitation with a view to a standing still. Thus immutability is rated higher than mutability, which implies a deficiency, a lack, a quest of the unchanging form. Nay, more, it is by this gap between the point where a thing is and the point where it should be, where it aspires to be, that movement and change will be defined and even measured. On this showing, duration becomes a debasement of being, time a deprivation of eternity. This whole system of metaphysics is involved in the Aristotelian conception of Deity. It consists in deifying both the social work which paves the way for language and the individual work of construction which needs patterns and models: the εἶδος (Idea or Form) is what corresponds to this twofold work; the Idea of Ideas or Thought of Thoughts is therefore Divinity itself. With the origin and meaning of Aristotle's God thus traced back we can but wonder how modern thinkers, when treating of the existence and the nature of God, hamper themselves with insoluble problems which arise only if God is studied from the Aristotelian point of view, and if they are pleased to call by that name a being whom mankind has never dreamed of invoking.

Now, is mystical experience able to solve these problems? It is easy to see the objections that such a notion will arouse. We have disposed of those which consist in asserting that no mystic is sound in the head and that all mysticism is a pathological state. The great mystics, the only ones that we are dealing with, have generally been men or women of action, endowed with superior common sense: it matters little that some of them had imitators who well deserved to be called "crazy," or that there are cases when they themselves felt the effect of extreme and prolonged strain of mind and will; many a man of genius has been in the same condition. But there is another series of objections, which it is impossible to overlook. For it is alleged that the experiences of the great mystics are individual and exceptional, that they cannot be verified by the ordinary man, that they cannot therefore be compared to a scientific experiment and cannot possibly solve problems. There is a great deal to be said on this point. In the first place, it is by no means certain that a scientific experiment, or more generally an observation recorded by science, can always be repeated or verified. In the days when Central Africa was a *terra incognita*, geography trusted to the account of one single explorer, if his honesty and competence seemed to be above suspicion. The route of Livingstone's journeys appeared for a long time on the maps and atlases. You may object that verification was potentially, if not actually, feasible, that other travellers could go and see if they liked, and that the map based on the indications of one traveller was a provisional one, waiting for subsequent exploration to make it definitive. I grant this: but the mystic too has gone on a journey that others can potentially, if not actually, undertake; and those who are actually capable of doing so are at least as many as those who possess the daring and energy of a Stanley setting out to find Livingstone. Indeed, that is an understatement. Along with the souls capable of following the mystic way to the end there are many who go at least part of the way: how numerous are those who take a few steps, either by an effort of will or from a natural disposition! William James used to say he had never experienced mystic states; but he added that if he heard them spoken of by a man who had experienced them "something within him echoed the call." Most of us are probably in the same case. It is no use invoking as evidence to the contrary the indignant protests of those who see nothing in mysticism but quackery and folly. Some people are doubtless utterly impervious to mystic experience, incapable of feeling or imagining anything of it. But we also meet with people to whom music is nothing but noise; and some of them will express their opinions of musicians with the same anger, the same tone of personal spite. No one would think of accepting this as an argument against music. Let us leave, then, these merely negative arguments and see whether the most superficial examination of mystic experience will not incline us favourably towards it.

We must first note the fact that mystics generally agree among themselves. This is striking in the case of the Christian mystics. To reach the ultimate identification with God, they go through a series of states. These may vary from mystic to mystic, but there is a strong resemblance between them. In any case, the path followed is the same, even admitting that the stopping-places by the way are at different intervals. They have in any case the same terminal point. In the descriptions of the final state we find the same expressions, the same images, the same comparisons, although the authors were generally unknown to each other. It will be replied that in some cases they had known one another, that furthermore there is a mystic tradition, and that all mystics may have felt its influence. We grant this, but the fact must be noted that the great mystics give little thought to this tradition; each one has his own originality, which is not intentional, which he has not sought, but which we feel is of fundamental importance to him; it means that he is the object of an exceptional favour, unmerited though it be. Now it may be objected that a community of religion suffices to explain the resemblance, that all Christian mystics have lived on the Gospels, that they all received the same theological teaching. But this would be to forget that, if the resemblance between the visions is indeed explainable by a common religion, these visions occupy but a small place in the lives of the great mystics; they are soon left behind, and treated as if they had been merely symbolical. As to theological teaching in general, it is true that they seem to accept it with utter docility, and in particular to obey their confessors; but, as has been shrewdly remarked, "they obey themselves alone, and a sure instinct leads them straight to the very man who can be relied upon to guide them in the way they want to go. If he should happen to depart from it, our mystics would not hesitate to shake off his authority, and, on the strength of their direct contact with the Deity, place their own liberty above all else."[5] It would indeed be interesting at this point to study closely the relations between the spiritual adviser and the soul seeking counsel. It would be found that, of the two, he that has meekly acquiesced in yielding to guidance has more than once, no less meekly, become the guide. But this is not for us the important point. All we want to make clear is that, if external resemblances between Christian mystics may be due to a common tradition or a common training, their deepseated agreement is a sign of an identity of intuition which would find its simplest explanation in the actual existence of the Being with whom they believe themselves to hold intercourse. So much the more so, then, if we consider that the other mysticisms, ancient or modern, go more or less far, stopping at this or that stage, but all point in the same direction.

Yet we may admit that mystical experience, left to

[5] M. de Montmorand, *Psychologie des mystiques catholiques orthodoxes* (Paris, 1920), p. 17.

itself, cannot provide the philosopher with complete certainty. It could be absolutely convincing only if he had come by another way, such as a sensuous experience coupled with rational inference, to the conclusion of the probable existence of a privileged experience through which man could get into touch with a transcendent principle. The occurrence in mystics of just such an experience would then make it possible to add something to the results already established, whilst these established results would reflect back on to the mystical experience something of their own objectivity. Experience is the only source of knowledge. But, since the intellectual record of the fact inevitably goes further than the raw fact, all experiences are far from being equally conclusive and from justifying the same certainty. Many lead us to merely probable conclusions. Yet probabilities may accumulate, and the sum-total be practically equivalent to certainty. We have alluded elsewhere to those "lines of fact" each one indicating but the direction of truth, because it does not go far enough: truth itself, however, will be reached if two of them can be prolonged to the point where they intersect. A surveyor measures the distance to an unattainable point by taking a line on it, now from one, now from the other of two points which he *can* reach. In our opinion this method of intersection is the only one that can bring about a decisive advance in metaphysics. By this means collaboration between philosophers can be established; metaphysics, like science, will progress by the gradual accumulation of results obtained, instead of being a complete take-it-or-leave-it system, always in dispute and always doomed to start afresh. Now it so happens that a thorough study of a certain order of problems, entirely different from religious problems, has led us to a conclusion which makes probable the existence of a singular privileged experience, such as a mystic experience. And, on the other hand, the mystical experience, studied for its own sake, supplies us with pointers that can be added and fitted to the knowledge obtained in an entirely different field, by an entirely different method. It is a case, then, of one supporting and complementing the other. Let us begin with the first point.

It was by following as closely as possible the evidence of biology that we reached the conception of a vital impetus and of a creative evolution. As we set it out at the beginning of the last chapter, this conception was by no means a hypothesis, such as can be found at the basis of any metaphysical system: it was a condensation of fact, a summing up of summings up. Now, whence came the impetus, and what was the principle behind it? If it sufficed unto itself, what was it in itself, and what meaning were we to ascribe to its manifestations as a whole? To such questions the facts under consideration supplied no direct answer; but we saw clearly from what direction the answer might come. For the energy thrown through matter appeared to us, as it were, below or above consciousness, in any case of the same order as consciousness. It had had to get round many obstacles, squeeze itself through others; above all, divide itself between diverging lines of evolution: at the extremity of the two main lines we ultimately found two modes of knowledge into which it had resolved itself in order to materialize: the instinct of insects, the intelligence of man. Instinct was intuitive; intelligence reflected and reasoned. It is true that intuition had had to debase itself to become instinct; it had become intent, as though hypnotized, on the interest of the species, and what had survived of its consciousness had assumed a somnambulistic form. But just as there subsisted around animal instinct a fringe of intelligence, so human intelligence preserved a halo of intuition. The latter, in man, had remained fully disinterested and conscious, but it was only a faint glow and did not radiate very far. Yet it is from this that the light must come, if ever the inner working of the vital impetus were to be made clear in its significance and in its object. For this intuition was turned inward; and if, in a first intensification, beyond which most of us did not go, it made us realize the continuity of our inner life, a deeper intensification might carry it to the roots of our being, and thus to the very principle of life in general. Now is not this precisely the privilege of the mystic soul?

This brings us to what we have just stated as our second point. The first question was to find out whether or no the mystics were merely "queer," if the accounts of their experiences were purely fanciful or not. But the question was soon settled, at least as far as the great mystics were concerned. The next thing was to find out whether mysticism was no more than a more fervent faith, an imaginative form such as traditional religion is capable of assuming in passionate souls, or whether, while assimilating as much as it can from this religion, while turning to it for confirmation, while borrowing its language, it did not possess an original content, drawn straight from the very well-spring of religion, independent of all that religion owes to tradition, to theology, to the Churches. In the first case, it would necessarily stand aloof from philosophy, for the latter ignores revelation which has a definite date, the institutions which have transmitted it, the faith that accepts it: it must confine itself to experience and inference. But, in the second case, it would suffice to take mysticism unalloyed, apart from the visions, the allegories, the theological language which express it, to make it a powerful helpmeet to philosophical research. Of these two conceptions of the relation that it maintains to religion, the second seems to us indubitably the right one. We must then find out in what measure mystic experience is a continuation of the experience which led us to the doctrine of the vital impetus. All the information with which it would furnish philosophy, philosophy would repay in the shape of confirmation.

Let us first note that the mystics ignore what we have called "false problems." It may perhaps be objected that they ignore *all* problems, whether real or false, and this is true enough. It is none the less certain that they supply us with an implicit answer to questions which force themselves upon the attention of philosophers, and that difficulties which should never have perplexed philosophy are implicitly regarded by the mystic as non-existent. We have shown elsewhere that part of metaphysics moves, consciously or not, around the question of knowing why anything exists—why matter, or spirit, or God, rather than nothing at all? But the question presupposes that reality fills a void, that underneath Being lies nothingness, that *de jure* there should be nothing, that we must therefore explain why there is *de facto* something. And this presupposition is pure illusion, for the idea of absolute nothingness has not one jot more meaning than a square circle. The absence of one thing being always the presence of another—which we prefer to leave aside because it is not the thing that interests us or the thing we were expecting—suppression is never anything more than substitution, a two-sided operation which we agree to look at from one side only: so that the idea of the abolition of everything is self-destructive, inconceivable; it is a pseudo-idea, a mirage conjured up by our imagination. But, for reasons we have stated elsewhere, the illusion is natural: its source lies in the depths of the understanding. It raises questions which are the main origin of metaphysical anguish. Now, for a mystic these questions simply do not exist, they are optical illusions arising, in the inner world, from the structure of human intelligence, they recede and disappear as the mystic rises superior to the human point of view. And, for similar reasons, the mystic will no more worry about the difficulties accumulated by philosophy around the "metaphysical" attributes of Deity: he has nothing to do with properties which are mere negations and can only be expressed negatively; he believes that he sees what God is, for him there is no seeing what God is not. It is therefore on the nature of God, immediately apprehended on the positive side, I mean on the side which is perceptible to the eyes of the soul, that the philosopher must question him.

The philosopher could soon define this nature, did he wish to find a formula for mysticism. God is love, and the object of love: herein lies the whole contribution of mysticism. About this twofold love the mystic will never have done talking. His description is interminable, because what he wants to describe is ineffable. But what he does state clearly is that divine love is not a thing of God: it is God Himself. It is upon this point that the philosopher must fasten who holds God to be a person, and yet wishes to avoid anything like a gross assimilation with man. He will think, for example, of the enthusiasms which can fire a soul, consume all that is within it, and henceforth fill the whole space. The individual then becomes one with the emotion; and yet he was never so thoroughly himself; he is simplified, unified, intensified. Nor has he ever been so charged with thought, if it be true, as we have said, that there are two kinds of emotion, the one below intellect, which is mere disturbance following upon a representation, the other above intellect, which precedes the idea and is more than idea, but which would burst into ideas if, pure soul that it is, it chose to give itself a body. What is there more systematically architectonic, more reflectively elaborate, than a Beethoven symphony? But all through the labour of arranging, rearranging, selecting, carried out on the intellectual plane, the composer was turning back to a point situated outside that plane, in search of acceptance or refusal, of a lead, an inspiration; at that point there lurked an indivisible emotion which intelligence doubtless helped to unfold into music, but which was in itself something more than music and more than intelligence. Just the opposite of infra-intellectual emotion, it remained dependent on the will. To refer to this emotion the artist had to make a constantly repeated effort, such as the eye makes to rediscover a star which, as soon as it is found, vanishes into the dark sky. An emotion of this kind doubtless resembles, though very remotely, the sublime love which is for the mystic the very essence of God. In any case, the philosopher must bear the emotion in mind when he compresses mystic intuition more and more in order to express it in terms of intelligence.

He may not write music, but he generally writes books; and the analysis of his own state of mind when he writes will help him to understand how the love in which the mystics see the very essence of divinity can be both a person and a creative power. He generally keeps, when writing, within the sphere of concepts and words. Society supplies ideas ready to hand, worked out by his predecessors and stored up in the language, ideas which he combines in a new way, after himself reshaping them to a certain extent so as to make them fit into his combination. This method will always produce some more or less satisfactory result, but still a result, and in a limited space of time. And the work produced may be original and vigorous; in many cases human thought will be enriched by it. Yet this will be but an increase of that year's income; social intelligence will continue to live on the same capital, the same stock. Now there is another method of composition, more ambitious, less certain, which cannot tell when it will succeed or even if it will succeed at all. It consists in working back from the intellectual and social plane to a point in the soul from which there springs an imperative demand for creation. The soul within which this demand dwells may indeed have felt it fully only once in its lifetime, but it is always there, a unique emotion, an impulse, an impetus received from the very depths of things. To obey it completely new words would have to be coined, new ideas would have to be created, but this would no longer be communicating something, it would not be writing. Yet the writer will attempt to realize the unrealizable. He will revert to the simple emotion, to the form which yearns to create its matter, and will go with it to meet ideas already made, words that already exist, briefly social segments of reality. All along the way he will feel it manifesting itself in signs born of itself, I mean in fragments of its own materialization. How can these elements, each unique of its kind, be made to coincide with words already expressing things? He will be driven to strain the words, to do violence to speech. And, even so, success can never be sure; the writer wonders at every step if it will be granted to him to go on to the end; he thanks his luck for every partial success, just as a punster might thank the words he comes across for lending themselves to his fun. But if he does succeed, he will have enriched humanity with a thought that can take on a fresh aspect for each generation, with a capital yielding ever-renewed dividends, and not just with a sum down to be spent at once. These are the two methods of literary composition. They may not, indeed, utterly exclude each other, yet they are radically different. The second one, as providing the image of the creation of matter by form, is what the philosopher must have in mind in order to conceive as creative energy the love wherein the mystic sees the very essence of God.

Has this love an object? Let us bear in mind that an emotion of a superior order is self-sufficient. Imagine a piece of music which expresses love. It is not love for any particular person. Another piece of music will express another love. Here we have two distinct emotional atmospheres, two different fragrances, and in both cases the quality of love will depend upon its essence and not upon its object. Nevertheless, it is hard to conceive a love which is, so to speak, at work, and yet applies to nothing. As a matter of fact, the mystics unanimously bear witness that God needs us, just as we need God. Why should He need us unless it be to love us? And it is to this very conclusion that the philosopher who holds to the mystical experience must come. Creation will appear to him as God undertaking to create creators, that He may have, besides Himself, beings worthy of His love.

We should hesitate to admit this if it were merely a question of humdrum dwellers on this corner of the universe called Earth. But, as we have said before, it is probable that life animates all the planets revolving round all the stars. It doubtless takes, by reason of the diversity of conditions in which it exists, the most varied forms, some very remote from what we imagine them to be; but its essence is everywhere the same, a slow accumulation of potential energy to be spent suddenly in free action. We might still hesitate to admit this, if we regarded as accidental the appearance amid the plants and animals that people the earth of a living creature such as man, capable of loving and making himself loved. But we have shown that this appearance, while not predetermined, was not accidental either. Though there were other lines of evolution running alongside the line which led to man, and though much is incomplete in man himself, we can say, while keeping closely to what experience shows, that it is man who accounts for the presence of life on our planet. Finally, we might well go on hesitating if we believed that the universe is essentially raw matter, and that life has been super-added to matter. We have shown, on the contrary, that matter and life, as we define them, are coexistent and interdependent. This being the case, there is nothing to prevent the philosopher from following to its logical conclusion the idea which mysticism suggests to him of a universe which is the mere visible and tangible aspect of love and of the need of loving, together with all the consequences entailed by this creative emotion: I mean the appearance of living creatures in which this emotion finds its complement; of an infinity of other beings without which they could not have appeared, and lastly of the unfathomable depths of material substance without which life would not have been possible.

No doubt we are here going beyond the conclusions we reached in *Creative Evolution.* We wanted then to keep as close as possible to facts. We stated nothing that could not in time be confirmed by the tests of biology. Pending that confirmation, we had obtained results which the philosophic method, as we understand it, justified us in holding to be true. Here we are in the field of probabilities alone. But we cannot reiterate too often that philosophic certainty admits of degrees, that it calls for intuition as well as for reason, and that if intuition, backed up by science, is to be extended, such extension can be made only by mystical intuition. In fact, the conclusions just set out complete naturally, though not necessarily, those of our former work. Granted the existence of a creative energy which is love, and which desires to produce from itself beings worthy to be loved, it might indeed sow space with worlds whose materiality, as the opposite of divine spirituality, would simply express the distinction between being created and creating, between the multifarious notes, strung like pearls, of a symphony and the indivisible emotion from which they sprang. In each of these worlds vital impetus and raw matter might thus be complementary aspects of creation, life owing to the matter it traverses its subdivision into distinct beings, and the potentialities it bears within it being mingled as much as the spatiality of the matter which displays them permits. This interpenetration has not been possible on our planet; everything conduces to the idea that whatever matter could be secured here for the embodiment of life was ill-adapted to favour life's impetus. The original impulsion therefore split into divergent lines of evolutionary progress, instead of remaining undivided to the end. Even along the line on which the essential of the impulsion travelled it ended by exhausting its effect, or rather the movement which started as straight ended as circular. In that circle humanity, the terminal point, revolves. Such was our conclusion. In order to carry it further otherwise than by mere guesswork, we should simply have to follow the lead of the mystic. That current of life which traverses matter, and which accounts for its existence, we simply took for granted. As for humanity, which stands at the extremity of the main line, we did not ask whether it had any other purpose but itself. Now, this twofold question is contained in the very answer given to it by mystical intuition. Beings have been called into existence who were destined to love and be loved, since creative energy is to be defined as love. Distinct from God, Who is this energy itself, they could spring into being only in a universe, and therefore the universe sprang into being. In that portion of the universe which is our planet—probably in our whole planetary system —such beings, in order to appear, have had to be wrought into a species, and this species involved a multitude of other species, which led up to it, or sustained it, or else formed a residue. It may be that in other systems there are only individuals radically differentiated— assuming them to be multifarious and mortal—and maybe these creatures too were shaped at a single stroke, so as to be complete from the first. On Earth, in any case, the species which accounts for the existence of all the others is only partially itself. It would never for an instant have thought of becoming completely itself, if certain representatives of it had not succeeded, by an individual effort added to the general work of life, in breaking through the resistance put up by the instrument, in triumphing over materiality—in a word in getting back to God. These men are the mystics. They have blazed a trail along which other men may pass. They have, by this very act, shown to the philosopher the whence and whither of life.

People are never tired of saying that man is but a minute speck on the face of the earth, the earth a speck in the universe. Yet, even physically, man is far from merely occupying the tiny space allotted to him, and with which Pascal himself was content when he condemned the "thinking reed" to be, materially, only a reed. For if our body is the matter to which our consciousness applies itself it is coextensive with our consciousness, it comprises all we perceive, it reaches to the stars. But this vast body is changing continually, sometimes radically, at the slightest shifting of one part of itself which is at its centre and occupies a small fraction of space. This inner and central body, relatively invariable, is ever present. It is not merely present, it is operative: it is through this body, and through it alone, that we can move other parts of the large body. And, since action is what matters, since it is an understood thing that we are present where we act, the habit has grown of limiting consciousness to the small body and ignoring the vast one. The habit appears, moreover, to be justified by science, which holds outward perception to be an epiphenomenon of corresponding intracerebral processes: so that all we perceive of the larger body is regarded as being a mere phantom externalized by the smaller one. We have previously exposed the illusion contained in this metaphysical theory.[6] If the surface of our organized small body (organized precisely with a view to immediate action) is the seat of all our actual movements, our huge inorganic body is the seat of our potential or theoretically possible actions: the percep-

[6] *Matière et Mémoire* (Paris, 1896). See the whole of Chap. I.

tive centres of the brain being the pioneers that prepare the way for subsequent actions and plan them from within, everything happens *as though* our external perceptions were built up by our brain and launched by it into space. But the truth is quite different, and we are really present in everything we perceive, although through ever varying parts of ourselves which are the abode of no more than potential actions. Let us take matters from this angle and we shall cease to say, even of our body, that it is lost in the immensity of the universe.

It is true that, when people speak of the littleness of man and the immensity of the universe, they are thinking of the complexity of the latter quite as much as of its size. A person appears as something simple; the material world is of a complexity that defies imagination: even the tiniest visible particle of matter is a world in itself. How then can we believe that the latter exists only for the sake of the former? Yet we can and must. For, when we find ourselves confronted with parts which we can go on counting without ever coming to an end, it may be that the whole is simple, and that we are looking at it from the wrong point of view. Move your hand from one point to another: to you who perceive it from the inside this is an indivisible movement. But I who perceive it from the outside, with my attention centred on the line followed, *I* say to myself that your hand has had to cover the first part of the interval, then the half of the second half, then the half of what was left, and so on: I could go on for millions of centuries, and never finish the enumeration of the acts into which, in my eyes, the movement you feel to be indivisible is split up. Thus the gesture which calls into being the human species, or, to use more general terms, the objects of love for the Creator, might well require conditions which require other conditions, and so on, endlessly, to infinity. We cannot think of this multiplicity without bewilderment; yet it is but the reverse of something indivisible. It is true that the infinite numbers into which we decompose a gesture of the hand are purely virtual, necessarily determined in their virtualness by the reality of the gesture, whereas the component parts of the universe, and the parts of these parts, are realities: when they are living beings, they possess a spontaneity which may even attain to free activity. Hence we are not affirming that the relation between the complex and the simple is the same in both cases. We only wanted to show by the comparison that complexity, even when unlimited, is no proof of importance, and that an existence that is simple may postulate a chain of conditions which never ends.

Such then will be our conclusion. Attributing the place we do to man, and the significance we do to life, it may well appear optimistic. The vision at once rises before us of all the suffering with which life is fraught, from the lowest stage of consciousness up to man. It would be no use for us to contend that among animals this suffering is by no means as great as people think; without going so far as the Cartesian theory of animal-machine, we may presume that pain is much diminished for beings possessing no active memory, who do not protract their past into their present, and who are not complete personalities; their consciousness is of a somnambulistic nature; neither their pleasure nor their pain produce the same deep and enduring reverberations as ours: do we count as real the pain we feel in a dream? Even in man, is not physical distress often due to imprudence or carelessness, or to overrefined tastes, or artificial needs? As for moral distress, it is as often as not our own fault, and in any case it would not be so acute if we had not exasperated our sensibility to the point of making it morbid; our pain is indefinitely protracted and multiplied by brooding over it. In a word, it would be easy to add a few paragraphs to the *Théodicée* of Leibnitz. But we have not the slightest inclination to do so. The philosopher may indulge in speculations of this kind in the solitude of his study; but what is he going to think about it in the presence of a mother who has just watched the passing of her child? No, suffering is a terrible reality, and it is mere unwarrantable optimism to define evil *a priori*, even reduced to what it actually is, as a lesser good. But there is an empirical optimism, which consists simply in noting two facts: first that humanity finds life, on the whole, good, since it clings to it; and then, that there is an unmixed joy, lying beyond pleasure and pain, which is the final state of the mystic soul. In this twofold sense, and from both points of view, optimism must be admitted, without any necessity for the philosopher to plead the cause of God. It will be said, of course, that if life is good on the whole, yet it would have been better without suffering, and that suffering cannot have been willed by a God of love. But there is nothing to prove that suffering was willed. We have pointed out that what, looked at from one side, appears as an infinite multiplicity of things, of which suffering is indeed one, may look from another side like an indivisible act, so that the elimination of one part would mean doing away with the whole. Now it will be suggested that the whole might have been different, and such that pain had no place in it; therefore that life, even if it is good, could have been better. And the conclusion will be drawn that, if a principle really exists, and if that principle is love, it is not omnipotent and it is therefore not God. But that is just the question. What exactly does "omnipotence" mean? We have shown that the idea of "nothing" is tantamount to the idea of a square circle, that it vanished under analysis, leaving only an empty word behind it, in fine that it is a pseudo-idea. May not the same apply to the idea of "everything," if this name is given not only to the sum-total of the real, but also to the totality of the possible? I can, at a stretch, represent something in my mind when I hear of the sum-total of existing things, but in the sum-total of the non-existent I can see nothing but a string of words. So that here again the objection is based on a pseudo-idea, a verbal entity. But we can go further still: the objection arises from a whole series of arguments implying a radical defect of method. A certain representation is built up *a priori*, and it is taken for granted that this is the idea of God; from thence are deduced the characteristics that the world ought to show; and if the world does not actually show them, we are told that God does not exist. Now, who can fail to see that, if philosophy is the work of experience and reasoning, it must follow just the reverse method, question experience as to what it has to teach us of a Being Who transcends tangible reality as He transcends human consciousness, and so appreciate the nature of God by reasoning on the facts supplied by experience? The nature of God will thus appear in the very reasons we have for believing in His existence: we shall no longer try to deduce His existence or non-existence from an arbitrary conception of His nature. Let agreement be reached on this point, and there will be no objection to talking about divine omnipotence. We find such expressions used by these very mystics to whom we turn for experience of the divine. They obviously mean by this an energy to which no limit can be assigned, and a power of creating and loving which surpasses all imagination. They certainly do not evoke a closed concept, still less a definition of God such as might enable us to conclude what the world is like or what it should be like.

The same method applies to all problems of the after-life. It is possible, with Plato, to lay down *a priori* a definition of the soul as a thing incapable of decomposition because it is simple, incorruptible because it is indivisible, immortal by virtue of its essence. This leads, by a process of deduction, to the idea of souls falling into Time, and thence to that of a return into Eternity. But what is to be the answer to those who deny the existence of the soul thus defined? And how could the problems touching a real soul, its real origin, its real fate, be resolved in accordance with reality, or even posited in terms of reality, when one has merely been speculating upon a possibly baseless conception of the soul, or, at the very best, defining conventionally the meaning of the word which society has inscribed on a slice of reality set apart for the convenience of conversation? The affirmation remains as sterile as the definition was arbitrary. The Platonic conception has not helped our knowledge of the soul by a single step, for all that it has been meditated upon for two thousand years. It was as complete and final as that of the triangle, and for the same reasons. How can we help seeing, however, that, if there really is a problem of the soul, it must be posited in terms of experience, and in terms of experience it must be progressively, and always partially, solved? We shall not revert to this subject, which we have dealt with elsewhere. Let us merely recall that the observation, by our senses and our consciousness, of normal facts and morbid states reveals to us the inadequacy of the physiological explanation of the memory, the impossibility of attributing the preservation of recollections to the brain, and, on the other hand, the possibility of following up, step by step, the successive expansions of memory, from the point where it contracts to allow the passage only of what is strictly necessary to the present action, up to the farthest plane where it spreads out a panorama of the whole indestructible past. We said metaphorically that we were proceeding thus from the summit to the base of the cone. It is only at its topmost point that the cone fits into matter; as soon as we leave the apex, we enter into a new realm. What is it? Let us call it the spirit, or again, if you will, let us refer to the soul, but in that case bear in mind that we are remoulding language and getting the word to encompass a series of experiences instead of an arbitrary definition. This experimental searching will suggest the possibility and even probability of the survival of the soul, since even here below we shall have observed something of its independence of the body, indeed we shall have almost felt it. This will be only one aspect of that independence; we still remain imperfectly informed of the conditions of the after-life, and especially regarding its duration: is it for a time, or for all eternity? But we shall at least have found something upon which experience can get a grip, and one indisputable affirmation will be made possible, as well as a future advance of our knowledge. So much for what we might call the experience on the lower plane. Let us now betake ourselves to the higher plane: we shall find an experience of another type, mystic intuition. And this is presumably a participation in the divine essence. Now, do these two experiences meet? Can the after-life, which is apparently assured to our soul by the simple fact that, even here below, a great part of this activity is independent of the body, be identical with that of the life into which, even here below, certain privileged souls insert themselves? Only a prolongation and a profound investigation of these two experiences will tell us; the problem must remain open. Still it is something to have obtained, on essential points, a probability which is capable of being transformed into a certainty, and for the rest, for the knowledge of the soul and of its destiny, the possibility of endless progress. It is true that at first this way out of the difficulty will satisfy neither of the two schools which do battle over the *a priori* definition of the soul, categorically asserting or denying. Those who deny, because they refuse to set up as a reality what is perhaps a baseless construction of the mind, will stick to their negation in the very teeth of the experience put before them, believing that they are still dealing with the same thing. Those who affirm will have nothing but contempt for ideas which are admittedly provisional and calling for improvement; they will see in them nothing

more than their own thesis, impaired and impoverished.
It will take them some time to understand that their
thesis had been extracted just as it stands from current
language. Society doubtless follows certain suggestions
of inner experience when it talks of the soul; but it has
made up this word, like all the others, for its own convenience. It has applied it to something distinct from the
body. The more radical the distinction, the better the
word answers its purpose: now it cannot be more radical
than when the qualities of the soul are taken to be
purely and simply the negations of those of matter. Such
is the idea that the philosopher has received only too
often, ready made, from society through language. It
appears to represent the acme of spirituality, just because
it goes to the very end of something. But this something
is only negation. There is nothing to be extracted from
nothingness, and knowledge of such a soul is, of course,
incapable of extension, nay, it rings hollow at the first
blow of an opposing philosophy. How much better to
turn back to the vague suggestions of consciousness from
which we started, to delve into them and follow them
up till we reach a clear intuition! Such is the method
we recommend. Once again, it will not please either side.
To apply it is to risk getting caught between the bark
and the tree. But no matter! The bark will split if the
wood of the old tree swells with a new flow of sap.

One of the results of our analysis has been to draw a sharp distinction, in the sphere of society, between the closed and the open. The closed society is that whose members hold together, caring nothing for the rest of humanity, on the alert for attack or defence, bound, in fact, to a perpetual readiness for battle. Such is human society fresh from the hands of nature. Man was made for this society, as the ant was made for the ant-heap. We must not overdo the analogy; we should note, however, that the hymenopterous communities are at the end of one of the two principal lines of animal evolution, just as human societies are at the end of the other, and that they are in this sense counterparts of one another. True, the first are stereotyped, whereas the others vary; the former obey instinct, the latter intelligence. But if nature, and for the very reason that she has made us intelligent, has left us to some extent with freedom of choice in our type of social organization, she has at all events ordained that we should live in society. A force of unvarying direction, which is to the soul what force of gravity is to the body, ensures the cohesion of the group by bending all individual wills to the same end. That force is moral obligation. We have shown that it may extend its scope in societies that are becoming open, but that it was made for the closed society. And we have shown also how a closed society can live, resist this or that dissolving action of intelligence, preserve and communicate to each of its members that confidence which is indispensable, only through a religion born of the myth-making function. This religion, which

we have called static, and this obligation, which is tantamount to a pressure, are the very substance of closed
society.

Never shall we pass from the closed society to the
open society, from the city to humanity, by any mere
broadening out. The two things are not of the same
essence. The open society is the society which is deemed
in principle to embrace all humanity. A dream dreamt,
now and again, by chosen souls, it embodies on every
occasion something of itself in creations, each of which,
through a more or less far-reaching transformation of
man, conquers difficulties hitherto unconquerable. But
after each occasion the circle that has momentarily
opened closes again. Part of the new has flowed into the
mould of the old; individual aspiration has become social pressure; and obligation covers the whole. Do these
advances always take place in the same direction? We
can take it for granted that the direction is the same,
the moment we agree that they are advances. For each
one is thus defined as a step forward. But this can be no
more than a metaphor, and if there were really a pre-
existent direction along which man had simply to advance, moral renovation would be foreseeable; there
would be no need, on each occasion, for a creative effort.
The truth is that it is always possible to take the latest
phase of renovation, define it by a concept, and say that
the others contained a greater or lesser quantity of what
the concept includes, that therefore they all led up to
that renovation. But things assume this form only in
retrospect; the changes were qualitative and not quanti-
tative; they defied all anticipation. In one respect, however, they had, in themselves, and not merely through
the medium of a conceptual interpretation, something
in common. All aimed at opening what was closed; and
the group, which after the last opening had closed on
itself, was brought back every time to humanity. Let us
go further: these successive efforts were not, strictly

speaking, the progressive realization of an ideal, since no idea, forged beforehand, could possibly portray a series of accretions each of which, creating itself, would create its own idea; and yet the diversity of these efforts could be summed up into one and the same thing: an impetus, which had ended in closed societies because it could carry matter no further along, but which later on is destined to be sought out and recaptured, not by the species, but by some privileged individual. This impetus is thus carried forward through the medium of certain men, each of whom thereby constitutes a species composed of a single individual. If the individual is fully conscious of this, if the fringe of intuition surrounding his intelligence is capable of expanding sufficiently to envelop its object, that is the mystic life. The dynamic religion which thus springs into being is the very opposite of the static religion born of the myth-making function, in the same way as the open society is the opposite of the closed society. But just as the new moral aspiration takes shape only by borrowing from the closed society its natural form, which is obligation, so dynamic religion is propagated only through images and symbols supplied by the myth-making function. There is no need to go back over these different points. I wanted simply to emphasize the distinction I have made between the open and the closed society.

We only have to concentrate on this distinction, and we shall see some of the big problems vanish, others assume a new shape. Whether we champion or impeach a religion, do we always take into account what is specifically religious in religion? We cherish or we dismiss a story which may have been found necessary for inducing a certain state of soul which can be propagated; but religion is essentially that very state. We discuss its definitions and its theories; and it has, indeed, made use of a metaphysic to give itself bodily substance; but it might, at a stretch, have assumed a different corporeal form, or even none at all. The mistake is to believe that it is possible to pass, by a mere process of enlargement or improvement, from the static to the dynamic, from demonstration or fabulation, even though it bear the stamp of truth, to intuition. The thing itself is thus confused with its expression or its symbol. This is the usual error of a sheer intellectualism. We find it, just the same, when we pass from religion to morality. There is a static morality, which exists, as a fact, at a given moment in a given society; it has become ingrained in customs, ideas, and institutions; its obligatory character is to be traced to nature's demand for a life in common. There is, on the other hand, a dynamic morality which is impetus, and which is related to life in general, creative of nature which created the social demand. The first obligation, in so far as it is a pressure, is infra-rational. The second, in so far as it is aspiration, is supra-rational. But intelligence intervenes. It seeks out the motive, that is to say the intellectual content, of each of these prescriptions; and, since intelligence is systematic, it imagines that the problem consists in reducing all moral motives to one. Now, if so, it is merely a matter of choosing one of them. General interest, personal interest, self-love, sympathy, pity, logical consistency, etc., there is no principle of action from which it is not possible to deduce more or less the morality that is generally accepted. It is true that the easiness of the operation, and the purely approximate character of the result, should put us on our guard. If almost identical rules of conduct are indifferently deducible from such divers principles, this is probably because no one of the principles was reduced to its specific characteristics. The philosopher went in search of his quarry in the social environment, where everything interpenetrates everything, where egoism and vanity are impregnated with sociability; it is in no way surprising, then, that he should find again in each principle the morality that he has put or left there. But morality itself he leaves unexplained, since he would have first had to delve into social life, in so far as it is a discipline demanded by nature, and then again to delve into nature herself taken as the creation of life in general. He would thus have reached the very root of morality, which eludes the search of a purely intellectualist philosophy; the latter can only proffer advice, adduce reasons, which we are perfectly free to combat with other reasons. As a matter of fact, such philosophy always implies that the motive it has taken up as a principle is "preferable" to the others, that there is a difference of value between motives, and that there exists a general ideal by reference to which the real is to be estimated. It thus provides itself with a refuge in the Platonic theory, with the Idea of Good dominating all others: the reasons for action could then, apparently, be ranged in order of merit beneath the Idea of Good, the best being those that come nearest to it, and the attraction of Good being the principle of obligation. But then the great difficulty is to say by what sign we are to recognize that this or that line of conduct is nearer or further from the ideal Good; if the sign were known, it would be the essential, and the Idea of Good would become unnecessary. It would be equally hard to explain how the ideal in question creates an imperative obligation, especially the strictest obligation of all, the obligation which attaches to custom in primitive and essentially closed societies. The truth is that an ideal cannot become obligatory unless it is already active, in which case it is made obligatory, not by the idea contained in it, but by its action. Or rather it is only the name we give to the supposedly ultimate effect of that action, felt to be continuous, the hypothetical terminal point of the movement which is already sweeping us forward. At the root of all theories, then, we find the two illusions we have time and again denounced. The first, a very general one, consists in the conception of movement as a gradual diminution of the space between the position of the moving object, which is immobility, and its terminal point considered as reached, which is immobility also, whereas positions are but mental snapshots of the indivisible movement: whence the impossibility of reestablishing the true mobility, that is to say, in this case, the aspirations and pressures directly or indirectly constituting obligation. The second illusion concerns more specially the evolution of life. Because an evolutionary process has been observed starting from a certain point, it is believed that this point must have been reached by the same evolutionary process, whereas the evolution may have been quite different, whereas even there may have been previously no evolution at all. Because we note a gradual enrichment of morality, we are apt to think that there is no such thing as a primitive irreducible morality, contemporary with the appearance of man. Yet we must posit this original morality at the same time as the human species, and assume that there was at the beginning a closed society.

Now, is the distinction between the closed and the open, which is necessary to resolve or remove theoretical problems, able to help us practically? It would be of little utility if the closed society had always been so constituted as to shut itself up again after each momentary opening. In that case, however untiringly we might delve back into the past, we should never reach the primitive; the natural would be a mere consolidation of the acquired. But, as we have just said, the truth is quite different. There is such a thing as fundamental nature, and there are acquisitions which, as they are superadded to nature, imitate it without becoming merged into it. Working back step by step we should get back to an original closed society, the general plan of which fitted the pattern of our species as the ant-heap fits the ant, but with this difference that in the second case it is the actual detail of the social organization which is given in advance, whereas in the other there exists only the main outline, a few directions, just enough natural prefiguration to provide immediately for the individual a suitable social environment. A knowledge of this plan would doubtless be to-day of mere historical interest, if the several dispositions had been ousted by others. But nature is indestructible. The French poet was wrong when he said: "Expel nature, she comes back at the double." There is no expelling her, she is there all the time. We have dwelt on the question of the transmissibility of acquired characteristics. It is highly improbable that a habit is ever transmitted; if this does occur, it is owing to a combination of many favourable conditions so accidental that it will certainly not recur often enough to implant the habit in the species. It is in customs, institutions, even in language, that moral acquisitions are deposited; they are then transmitted by unceasing education; it is in this way that habits which pass on from generation to generation end by being considered as hereditary. But everything conspires to encourage the wrong explanation: misdirected pride, superficial optimism, a mistaken idea of the real nature of progress, lastly and above all, a very widespread confusion between the inborn tendency, which is indeed transmissible from parent to child, and the acquired habit that has frequently become grafted on to the natural tendency. There is no doubt but that this belief has influenced positive science itself, which accepted it from common sense, in spite of the small number and the questionable character of the facts called upon to support it, and then handed it back to common sense after having reinforced it with its own undisputed authority. There is nothing more instructive on this point than the biological and psychological work of Herbert Spencer. It is based almost entirely on the idea of the hereditary transmission of acquired characteristics. And, in the days of its popularity, it impregnated scientists' doctrines of evolution. Now, this idea was, in Spencer, nothing more than the general application of a thesis, presented in his first works, on social progress: his interest had at first been exclusively centred on the study of societies; it was only later that he came to deal with the phenomena of life. So that a sociology which thinks it is borrowing from biology the idea of hereditary transmission of the acquired is only taking back what it lent. This unproven philosophical theory has assumed a false air of scientific assurance on its way through science, but it remains mere philosophy, and is further than ever from being proved. So let us keep to ascertained facts and to the probabilities suggested by them: in our opinion, if you eliminated from the man of to-day what has been deposited in him by unceasing education, he would be found to be identical, or nearly so, with his remotest ancestors. [1]

What conclusion are we to deduce from this? Since the dispositions of the species subsist, immutable, deep within all of us, it is impossible that moralists and sociologists should not find it necessary to take them into account. True, it has been given only to a chosen few to dig down, first beneath the strata of the acquired, then beneath nature, and so get back into the very impetus of life. If such an effort could be made general,

[1] We say "nearly" because we must take into account the variations which the living creature plays, as it were, on the theme supplied by his progenitors. But these variations, being accidental, and taking place in any direction, cannot be added together, in the lapse of time, to modify the species. On the thesis of the transmissibility of acquired characteristics, and on the evolutionism which certain biologists would found upon it, see *Creative Evolution* (Chap. I).

Let us add that, as we have already remarked, the sudden leap forward which ended in the human species may have been attempted at more than one point in space and time and only partially succeeded, thus giving rise to "men" to whom we may, if we like, give that name, but who are not necessarily our ancestors.

the impetus would not have stopped short at the human species, nor consequently at the closed society, as if before a blank wall. It is none the less true that these privileged ones would fain draw humanity after them; since they cannot communicate to the world at large the deepest elements of their spiritual condition, they transpose it superficially; they seek a translation of the dynamic into the static which society may accept and stabilize by education. Now they can succeed only in the measure in which they have taken nature into consideration. Humanity as a whole cannot bend nature to its will. But it can get round it. And this is possible only if its general configuration is known. The task would be a difficult one if it obliged us to undertake the study of psychology in general. But we are dealing here with only one particular point, human nature in so far as it is predisposed to a certain social form. We suggest that there is a natural human society, vaguely prefigured in us, that nature has taken care to supply us with a diagram of it beforehand, while leaving all latitude to our intelligence and our will to follow its indications. The diagram, vague and incomplete, corresponds, in the realm of reasonable and free activity, to what is, in the case of instinct, the clear-cut design of the ant-hill or the hive at the other terminal point of evolution. So that all we have to do is to get back to the simple original sketch.

But how is it to be found, with the acquired overlaying the natural? We should be at a loss to give the answer if we had to supply an automatically applicable method of research. The truth is that we have to grope our way tentatively, by a system of cross-checking, following simultaneously several methods, each of which will lead only to possibilities or probabilities: by their mutual interplay the results will neutralize or reinforce one another, leading to reciprocal verification and correction. Thus, we shall take "primitive peoples" into account, without forgetting that here also a layer of acquisitions covers nature, though it may be thinner than in our own case. We shall observe children, but not forget that nature has made provision for differences of age, and that child nature is not necessarily human nature; above all, the child is imitative, and what appears to us as spontaneous is often the effect of an education we have unwittingly been giving him. But the main and essential source of information is bound to be introspection. We must search for the bedrock of sociability, and also of unsociability, which would be perceptible to our consciousness, if established society had not imbued us with habits and dispositions which adjust us to it. Of these strata we are no longer aware, save at rare intervals, and then in a flash. We must recapture that moment of vision and abide by it.

Let us begin by saying that man was designed for very small societies. And it is generally admitted that primitive communities were small. But we must add that the original state of mind survives, hidden away beneath the habits without which indeed there would be no civilization. Driven inwards, powerless, it yet lives on in the depths of consciousness. If it does not go so far as to determine acts, yet it manifests itself in words. In a great nation certain districts may be administered to the general satisfaction; but where is the government that the governed go so far as to call a good one? They think they have praised it quite enough when they say it is not so bad as the others and, in this sense only, the best. Here the disapproval is congenital. In fact, the art of governing a great people is the only one for which there exists no technical training, no effective education, especially when we come to the highest posts. The extreme scarcity of political leaders of any calibre is owing to the fact that they are called upon to decide at any moment, and in detail, problems which the increased size of societies may well have rendered insoluble. Study the history of the great modern nations: you will find plenty of great scientists, great artists, great soldiers, great specialists in every line—but how many great statesmen?

Yet nature, which ordained small societies, left them an opening for expansion. For she also ordained war, or at least she made the conditions of man's life such that war was inevitable. Now, the menace of war can determine several small societies to unite against a common danger. It is true that these unions are rarely lasting. In any case they lead to an assemblage of societies which is of the same order of magnitude as each single unit. It is rather in another sense that war is the origin of empires. These are born of conquest. Even if the war at the outset was not one of conquest, that is what it becomes ultimately, because the victor will have found it so convenient to appropriate the lands of the vanquished, and even their populations, and thus profit by their labour. In this way the great Eastern empires of bygone days were formed. They fell into decay under various influences, but in reality because they were too unwieldy to live. When the victor grants to the conquered populations a semblance of independence, the grouping lasts longer: witness the Roman Empire. But that the primitive instinct persists, that it exercises a disintegrating effect, there is no doubt. Leave it to operate, and the political construction crumbles. It was thus that the feudal system came into being in different countries, as the result of different events, under different conditions; the only common factor was the suppression of the force which was preventing the breaking-up of society; the break-up then took place spontaneously. If great nations have been able to build themselves up firmly in modern times, this is because constraint, a cohesive force working from without and from above on the complex whole, has little by little given way to a principle of unity arising from the very heart of each of the elementary societies grouped together, that is to say, from the very seat of the disruptive forces to which an uninterrupted resistance has to be opposed. This principle, the only one that can possibly neutralize the tendency to disruption, is patriotism. The ancients were well acquainted with it; they adored their country, and it is one of their poets who said that it is sweet to die for her. But it is a far cry from that attachment to the city, a group still devoted to a god who stands by it in battle, to the patriotism which is as much a pacific as a warlike virtue, which may be tinged with mysticism, which mingles no calculations with its religion, which overspreads a great country and rouses a nation, which draws to itself the best in all souls, which is slowly and reverently evolved out of memories and hopes, out of poetry and love, with a faint perfume of every moral beauty under heaven, like the honey distilled from flowers. It took as noble a sentiment as this, imitating the mystic state, to overcome so deep-seated a sentiment as the selfishness of the tribe.

Now what is the régime of a society fresh from the hands of nature? It is possible that humanity did in fact begin as scattered and isolated family groups. But these were mere embryonic societies, and the philosopher should no more seek in them the essential tendencies of social life than the naturalist should study the habits of a species by confining his attention to the embryo. We must take society when it is complete, that is to say, capable of defending itself, and consequently, however small, organized for war. What then, in this precise sense, will its natural government be? If it were not desecrating the Greek words to apply them to a state of savagery, we should say that it is monarchic or oligarchic, probably both. These two systems are indistinguishable in the rudimentary state: there must be a chief, and there is no community without privileged individuals, who borrow from or give to the chief something of his prestige, or rather who draw it, as he does, from some supernatural power. Authority is absolute on one side, obedience absolute on the other. We have said time and again that human societies and hymenopterous societies stand at the extremities of the two principal lines of biological evolution. Heaven forbid that we should assimilate them to each other! Man is intelligent and free. But we must always remember that social life was part of the structural plan of the human species just as in that of the bee, that it was a necessary part, that nature could not rely exclusively on our free will, that accordingly she had to see to it that one or a few individuals should command and the rest obey. In the insect world, the diversity of social function is bound up with a difference of organization; you have "polymorphism." Shall we then say that in human societies we have "dimorphism," no longer both physical and psychical as in the insect, but psychical only? We think so, though it must be understood that this dimorphism does not separate men into two hard and fast categories, those that are born leaders and those that are born subjects. Nietzsche's mistake was to believe in a separation of this kind: on the one hand "slaves," on the other "masters." The truth is that dimorphism generally makes of each of us both a leader with the instinct to command and a subject ready to obey, although the second tendency predominates to the extent of being the only one apparent in most men. It is comparable to that of insects in that it implies two organizations, two indivisible systems of qualities (certain of which would be defects in the moralist's eyes): we plump for the one system or the other, not in detail, as would be the case if it were a matter of contracting habits, but at a single stroke, kaleidoscope-fashion, as is bound to result from a natural dimorphism exactly comparable to that of the embryo in its choice between two sexes. We have a clear vision of this in times of revolution. Unassuming citizens, up to that moment humble and obedient, wake up one fine day with pretensions to be leaders of men. The kaleidoscope which had been held steady has now shifted one notch and lo! a complete metamorphosis! The result is sometimes good: great men of action have been revealed who were themselves unaware of their real capacity. But it is generally unfortunate. Within honest and gentle men there rushes up from the depths a ferocious personality, that of the leader who is a failure. And here we have a characteristic trait of that "political animal," man.

We shall not go so far, indeed, as to say that one of the attributes of the leader dormant within us is ferocity. But it is certain that nature, at once destructive of individuals and productive of species, must have willed the ruthless leader if she provided for leaders at all. The whole of history bears witness to this. Incredible wholesale slaughter, preceded by ghastly tortures, has been ordered in absolute cold blood by men who have themselves handed down the record of these things, graven in stone. It may be argued that such things happened in very remote times. But if the form has changed, if Christianity has put an end to certain crimes, or at least obtained that they be not made a thing to boast of, murder has all too often remained the *ratio ultima*, if not *prima*, of politics. An abomination no doubt, but imputable to nature as much as to man. For nature has at her disposal neither imprisonment nor exile; she knows only sentence of death. We may be allowed perhaps to recall a memory. It so happened that we met certain distinguished foreigners, coming from far-off lands, but dressed as we were, speaking French as we did, moving about, affable and amiable, among us. Shortly after we learned from a daily paper that, once back in their country and affiliated to opposite parties, one of them had had the other hanged, with all the paraphernalia of justice, simply to get rid of an awkward opponent. The tale was illustrated with a photograph of the gallows. The accomplished man of the world was dangling, half-naked, before the gaping crowd. Horrible, most horrible! Civilized men all, but the original political instinct had blown civilization to the winds and laid bare the nature underneath. Men who would think themselves bound to make the punishment fit the offence, if they had to deal with a guilty man, go to the extreme of killing an innocent person at the call of political expediency. Similarly do the worker bees stab the drones to death when they consider that the hive needs them no longer.

But let us leave aside the temperament of the "leader" and consider the respective sentiments of ruler and ruled. These sentiments will be clearer where the line of demarcation is more distinct, in a society already considerable, but which has grown without radically modifying the "natural society." The governing class, in which we include the king if there is a king, may have been recruited in the course of history by different methods; but it always believes itself to belong to a superior race. There is nothing surprising in this. What might surprise us more, if we were not familiar with the dimorphism of social man, is that the people themselves should be convinced of this innate superiority. Doubtless the oligarchy is careful to foster this sentiment; and if it owes its origin to war, it will have faith and compel others to have faith in its own congenital military virtues, handed down from father to son. And indeed it maintains a real superiority of strength, thanks to the discipline it imposes on itself, and to the measures it takes to prevent the inferior class from organizing itself in its turn. Yet, in such a case, experience should show the ruled that their rulers are men like themselves. But instinct resists. It begins to waver only when the upper class itself invites it to do so. Sometimes the upper class does this unwittingly, through obvious incapacity, or by such crying abuses that it undermines the faith placed in it.

At other times the invitation is intentional, certain members of the class turning against it, often from personal ambition, sometimes from a sentiment of justice: by stooping down towards the lower classes, they dispel the illusion fostered by distance. It was in this way that some of the nobles collaborated in the French Revolution of 1789, which abolished the privilege of birth. Generally speaking, the initiative of assaults against inequality—justified or unjustified—has come rather from the upper classes, from those that were better off, and not from the lower, as might have been expected if it were merely a matter of conflict between class interests. Thus it was the upper middle class, and not the working classes, who played the leading part in the Revolutions of 1830 and 1848, aimed (the second in particular) against the privilege of wealth. Later it was men of the educated classes who demanded education for all. The truth is that, if an aristocracy believes naturally, religiously, in its native superiority, the respect it inspires is no less religious, no less natural.

It is easy, then, to understand that humanity should have arrived at democracy as a later development (for they were false democracies, those cities of antiquity, based on slavery, relieved by this fundamental iniquity of the biggest and most excruciating problems). Of all political systems, it is indeed the furthest removed from nature, the only one to transcend, at least in intention, the conditions of the "closed society." It confers on man inviolable rights. These rights, in order to remain inviolate, demand of all men an incorruptible fidelity to duty. It therefore takes for its matter an ideal man, who respects others as he does himself, inserting himself into obligations which he holds to be absolute, making them coincide so closely with this absolute that it is no longer possible to say whether it is the duty that confers the right or the right which imposes the duty. The citizen thus defined is both "law-maker and subject," as Kant has it. The citizens as a whole, the people, are therefore sovereign. Such is democracy in theory. It proclaims liberty, demands equality, and reconciles these two hostile sisters by reminding them that they are sisters, by exalting above everything fraternity. Looked at from this angle, the republican motto shows that the third term dispels the oft-noted contradiction between the two others, and that the essential thing is fraternity: a fact which would make it possible to say that democracy is evangelical in essence and that its motive power is love. Its sentimental origins could be found in the soul of Rousseau, its philosophic principles in the works of Kant, its religious basis in both Kant and Rousseau: we know how much Kant owed to his pietism, and Rousseau to an interplay of Protestantism and Catholicism. The American Declaration of Independence (1776), which served as a model for the Declaration of the Rights of Man in 1791, has indeed a Puritan ring: "We hold these truths to be self-evident . . . that all men are endowed by their Creator with certain unalienable rights, etc." Objections occasioned by the vagueness of the democratic formula arise from the fact that the original religious character has been misunderstood. How is it possible to ask for a precise definition of liberty and of equality when the future must lie open to all sorts of progress, and especially to the creation of new conditions under which it will be possible to have forms of liberty and equality which are impossible of realization, perhaps of conception, to-day? One can do no more than trace the general outlines; their content will improve as and when fraternity provides. *Ama, et fac quod vis.* The formula of non-democratic society, wishing its motto to tally, word for word, with that of democracy, would be "authority, hierarchy, immobility." There you have then democracy in its essence. Of course it must be considered only as an ideal, or rather a signpost indicating the way in which humanity should progress. In the first place, it was more than anything else as a protest that it was introduced into the world. Every sentence of the Declaration of the Rights of Man is a challenge to some abuse. The main thing was to put an end to intolerable suffering. Summing up the grievances set forth in the memoirs presented to the *États Généraux*, Émile Faguet has written somewhere that the French Revolution was not made for the sake of liberty and equality, but simply because "people were starving." Supposing this to be true, we must explain why it was at a given time that people refused to go on "starving." It is none the less true that, if the French Revolution formulated things as they should be, the object was to do away with things as they were. Now, it sometimes happens that the intention with which an idea is started remains invisibly attached to it, like the direction to the arrow. The democratic precepts, first enunciated with a definite idea of protest, provide evidence of their origin. They are found convenient to prevent, to reject, to overthrow; it is not easy to gather from them the positive indiction of what is to be done. Above all, they are applicable only if transposed, absolute and semi-evangelical as they originally were, into terms of purely relative morality or rather of general utility; and the transposition always risks turning into an incurvation in the direction of private interest. But it is not necessary to catalogue the objections raised against democracy nor indeed the replies to those objections. We merely wanted to show, in the democratic mind, a mighty effort in a direction contrary to that of nature.

Now, we have pointed to certain features of natural society. Taken together, they compose a countenance whose expression can be easily interpreted. Self-centredness, cohesion, hierarchy, absolute authority of the chief, all this means discipline, the war-spirit. Did nature will war? Let us repeat once again that nature willed nothing at all, if we mean by will a faculty of making particular decisions. But she cannot posit an animal species without implicitly outlining the attitudes and movement which arise from its structure and extend that structure. It is in this sense that she willed war. She endowed man with a tool-making intelligence. Instead of supplying him with tools, as she did for a considerable number of the animal species, she preferred that he should make them himself. Now man is necessarily the owner of his tools, at any rate while he is using them. But since they are things apart from him, they can be taken away from him; it is easier to take them ready-made than to make them. Above all, they are meant to act on some specific matter, meant to be used for hunting or fishing, for example; the group of which he is a member may have fixed its choice on a forest, a lake, a river; another group may find it more convenient to settle in that very same place than to look further afield. There is now nothing for it but to fight the matter out. We have taken the case of a hunting forest, or a lake for fishing; it may just as well be a matter of fields to be cultivated, women to be seized, slaves to be carried off. In the same way reasons will be brought forward to justify such dealings. But no matter the thing taken, the motive adduced: the origin of war is ownership, individual or collective, and since humanity is predestined to ownership by its structure, war is natural. So strong, indeed, is the war instinct, that it is the first to appear when we scratch below the surface of civilization in search of nature. We all know how little boys love fighting. They get their heads punched. But they have the satisfaction of having punched the other fellow's head. It has been justly said that childhood's games are the preparatory training to which nature prompts them, with a view to the task laid on grown men. But we can go further, and look on most of the wars recorded in history as preparatory training or sport. When we consider the futility of the motives which brought about a goodly number of them, we are reminded of the duellists in *Marion Delorme* running each other through the body "for no reason, for the fun of the thing," or else the Irishman cited by Lord Bryce, who could not see two men exchanging fisticuffs in the street without asking, "Is this a private affair, or may anyone join in?" On the other hand, if we put side by side with these casual scraps those decisive wars which led to the annihilation of a whole people, we realize that the second account for the first: a war-instinct was inevitable, and because it existed to meet the contingency of those savage wars, which we might call natural, a number of incidental wars have occurred, simply to prevent the sword from rusting. Think now of the enthusiasm of a people at the outbreak of a war! This is doubtless, to a certain extent, a defensive reaction against fear, an automatic stimulation of courage. But there is also the feeling that we were made for a life of risk and adventure, as though peace were but a pause between two wars. The enthusiasm quickly dies down, for the suffering is considerable. If we leave out the last war, however, where the horror was beyond anything we believed possible, it is strange to see how soon the sufferings of war are forgotten in time of peace. It is asserted that woman is provided with a special psychical mechanism which causes her to forget the pains of childbirth: a too complete recollection might prevent her from having another child. Some mechanism of the same order really seems to be operative in favour of the horrors of war, especially among young nations. Nature has taken yet further precautions in this direction. She has interposed between foreigners and ourselves a cunningly woven veil of ignorance, preconceptions and prejudices. That we should know nothing about a country to which we have never been is not surprising. But that, being ignorant of it, we should criticize it, and nearly always unfavourably, is a fact which calls for explanation. Anyone who has lived outside his own country, and has later tried to initiate his countrymen into what we call a foreign "mentality," has felt in them an instinctive resistance. The resistance is not any stronger the more remote the country. Very much the contrary, it varies rather in inverse ratio to the distance. It is those whom we have the greatest chance of meeting whom we least want to know. Nature could have found no surer way of making every foreigner a virtual enemy, for if perfect mutual knowledge does not necessarily conduce to a fellow-feeling, it at least precludes hate. We had examples of this during the war. A professor of German was just as patriotic as any other Frenchman, just as ready to lay down his life, just as "worked up" even against Germany; yet it was not the same thing. One corner was set apart. Anyone who is thoroughly familiar with the language and literature of a people cannot be wholly its enemy. This should be borne in mind when we ask education to pave the way for international understanding. The mastery of a foreign tongue, by making possible the impregnation of the mind by the corresponding literature and civilization, may at one stroke do away with the prejudice ordained by nature against foreigners in general. But this is not the place to enumerate all the visible outward effects of the latent prejudice. Let us only say that the two opposing maxims, *Homo homini deus* and *Homo homini lupus*, are easily reconcilable. When we formulate the first, we are thinking of some fellow-countryman. The other applies to foreigners.

We have just said that besides incidental wars there are essential wars, for which the war-instinct, apparently, was made. Among these are the great conflicts of our own times. The object is less and less conquest for conquest's sake. Peoples no longer go to war for the sake of wounded pride, prestige or glory. They fight to avoid starvation, so they say—in reality to maintain a certain standard of living, below which they believe that life would not be worth while. Gone is the idea of the delegating of the fighting to a limited number of soldiers chosen to represent the nation. Gone anything resembling a duel. All must fight against all, as did the hordes of the early days. Only, the fighting is done with arms forged by our civilization, and the slaughter surpasses in horror anything the ancients could have even dreamed of. At the pace at which science is moving, that day is not far off when one of the two adversaries, through some secret process which he was holding in reserve, will have the means of annihilating his opponent. The vanquished may vanish off the face of the earth.

Are things bound to follow their natural course? Men whom we unhesitatingly rank among the benefactors of humanity have fortunately interposed. Like all great optimists they began by assuming as solved the problem to be solved. They founded the League of Nations. Now, the results already obtained are more than we dared to hope. For the difficulty of abolishing war is greater even than is generally realized by most people who have no faith in its abolition. Pessimists though they are, they yet agree with the optimists in considering the case of two peoples on the verge of war as similar to that of two individuals with a quarrel; only in their opinion it will be materially impossible to compel the former, like the latter, to bring this difference before the court and accept its decision. Yet there is a radical distinction. Even if the League of Nations had at its disposal a seemingly adequate armed force (and even so the recalcitrant nation would still have over the League the advantage of the initial impetus; even so the unexpectedness of a scientific discovery would render increasingly unforeseeable the nature of the resistance the League of Nations would have to organize), it would come up against the deep-rooted war-instinct underlying civilization; whereas individuals who leave to the judge the business of settling a dispute are in some obscure way encouraged to do so by the instinct of discipline immanent in the

closed society: a quarrel has momentarily upset their
normal position which was a complete insertion into society; but they come back to this position, as the pendulum swings back to the vertical. So that the difficulty
is far greater. Is it vain, however, to try and overcome
it?

We think not. The object of the present work was to
investigate the origins of morality and religion. We have
been led to certain conclusions. We might leave it at
that. But since at the basis of our conclusions was a
radical distinction between the closed and the open society, since the tendencies of the closed society have,
in our opinion, persisted, ineradicable, in the society
that is on the way to becoming an open one, since all
these instincts of discipline originally converged towards
the war-instinct, we are bound to ask to what extent the
primitive instinct can be repressed or circumvented, and
answer by a few supplementary considerations a question which occurs to us quite naturally.

For, though the war-instinct does exist independently,
it none the less hinges on rational motives. History tells
us that these motives have been extremely varied. They
become increasingly few as war becomes more terrible.
The last war, together with those future ones which we
can dimly foresee, if we are indeed doomed to have
more wars, is bound up with the industrial character of
our civilization. If we want to get an outline, simplified
and stylized, of modern conflicts, we shall have to begin
by picturing nations as purely agricultural populations.
They live on the produce of their soil. Suppose they
have just enough to feed themselves. They will increase
in proportion as they obtain a higher yield from their
soil. So far, so good. But if there be a surplus of population, and if this surplus population refuses to overflow
into the world outside, or cannot do so because foreign
countries close their doors, where will it find its food?
Industry is called upon to rectify the situation. The sur-

plus population will become factory-workers. If the country does not possess the motive power for its machines, the iron to make them, the raw material for its manufactured goods, it will try to borrow them from foreign countries. It will pay its debts, and receive the food it cannot obtain through home production, by sending back manufactured products to other countries. The factory-workers will thus become "internal emigrants." The foreign country provides them with employment, just as if they had actually settled within its frontiers; it prefers to leave them—or perhaps they prefer to stay—where they are; but on foreign countries they are dependent. If these countries cease to accept their products, or cease to supply them with the material for manufacture, they are just condemned to starve to death —unless they decide, carrying the whole country with them, to go and seize what is refused to them. That means war. It goes without saying that things never happen so simply as that. Without being exactly in danger of starving to death, people consider that life is not worth living if they cannot have comforts, pleasures, luxuries; the national industry is considered insufficient if it provides for a bare existence, if it does not provide affluence; a country considers itself incomplete if it has not good ports, colonies, etc. All this may lead to war. But the outline we have just traced sufficiently emphasizes the main causes: increase in population, closing of markets, cutting off of fuel and raw materials.

To eliminate these causes or mitigate their effect, such is the essential task of an international organism with the abolition of war as its aim. The gravest of all is overpopulation. In a country with too low a birth-rate, like France, the State should doubtless encourage the increase of population: a certain French economist, though the most thorough-going opponent of State intervention, used to demand that a bonus be granted to families for every child after the third. But then, conversely, would it not be possible, in over-populated countries, to impose more or less heavy taxes on every supernumerary child? The State would have the right to interfere, to establish the paternity, in short, take measures which under other circumstances would be inquisitorial, since the State is tacitly expected to guarantee the food supply of the country and hence that of the child that has been brought into the world. We recognize the difficulty of fixing an official limit to the population, even if the figure be elastic. If we give the outline of a solution, it is merely to point out that the problem does not strike us as insoluble: more competent thinkers will find something better. But one fact is certain: Europe is over-populated, the world will soon be in the same condition, and if the self-reproduction of man is not "rationalized," as his labour is beginning to be, we shall have war. In no other matter is it so dangerous to rely upon instinct. Antique mythology realized this when it coupled the goddess of love with the god of war. Let Venus have her way, and she will bring you Mars. You will not escape regimentation (an unpleasant word, but an unavoidable thing). What will happen when problems almost equally grave arise, such as the distribution of raw materials, the more or less unrestricted movement of products, the general problem of dealing justly with opposing demands represented by both sides as vital? It is a dangerous mistake to think that an international institution can obtain permanent peace without having the authority to intervene in the legislation of the various countries, and even perhaps in their government. Maintain the principle of the sovereignty of the State if you will: it is bound to be whittled down in its application to individual cases. We repeat, no single one of these difficulties is insurmountable, if an adequate portion of humanity is determined to surmount them. But we must face up to them, and realize what has to be given up if war is to be abolished.

Now, would it not be possible to shorten the road before us, or even to smooth away all the difficulties at once, instead of negotiating them one by one? Let us set aside the main question, that of population, which will have to be resolved for its own sake, whatever happens. The others arise principally from the direction taken by our existence since the great expansion of industry. We demand material comfort, amenities and luxuries. We set out to enjoy ourselves. What if our life were to become more ascetic? Mysticism is undoubtedly at the origin of great moral transformations. And mankind seems to be as far away as ever from it. But who knows? In the course of our last chapter we fancied we had caught sight of a possible link between the mysticism of the West and its industrial civilization. The matter needs to be gone into thoroughly. Everybody feels that the immediate future is going to depend largely on the organization of industry and the conditions it will impose or accept. We have just seen that the problem of peace between nations is contingent on this problem. That of peace at home depends on it just as much. Must we live in fear, or may we live in hope? For a long time it was taken for granted that industrialism and mechanization would bring happiness to mankind. Today one is ready to lay to their door all the ills from which we suffer. Never, it is said, was humanity more athirst for pleasure, luxury and wealth. An irresistible force seems to drive it more and more violently towards the satisfaction of its basest desires. That may be, but let us go back to the impulsion at the origin. If it was a strong one, a slight deviation at the beginning may have been enough to produce a wider and wider divergence between the point aimed at and the object reached. In that case, we should not concern ourselves so much with the divergence as with the impulsion. True, things never get done of themselves. Humanity will change only if it is intent upon changing. But perhaps it has already prepared the means of doing so. Perhaps it is nearer the goal than it thinks. Since we have brought a charge against industrial effort, let us examine it more closely. This will form the conclusion of the present work.

The alterations of ebb and flow in history have often been discussed. All prolonged action, it would seem, brings about a reaction in the opposite direction. Then it starts anew, and the pendulum swings on indefinitely. True, in this case the pendulum is endowed with memory, and is not the same when it swings back as on the outward swing, since it is then richer by all the intermediate experience. This is why the image of a spiral movement, which has sometimes been used, is perhaps more correct than that of the oscillations of a pendulum. As a matter of fact, there are psychological and social causes which we might *a priori* predict will be productive of such effects. The uninterrupted enjoyment of an eagerly-sought advantage engenders weariness or indifference; it seldom fulfils completely its promise; it brings with it unforeseen drawbacks; it ends by making conspicuous the good side of what has been given up and arousing a desire to get it back. The desire will be found principally in the rising generations, who have not experienced the ills of the past, and have not had to extricate themselves from them. Whereas the parents congratulate themselves on the present state of things as an acquisition for which they remember paying dearly, the children give it no more thought than the air they breathe; on the other hand, they are alive to disadvantages which are nothing but the reverse side of the advantages so painfully won for them. Thus may arise a wish to put the clock back. Such actions and reactions are characteristic of the modern State, not by reason of any historical fatality, but because parliamentary government was conceived in part with the very object of providing a channel for discontent. The powers that be receive but moderate praise for the good they do; they are there to do it: but their slightest mistake is scored; and all mistakes are stored up until their accumulated weight causes the government to fall. If there are two opposing parties and two only, the game will go on with perfect regularity. Each team will come back into power, bringing with it the prestige of principles which have apparently remained intact during the period in which it had no responsibility to bear: principles sit with the Opposition. In reality the Opposition will have profited, if it is intelligent, by the experience it has left the party in power to work out; it will have more or less modified the content of its ideas and hence the significance of its principles. Thus progress becomes possible, in spite of the swing of the pendulum, or rather because of it, if only men care about it. But, in such cases, the oscillation between the two opposite extremes is the result of certain very simple contrivances set up by society, or certain very obvious tendencies of the individual. It is not the effect of a paramount necessity towering above the particular causes of alternation and dominating human events in general. Does such a necessity exist?

We do not believe in the fatality of history. There is no obstacle which cannot be broken down by wills sufficiently keyed up, if they deal with it in time. There is thus no unescapable historic law. But there are biological laws; and the human societies, in so far as they are partly willed by nature, pertain to biology on this particular point. If the evolution of the organized world takes place according to certain laws, I mean by virtue of certain forces, it is impossible that the psychological evolution of individual and social man should entirely renounce these habits of life. Now we have shown elsewhere that the essence of a vital tendency is to develop fan-wise, creating, by the mere fact of its growth, divergent directions, each of which will receive a certain portion of the impetus. We added that there was nothing mysterious about this law. It simply expresses the fact that a tendency is the forward thrust of an indistinct multiplicity, which is, moreover, indistinct, and multiplicity, only if we consider it in retrospect, when the multitudinous views taken of its past undivided character allow us to see it composed of elements which were actually created by its development. Let us imagine that orange is the only colour that has as yet made its appearance in the world. Would it be already a composite of yellow and red? Obviously not. But it *will have been* composed of yellow and red when these two colours are born in their turn; from that hour the original orange colour can be looked at from the twofold point of view of red and yellow; and if we supposed, by a trick of fancy, that yellow and red appeared through an intensification of orange, we should have a very simple example of what we call fan-wise growth. But there is no real necessity for fancy and comparisons. All we need is to look at life without letting any idea of artificial synthesis supervene. Some psychologists hold the act of volition to be a composite reflex, others are inclined to see in the reflex activity a curtailment of volition. The truth is that the reflex and the voluntary actions embody two views, now rendered possible, of a primordial, indivisible activity, which was neither the one nor the other, but which becomes retroactively, through them, both at once. We could say the same of instinct and intelligence, of animal life and vegetable life, of many other pairs of divergent and complementary tendencies. Only, in the general evolution of life, the tendencies thus created by a process of dichotomy are to be found in species different from one another; they have set forth, each independently, to seek their fortunes in the world; and the material form they have assumed prevents them from reuniting to bring back again, stronger than it was, more complex, more fully evolved, the original tendency. Not so in the evolution of the psychical and social life. Here the tendencies, born of the process of splitting, develop in the same individual, or in the same society. As a rule, they can be developed only in succession. If there are two of them, as is generally the case, one of them will be clung to first; with this one we shall move more or less forward, generally as far as possible; then, with what we have acquired in the course of this evolution, we shall come back to take up the one we left behind. That one will then be developed in its turn, the former being neglected, and our new effort will be continued until, reinforced by new acquisitions, we can take up the first one again and push it further forward still. Since, during the operation, we are entirely given up to one of the two tendencies, since it alone counts, we are apt to say that it alone is positive and that the other was only its negation; if we like to put things in this way, the other is, as a matter of fact, its opposite. It will then be said—and this will be more or less true according to circumstances—that the progress was due to an oscillation between the two opposites, the situation moreover not being the same and a gain having been realized by the time the pendulum has swung back to its original position. But it does sometimes happen that the expression is entirely accurate, and that there *is* really oscillation between two opposites. This is when a tendency, advantageous in itself, cannot be moderated otherwise than by the action of a counter-tendency, which hence becomes advantageous also. It would seem as though the wise course, then, would be a co-operation of the two tendencies, the first intervening when circumstances require, the other restraining it when it threatens to go too far. Unfortunately, it is difficult to say where exaggeration and danger begin. Sometimes the mere fact of going further than appeared reasonable leads to new surroundings, creates a new situation which removes the danger, at the same time emphasizing the advantage. This is especially the case with the very general tendencies which determine the trend of a society, and whose development necessarily extends over a more or less considerable number of generations. An intelligence, even a superhuman one, cannot say where this will lead to, since action on the move creates its own route, creates to a very great extent the conditions under which it is to be fulfilled, and thus baffles all calculation. In such a case, one pushes further and further afield, often stopping only on the very brink of disaster. The counter-tendency then steps into the place that has been vacated; alone, in its turn, it will go as far as it can go. If the other was called action, then this will be reaction. As the two tendencies, if they had journeyed together, would have moderated each other, as their interpenetration in an undivided primitive tendency is the very definition of moderation, the mere fact of taking up all the room imparts to each of them such an impetus that it bolts ahead as the barriers collapse one by one; there is something frenzied about it. Now we must not make exaggerated use of the word "law" in a field which is that of liberty, but we may use this convenient term when we are confronted with important facts which show sufficient regularity. So we will call *law of dichotomy* that law which apparently brings about a materialization, by a mere splitting up, of tendencies which began by being two photographic views, so to speak, of one and the same tendency. And we propose to designate *law of twofold frenzy* the imperative demand, forthcoming from each of the two tendencies as soon as it is materialized by the splitting, to be pursued to the very end—as if there was an end! Once more, it is difficult not to wonder whether the simple tendency would not have done better to grow without dividing in two, thus being kept within bounds by the very coincidence of its propulsive force with the power of stopping, which would then have been virtually, but not actually, a distinct and contrary force of impulsion. There would have been, then, no risk of stumbling into absurdity; there would have been an insurance against disaster. Yes, but this would not have given the maximum of creation, in quantity and in quality. It is necessary to keep on to the bitter end in one direction, to find out what it will yield: when we can go no further, we turn back, with all we have acquired, to set off in the direction from which we had turned aside. Doubtless, looking from the outside at these comings and goings we see only the antagonism of the two tendencies, the futile attempt of the one to thwart the other, the ultimate defeat of the second and the revenge of the first: man loves the dramatic; he is strongly inclined to pick out from a whole more or less extended period of history those characteristics which make of it a struggle between two parties, two societies or two principles, each of them in turn coming off victorious. But the struggle is here only the superficial aspect of an advance. The truth is that a tendency on which two different views are possible can put forth its maximum, in quantity or quality, only if it materializes these two possibilities into moving realities, each one of which leaps forward and monopolizes the available space, while the other is on the watch unceasingly for its own turn to come. Only thus will the content of the original tendency develop, if indeed we can speak of a content when no one, not even the tendency itself if it achieved consciousness, could tell what will issue from it. It supplies the effort, and the result is a surprise. Such are the workings of nature; the struggles which she stages for us do not indicate pugnacity so much as curiosity. And it is precisely when it imitates nature, when it yields to the original impulsion, that the progress of humanity assumes a certain regularity and conforms—though very imperfectly, be it said—to such laws as those we have stated. But the time has come to close this all too long parenthesis. Let us merely show how our two laws would apply in the case which led us to open it.

We were dealing with the concern for comfort and luxury which has apparently become the main preoccupation of humanity. In considering how it has developed the spirit of invention, how so many inventions are the application of science, and how science is destined to extend its scope indefinitely, we should be tempted to believe in indefinite progress in the same direction. Never, indeed, do the satisfactions with which new inventions meet old needs induce humanity to leave things at that; new needs arise, just as imperious and increasingly numerous. We have seen the race for comfort proceeding faster and faster, on a track along which are surging ever denser crowds. To-day it is a stampede. But should not this very frenzy open our eyes? Was there not some other frenzy to which it has succeeded, and which developed in the opposite direction an activity of which the present frenzy is the complement? In point of fact, it is from the fifteenth or sixteenth century onward that men seemed to aspire to easier material conditions. Throughout the Middle Ages, an ascetic ideal had predominated. There is no need to recall the exaggerations to which it led; here already you had frenzy. It may be alleged that asceticism was confined to a very small minority, and this is true. But just as mysticism, the privilege of a few, was popularized by religion, so concentrated asceticism, which was doubtless exceptional, became diluted for the rank and file of mankind into a general indifference to the conditions of daily existence. There was for one and all an absence of comfort which to us is astonishing. Rich and poor did without superfluities which we consider as necessities. It has been pointed out that if the lord lived better than the peasant, we must understand by this that he had more abundant food.[2] Otherwise, the difference was slight. Here we are, then, in the presence of two divergent tendencies which have succeeded each other and have behaved, both of them, frantically. So, we may presume that they correspond to two opposing manifestations of one primordial tendency, which in this way contrived to evolve from itself, in quantity and quality, everything that it was capable of, even more than it had to give, proceeding along each of the two roads, one after the other, getting back into one direction with everything that had been picked up by the way in the other. That signifies oscillation and progress, progress by oscillation. And we should expect, after the ever-increasing complexity of life, a return to simplicity. This return is obviously not a certainty; the future of humanity remains indeterminate, precisely because it is on humanity that it depends. But if, ahead of us, lie only possibilities or probabilities, which we shall examine presently, we cannot say the same for the past: the two opposite developments which we have just indicated are indeed those of a single original tendency.

And indeed the history of ideas bears witness to it. Out of Socratic thought, pursued in two different directions which in Socrates were complementary, came the Cyrenaic and the Cynic doctrines: the one insisted that we should demand from life the greatest possible number of satisfactions, the other that we should learn to do without them. They developed into Epicureanism and Stoicism with their two opposing tendencies, laxity and tension. If there were the least doubt about the common essence of the two mental attitudes to which these principles correspond, it would suffice to note that, in the Epicurean school itself, along with popular Epicureanism which was at times the unbridled pursuit of pleasure, there was the Epicureanism of Epicurus, ac-

2 See Gina Lombroso's interesting work, *La Rançon du machinisme* (Paris, 1930).

cording to which the supreme pleasure was to need no pleasures. The truth is that the two principles are at the heart of the traditional conception of happiness. Here is a word which is commonly used to designate something intricate and ambiguous, one of those ideas which humanity has intentionally left vague, so that each individual might interpret it after his own fashion. But in whatever sense it is understood, there is no happiness without security—I mean without the prospect of being able to rely on the permanence of a state into which one has settled oneself. This assurance is to be found either in the mastering of things, or in the mastering of self which makes one independent of things. In both cases there is delight in one's strength, whether inwardly perceived or outwardly manifested: the one may lead to pride, the other to vanity. But the simplification and complication of life do indeed follow from a "dichotomy," are indeed apt to develop into "double frenzy," in fact have all that is required to alternate periodically.

This being so, as we have said above, there is nothing improbable in the return to a simpler life. Science itself might show us the way. Whereas physics and chemistry help us to satisfy and encourage us to multiply our needs, it is conceivable that physiology and medical science may reveal more and more clearly to us all the dangers of this multiplication, all the disappointments which accompany the majority of our satisfactions. I enjoy a well-prepared dish of meat; to a vegetarian, who used to like it as much as I do, the mere sight of meat is sickening. It may be alleged that we are both right, and that there is no more arguing about taste than about colour. Perhaps: but I cannot help noting that my vegetarian is thoroughly convinced he will never revert to his old inclinations, whereas I am not nearly so sure that I shall always stick to mine. He has been through both experiments; I have only tried one. His repulsion grows stronger as he fixes his attention on it, whereas my satisfaction is largely a matter of inattention and tends to pale in a strong light. I do believe it would fade away altogether, if decisive experiments came to prove, as it is not impossible they will, that I am directly and slowly poisoning myself by eating meat.[3] I was taught in my school days that the composition of foodstuffs was known, the requirements of our organs also, that it was possible to deduce from this the necessary and sufficient ration to maintain life. The master would have been very much surprised to hear that chemical analysis did not take into account "vitamins" whose presence in food is indispensable to health. It will probably be found that more than one malady, for which medical science has no cure, takes its remote origin from "deficiencies" of which we have no inkling. The only sure means of absorbing all we need would be to have our food subjected to no preparation, perhaps even (who knows) not cooked at all. Here again the belief in the heredity of acquired habits has done great harm. It is commonly said that the human stomach has lost the habit, that we could not feed ourselves nowadays like primitive man. This is true, if taken as meaning that we have left certain natural tendencies lie dormant from our infancy, and that it would be difficult to reawaken them in middle age. But that we are born modified is hardly probable: even if our stomach is different from that of our prehistoric ancestors, the difference is not due to mere habit contracted down the ages. It will not be long before science enlightens us on all these points. Let us suppose that it does so in the sense we foresee: the mere reform of our food supply would have immeasurable reactions on our industry, our trade, our agriculture, all of which it would considerably simplify. What

[3] We hasten to state that we have no particular knowledge of this subject. We have chosen the example of meat as we might have that of any other usual food.

about our other needs? The demands of the procreative senses are imperious, but they would be quickly settled if we hearkened to nature alone. The trouble is that around a violent but paltry sensation, taken as the fundamental, humanity has made rise an endlessly increasing number of overtones: so rich a variety of timbres that almost any object struck on some particular point now gives out the sound that has become an obsession. Thus the senses are constantly being roused by the imagination. Sex-appeal is the keynote of our whole civilization. Here again science has something to say, and it will say it one day so clearly that all must listen: there will no longer be pleasure in so much love of pleasure. Woman will hasten the coming of this time according as she really and sincerely strives to become man's equal, instead of remaining the instrument she still is, waiting to vibrate under the musician's bow. Let the transformation take place: our life will be both more purposeful and more simple. What woman demands in the way of luxuries in order to please man, and, at the rebound, to please herself, will become to a great extent unnecessary. There will be less waste, and less enviousness. Luxury, pleasure and comfort are indeed closely akin, though the connexion between them is not what it is generally supposed to be. It is our way to arrange them in a certain gradation, we are supposed to move up the scale from comfort to luxury: when we have made sure of our comfort we want to cap it with pleasures, then comes love of luxury on top of all. But this is a purely intellectualist psychology, which imagines that our feelings can be measured exactly by their objects. Because luxuries cost more than mere conveniences, and pleasure more than comfort, they are supposed to be keeping pace with goodness knows what corresponding desire. The truth is that it is generally for the sake of our luxuries that we want our comforts, because the comforts we lack look to us like luxuries, and because we want to imitate and equal those people who can afford them. In the beginning was vanity. How many delicacies are sought after solely because they are expensive! For years civilized people spent a great part of their efforts abroad in procuring spices. It is amazing to think that this was the supreme object of navigation, so perilous in those days; that for this thousands of men risked their lives; that the courage, the energy and the spirit of adventure, of which the discovery of America was a mere incident, were mainly employed in the search for ginger, cloves, pepper and cinnamon. Who troubles about these flavourings which so long tasted delicious, now that they can be had for a few pence from the grocer round the corner? Such facts as these are sad reading for the moralist. But reflect a moment, they contain cause for hope as well. The continual craving for creature comforts, the pursuit of pleasure, the unbridled love of luxury, all these things which fill us with so much anxiety for the future of humanity, because it seems to find in them solid satisfactions, all this will appear as a balloon which man has madly inflated, and which will deflate just as suddenly. We know that one frenzy brings on the counter-frenzy. More particularly, the comparison of present-day facts with those of the past is a warning to us to regard as transient tastes which appear to be permanent. Since to-day the supreme ambition for so many men is to have a car, let us recognize the incomparable services rendered by motor-cars, admire the mechanical marvel they are, hope that they will multiply and spread wherever they are needed, but let us say to ourselves that a short time hence they may not be so greatly in demand just as an amenity or "for swank," though the chances are that they may not be quite so neglected, and we hope not, as cloves and cinnamon are to-day.

Here we come to the essential point of our discussion. We have just cited an example of the craving for luxuries arising from a mechanical invention. Many are of the opinion that it is mechanical invention in general which has developed the taste for luxuries, and indeed for mere comfort. Nay, if it is generally admitted that our material needs will go on indefinitely growing more numerous and more imperious, this is because there seems to be no reason why humanity should abandon the path of mechanical invention, once it has started on it. Let us add that, the more science advances, the more inventions are suggested by its discoveries; in many cases from theory to application is but a step; and since science cannot stop, it really does look indeed as though there could be no end to the satisfying of our old needs and the creation of new ones. But we must first ascertain whether the spirit of invention necessarily creates artificial needs, or whether in this case it is not the artificial need which has guided the spirit of invention.

The second hypothesis is by far the more probable. It is confirmed by recent research on the origin of mechanization.[4] The fact has been recalled that man has always invented machines, that antiquity has remarkable ones to show, that many a clever mechanical device was thought of long before the development of modern science, and, at a later stage, independently of it: even to-day a mere workman, without scientific culture, will hit on improvements which have never occurred to skilled engineers. Mechanical invention is a natural gift. Doubtless its effects were limited so long as it was confined to utilizing actual, and as it were visible, forces: muscular effort, wind or water power. The machine developed its full efficiency only from the day when it became possible to place at its service, by a simple process of releasing, the potential energies stored up for

---

[4] We again refer the reader to Gina Lombroso's fine work. Cf. also Mantoux, *La Révolution industrielle au dix-huitième siècle*.

millions of years, borrowed from the sun, deposited in coal, oil, etc. But that was the day when the steam-engine was invented, and we know that this invention was not the outcome of theoretical considerations. Let us hasten to add that the progress made, slow enough at first, assumed giant proportions as soon as science took a hand. It is none the less true that the spirit of mechanical invention, which runs between narrow banks so long as it is left to itself, but expands indefinitely after its conjunction with science, remains distinct from it, and could, if need be, do without it. Similarly we have the Rhone entering the Lake of Geneva, apparently mingling with its waters, but showing, when it leaves it again, that it has preserved its independence.

There has not been then, as some people are inclined to believe, a demand on the part of science, imposing on men, by the mere fact of its development, increasingly artificial needs. If that were so, humanity would be doomed to a growing materiality, for the progress of science will never cease. But the truth is that science has given what was asked of it, and has not in this case taken the initiative; it is the spirit of invention which has not always operated in the best interests of humanity. It has created a mass of new needs; it has not taken the trouble to ensure for the majority of men, for all if that were possible, the satisfaction of old needs. To put it more clearly: though not neglecting the necessary, it has thought too much about the superfluous. It may be said that these two terms are hard to define, and that what are luxuries to some people are necessities to others. True, and it would be easy enough here to lose one's way amid subtle and fine distinctions. But there are cases where subtlety should be cast aside and a broad view taken. Millions of men never get enough to eat. There are some who starve to death. If the land produced much more, there would be far fewer chances of not getting enough to eat,[5] or of starving to death. Over-production here is but a *deceptio visus*. If mechanization is in any way to blame, it is for not having sufficiently devoted itself to helping man in his agricultural labour. It will be said that agricultural implements exist and are now widely used. I grant it, but all that mechanization has done here to lighten man's burden, all that science has done on its side to increase the yield of the soil, amounts to comparatively little. We feel strongly that agriculture, which nourishes man, should dominate all else, in any case be the first concern of industry itself. Generally speaking, industry has not troubled enough about the greater or lesser importance of needs to be satisfied. It simply complied with public taste, and manufactured with no other thought than that of selling. Here as elsewhere, we should like to see a central, organizing intelligence, which would co-ordinate industry and agriculture and allot to the machine its proper place, I mean the place where it can best serve humanity. Thus, when the case against mechanization is stated, the main grievance is often left out. The charge is first that it converts the workman into a mere machine, and then that it leads to a uniformity of production which shocks the aesthetic sense. But if the machine procures for the workman more free time, and if the workman uses this increase of leisure for something else than the so-called pleasures which an ill-directed industry has put within the reach of all, he will develop his intelligence as he chooses, instead of remaining content with the development which would have been imposed upon him, and necessarily maintained within very narrow limits, by a return (impossible in fact) to tools,

[5] There are doubtless periods of "over-production" which extend to agricultural products and may even start from these. But they are obviously not due to the fact that there is too much food for the consumption of mankind. The fact is simply that, production in general not being properly organized, there is no way of exchange.

were machines abolished. As regards uniformity of products, the disadvantage would be negligible, if the economy of time and labour thus realized by the mass of the nation permitted the furtherance of intellectual culture and the development of true originality. An author, writing about the Americans, criticizes them for all wearing the same hat. But the head should come before the hat. Allow me to furnish the interior of my head as I please, and I shall put up with a hat like everybody else's. Such is not our grievance against mechanization. Without disputing the services it has rendered to man by greatly developing the means of satisfying real needs, we reproach it with having too strongly encouraged artificial ones, with having fostered luxury, with having favoured the towns to the detriment of the countryside, lastly with having widened the gap and revolutionized the relations between employer and employed, between capital and labour. These effects, indeed, can all be corrected, and then the machine would be nothing but a great benefactor. But then, humanity must set about simplifying its existence with as much frenzy as it devoted to complicating it. The initiative can come from humanity alone, for it is humanity and not the alleged force of circumstances, still less a fatality inherent to the machine, which has started the spirit of invention along a certain track.

But did humanity wholly intend this? Was the impulsion it gave at the beginning exactly in the same direction that industrialism has actually taken? What is at the outset only an imperceptible deviation becomes in the end a considerable divergence, if the road has been straight and the journey long. Now, there is no doubt that the earliest features of what was destined later to become mechanization were sketched out at the same time as the first yearnings after democracy. The connexion between the two tendencies becomes plainly visible in the eighteenth century. It is a striking feature of the

"Encyclopaedists." Should we not, then, suppose that it was a breath of democracy which urged the spirit of invention onward, that spirit as old as humanity, but insufficiently active so long as it was not given the necessary scope? There was surely no thought then of luxuries for all, or even of comforts for all. But there might have been the desire of an assured material existence, of dignity in security for all. Was this a conscious wish? We do not believe in the unconscious in history: the great undercurrents of thought of which so much has been written are due to the fact that masses of men have been carried along by one or several individuals. These individuals knew what they were doing, but did not foresee all the consequences. We, who know what followed, cannot help transferring back the image of it to the beginning: the present, reflected back into the past and perceived inside it as though in a mirror, is then what we call the unconscious of the past. The retroactivity of the present is at the origin of many philosophical delusions. We shall be careful, then, not to attribute to the fifteenth, sixteenth and eighteenth centuries (and still less the seventeenth, which is so different and has been considered as a sublime parenthesis) a concern for democratic ideas comparable to our own. Neither shall we attribute to them the vision of the power which lay hidden in the spirit of invention. It is none the less true that the Reformation, the Renaissance and the first symptoms or precursory signs of the great inventive impetus date from the same period. It is not impossible that there were here three reactions, interrelated, against the form taken until then by the Christian ideal. This ideal subsisted just the same, but it showed like a heavenly body that had up to then always turned the same face towards man: people now began to catch a glimpse of the other side, though they did not always realize that it was the same body. That mysticism evokes asceticism there is no doubt. Both the one and the other will ever be peculiar to the few. But that true, complete, active mysticism aspires to radiate, by virtue of the charity which is its essence, is none the less certain. How could it spread, even diluted and enfeebled as it must necessarily be, in a humanity obsessed by the fear of hunger? Man will rise above earthly things only if a powerful equipment supplies him with the requisite fulcrum. He must use matter as a support if he wants to get away from matter. In other words, the mystical summons up the mechanical. This has not been sufficiently realized, because machinery, through a mistake at the points, has been switched off on to a track at the end of which lies exaggerated comfort and luxury for the few, rather than liberation for all. We are struck by the accidental result, we do not see mechanization as it should be, as what it is in essence. Let us go further still. If our organs are natural instruments, our instruments must then be artificial organs. The workman's tool is the continuation of his arm, the tool-equipment of humanity is therefore a continuation of its body. Nature, in endowing us with an essentially tool-making intelligence, prepared for us in this way a certain expansion. But machines which run on oil or coal or "white coal," and which convert into motion a potential energy stored up for millions of years, have actually imparted to our organism an extension so vast, have endowed it with a power so mighty, so out of proportion to the size and strength of that organism, that surely none of all this was foreseen in this structural plan of our species: here was a unique stroke of luck, the greatest material success of man on the planet. A spiritual impulsion had been given, perhaps, at the beginning: the extension took place automatically, helped as it were by a chance blow of the pick-axe which struck against a miraculous treasure underground.[6] Now, in this body, distended out of all proportion, the soul re-

---

[6] We are speaking figuratively, of course. Coal was known long before the steam-engine turned it into a treasure.

mains what it was, too small to fill it, too weak to guide it. Hence the gap between the two. Hence the tremendous social, political and international problems which are just so many definitions of this gap, and which provoke so many chaotic and ineffectual efforts to fill it. What we need are new reserves of potential energy— moral energy this time. So let us not merely say, as we did above, that the mystical summons up the mechanical. We must add that the body, now larger, calls for a bigger soul, and that mechanism should mean mysticism. The origins of the process of mechanization are indeed more mystical than we might imagine. Machinery will find its true vocation again, it will render services in proportion to its power, only if mankind, which it has bowed still lower to the earth, can succeed, through it, in standing erect and looking heavenwards.

In a long series of writings, which for depth and forcefulness are beyond praise, M. Ernest Seillière shows how national ambitions claim for themselves divine missions: "imperialism" naturally becomes "mysticism." If we give to this latter word the sense M. Ernest Seillière[7] attributes to it, and which his many books have made abundantly clear, the fact is undeniable; by noting it, by linking it up with its causes and following it in its effects, the author makes an invaluable contribution to the philosophy of history. But he himself would probably be of the opinion that mysticism taken in this sense, and indeed understood in this way by "imperialism" such as he exhibits it, is but a counterfeit of true mysticism, the mysticism of "dynamic religion" which we studied in the last chapter. We believe the counterfeiting to have taken place in the following way. It was a borrowing from the "static religion" of the ancients, stripped of its old tags and left in its static form with the new label supplied by dynamic religion. There was indeed nothing

[7] A meaning only part of which we deal with here, as also in the case of the word "imperialism."

fraudulent in this imitation; it was almost unintentional. For we must remember that "static religion" is natural to man, and that nature does not alter. The innate beliefs of our ancestors subsist in the depths of our inner selves; they reappear as soon as they are no longer inhibited by opposing forces. Now, one of the essential characteristics of ancient religions was the idea of a link between the human groups and the deities attached to them. The gods of the city fought with and for the city. This belief is incompatible with true mysticism, I mean with the feeling which certain souls have that they are the instruments of God who loves all men with an equal love, and who bids them to love each other. But, rising from the darkest depths of the soul to the surface of consciousness, and meeting there with the image of true mysticism as the modern mystics have revealed it to the world, it instinctively decks itself out in this garb; it endows the God of the modern mystic with the nationalism of the ancient gods. It is in this sense that imperialism becomes mysticism. So that if we keep to true mysticism, we shall judge it incompatible with imperialism. At the most it will be admitted, as we have just put it, that mysticism cannot be disseminated without encouraging a very special "will to power." This will be a sovereignty, not over men, but over things, precisely in order that man shall no longer have so much sovereignty over man.

Let a mystic genius but appear, he will draw after him a humanity already vastly grown in body, and whose soul he has transfigured. He will yearn to make of it a new species, or rather deliver it from the necessity of being a species; for every species means a collective halt, and complete existence is mobility in individuality. The great breath of life which swept our planet had carried organization as far along as nature, alike docile and recalcitrant, permitted. Nature—let us repeat it—is the name we give to the totality of compliances and resistances which life encounters in raw matter—a totality which we treat, just as the biologist does, *as though* intentions could be attributed to it. A body compact of creative intelligence, and, round about that intelligence, a fringe of intuition, was the most complete thing nature had found it possible to produce. Such was the human body. There the evolution of life stopped. But now intelligence, raising the construction of instruments to a degree of complexity and perfection which nature (so incapable of mechanical construction) had not even foreseen, pouring into these machines reserves of energy which nature (so heedless of economy) had never even thought of, has endowed us with powers beside which those of our body barely count: they will be altogether limitless when science is able to liberate the force which is enclosed, or rather condensed, in the slightest particle of ponderable matter. The material barrier then has well nigh vanished. To-morrow the way will be clear, in the very direction of the breath which had carried life to the point where it had to stop. Let once the summons of the hero come, we shall not all follow it, but we shall all feel that we ought to, and we shall see the path before us, which will become a highway if we pass along it. At the same time, for each and every philosophy the mystery of the supreme obligation will be a mystery no longer: a journey had been begun, it had had to be interrupted; by setting out once more we are merely willing again what we had willed at the start. It is always the stop which requires explanation, and not the movement.

But perhaps it will be just as well not to count too much on the coming of a great privileged soul. Failing that, some other influences might divert our attention from the baubles that amuse us, and the vain shadows for which we fight.

What influence? We have seen how the talent of invention, assisted by science, put unsuspected energies at man's disposal. We were alluding here to physico-chemical energies, and to a science that was concerned with matter. But what about things spiritual? Has spirit been scientifically investigated as thoroughly as it might have been? Do we know to what results such investigation might lead? Science attended first to matter; for three whole centuries it had no other object; even to-day, when we leave the word unqualified, it is understood that we mean the science of matter. We have given the reasons for this on another occasion. We have indicated why the scientific study of matter preceded that of the spirit. The most pressing needs had to be taken first. Geometry existed already; it had been considerably advanced by the ancients; the thing was to extract from mathematics all it could give in explanation of the world in which we live. Nor was it desirable, indeed, to begin by the science of the spirit; it would not have attained, unaided, the precision, the rigour, the demand for proof, which have spread from geometry to physics, to chemistry, to biology, until such time as they might rebound on to the science of the spirit. And yet, on the other hand, it has certainly suffered to some extent from coming so late. For human intelligence has thus been left time to get scientific support for, and thus invest with unquestionable authority, its habit of looking at things as if they all occupied so much space, of explaining everything in terms of matter. Suppose, then, that it now turns its attention to the soul? It will picture the life of the soul too as if it were spread out in space; it will extend to this new object the image it kept of the old: hence the errors of an atomistic psychology, which does not take into account the mutual overlapping of psychic states; hence the futile efforts of a philosophy that claims to attain to the spirit without seeking it in enduring time. Suppose, again, that we take the relation of the body to the soul. The confusion is graver still. Not only has it started metaphysics on a false scent, it has diverted science from the observation of certain facts, or rather

FOUR *Final Remarks*   314

it has prevented certain sciences from being born, causing them to be excommunicated beforehand in the name of I know not what dogma. For it was agreed that the material accompaniment of mental activity was its equivalent: every reality being supposed to have its basis in space, nothing more is to be found in the mind, so they said, than what a superhuman physiologist could read in the corresponding brain. Note that this thesis is a pure metaphysical hypothesis, an arbitrary interpretation of facts. But no less arbitrary is the spiritualistic metaphysics opposed to it, according to which each mental state is supposed to use a cerebral state which serves merely as its instrument; for this metaphysics, too, mental activity is coextensive with cerebral activity and corresponds to it at every point in our present life. The second theory is indeed influenced by the first, having always lain under its spell. Now, we have attempted to prove, by removing the preconceived ideas accepted on both sides, by adhering as closely as possible to the configuration of facts, that the part played by the body is something quite different. The activity of the spirit has indeed a material concomitant, but one which corresponds only to part of it; the rest lies buried in the unconscious. The body is indeed for us a means of action, but it is also an obstacle to perception. Its rôle is to perform the appropriate action on any and every occasion; for this very reason it must keep consciousness clear both of such memories as would not throw any light on the present situation, and also of the perception of objects over which we have no control.[8] It is, as you like to take it, a filter or a screen. It maintains in a virtual state anything likely to hamper the action by becoming actual. It helps us to see straight in front of us in the

[8] We have shown above how a sense such as that of sight carries further, because its instrument makes this extension inevitable (see p. 160. Cf. *Matière et mémoire,* the whole of Chap. I).

interests of what we have to do; and, on the other hand,
it prevents us from looking to right and left for the mere
sake of looking. It plucks for us a real psychical life out
of the immense field of dreams. In a word, our brain is
intended neither to create our mental images nor to
treasure them up; it merely limits them, so as to make
them effective. It is the organ of *attention to life*. But
this means that there must have been provided, either
in the body or in the consciousness limited by the body,
some contrivance expressly designed to screen from
man's perception objects which by their nature are beyond the reach of man's action. If these mechanisms get
out of order, the door which they kept shut opens a little
way: there enters in something of a "without" which
may be a "beyond." It is with these abnormal perceptions that "psychical research" is concerned. To a certain
extent the opposition it encounters is intelligible. It is a
science that rests on human evidence, and human evidence can always be disputed. The typical scientist is in
our eyes the physicist; his attitude of fully justified confidence towards matter, which is obviously not out to
deceive him, has become for us characteristic of all
science. We are reluctant to go on treating as scientific
a form of investigation which requires of the investiga-
tors that they be ever on the lookout for trickery. Their
distrust makes us uneasy, their trust still more so: we
know how soon one is apt to relax one's guard; that it is
so perilously easy to glide from curiosity to credulity.
Consequently, certain reluctances, as we said just now,
are readily explained. But the flat denial which some
true scientists oppose to "psychical research" would
never be understood, where it not that, above all, they
regard the facts reported as "improbable"; "impossible"
they would say, if they did not know that there exists no
conceivable means of establishing the impossibility of a
fact; they are none the less convinced, in the main, of
that impossibility. And they are convinced of it because

they believe to be undeniable, definitely established, a certain relation between the organism and consciousness, between body and spirit. Now we have just seen that this relation is purely hypothetical, that it is not proved by science, but postulated by a certain metaphysics. The facts suggest a very different hypothesis; and if this is admitted, the phenomena recorded by "psychical research," or at least some of them, become so likely that we should rather be surprised at the time they have had to wait before they were studied. We shall not here go over again a matter we have discussed elsewhere. Let us merely say, to take what seems to us the most strongly established fact, that if, for example, the reality of "telepathic phenomena" is called in doubt after the mutual corroboration of thousands of statements which have been collected on the subject, it is human evidence in general that must, in the eyes of science, be declared to be null and void: what, then, is to become of history? The truth is that one must make a selection among the results which "psychical research" puts before us; that science itself by no means considers them all of equal value; it distinguishes between what seems to it as certain and what is simply probable or, at most, possible. But, even if one retains only a portion of what it would fain look upon as certain, enough remains for us to divine the immensity of the *terra incognita* that it has just begun to explore. Suppose that a gleam from this unknown world reaches us, visible to our bodily eyes. What a transformation for humanity, generally accustomed, whatever it may say, to accept as existing only what it can see and touch! The information which would then reach us would perhaps concern only the inferior portion of the souls, the lowest degree of spirituality. But this would be sufficient to turn into a live, acting reality a belief in the life beyond, which is apparently met with in most men, but which for the most part remains verbal, abstract, ineffectual. To know to what extent it does count, it suffices to see how we plunge into pleasure: we should not cling to it so desperately, did we not see in it so much ground gained over nothingness, a means whereby we can snap our fingers at death. In truth, if we were sure, absolutely sure, of survival, we could not think of anything else. Our pleasures would still remain, but drab and jejune, because their intensity was merely the attention that we centred upon them. They would pale like our electric lamps before the morning sun. Pleasure would be eclipsed by joy.

Joy indeed would be that simplicity of life diffused throughout the world by an ever-spreading mystic intuition; joy, too, that which would automatically follow a vision of the life beyond attained through the furtherance of scientific experiment. Failing so thoroughgoing a spiritual reform, we must be content with shifts and submit to more and more numerous and vexatious regulations, intended to provide a means of circumventing each successive obstacle that our nature sets up against our civilization. But, whether we go bail for small measures or great, a decision is imperative. Mankind lies groaning, half crushed beneath the weight of its own progress. Men do not sufficiently realize that their future is in their own hands. Theirs is the task of determining first of all whether they want to go on living or not. Theirs the responsibility, then, for deciding if they want merely to live, or intend to make just the extra effort required for fulfilling, even on their refractory planet, the essential function of the universe, which is a machine for the making of gods.